LANGUAGE DEVELOPMENT

IN DEAF AND

PARTIALLY HEARING

CHILDREN

LANGUAGE DEVELOPMENT

IN DEAF AND

PARTIALLY HEARING

CHILDREN

By

D. M. C. DALE B.A., Dip. Ed., Ph.D.

Department of Child Development

University of London Institute of Education

CHARLES C THOMAS • PUBLISHER

Springfield • Illinois • U. S. A.

Published and Distributed Throughout the World by

CHARLES C THOMAS • PUBLISHER

Bannerstone House

301-327 East Lawrence Avenue, Springfield, Illinois, U.S.A.

© *1974, by* CHARLES C THOMAS • PUBLISHER

ISBN 0-398-03164-9

Library of Congress Catalog Card Number: 74-3254

Library of Congress Cataloging in Publication Data

Dale, Dion Murray Crosbie.
   Language development in deaf and partially hearing
children.

   Bibliography: p.
   1. Deaf—Education—English language. I. Title.
[DNLM: 1. Deafness—In infancy and childhood.
2. Education, Special. 3. Hearing disorders—In
infancy and childhood. 4. Language development.
HV2440 D139L 1974]
HV2440.D35   371.9′12′4   74-3254
ISBN 0-398-03164-9

Printed in the United States of America

CC-11

INTRODUCTION

Most deaf children begin their school careers with language which is grossly retarded and in not a few cases, is nonexistent. In addition, it takes longer to teach a given point to deaf children than to those who are not so handicapped, and deaf children learn so little from incidental conversations that time must be given to presenting colloquial language both at home and in school. It can be seen, therefore, how important it is to ensure that the precious time devoted to language work by parents and teachers, is not squandered. Assistance to this end is the major aim of this book. The first five chapters cover teaching methods and practices which apply to the development of language in deaf or partially hearing children; the next three chapters contain topics which have been found helpful in presenting language to hearing impaired children of various ages.

It is hoped that many of the suggestions will be of practical assistance to teachers in training, inexperienced teachers, parents, and houseparents. Some might also act as a catalyst for the experienced teacher who feels he or she has begun to run out of steam, or worse, has nothing more to learn. If during the past three or four years one's teaching has not included regular two way contact with the homes of the children, carefully prepared class visits, a nearby class of normally hearing children, a camera, a language master, an amplified tape recorder, a spirit duplicator, filmstrips, a cine loop projector, television programmes, or diaries of home and school activities, it may be helpful to learn that a growing number of teachers of deaf children have done so; and they, the children and their parents and houseparents have enjoyed the experiences and are convinced of the value of such procedures.

It is more correct to say that language is *presented* to the children in school than it is to say that it is *taught* to them. The full comprehension and use of language is only achieved by regular practice in everyday situations. For this reason, the closest possible communication between homes and schools (and hostels) is stressed constantly throughout this book.

D. M. C. DALE

v

ACKNOWLEDGMENTS

In 1968 and 1969, Mr. Raymond Chapman-Taylor, a senior inspector of schools, carried out a most useful survey of language teaching in 17 schools for deaf and partially hearing children and in 29 units for these children in ordinary schools, in the South of England and Wales. Observations of classroom practice were made and interviews with 267 teachers of deaf children were conducted. Almost half of the examples of lessons given in Chapters 6, 7 and 8 have come from this investigation. I am most grateful to Mr. Chapman-Taylor, to the teachers and children in these schools, and to the National Deaf Children's Society who financed the survey.

Ex-pupils of schools for deaf children, students, teachers, and colleagues in the Institute of Education have offered suggestions and made valuable criticisms of various parts of the text.

D.M.C.D.

CONTENTS

Page

Introduction v

Acknowledgments vi

Part I
LANGUAGE DEVELOPMENT

Chapter

I.   DEVELOPING LANGUAGE IN DEAF CHILDREN 3

II. PARENTS AND HOUSEPARENTS 31

III. VISUAL AIDS 47

IV. ANIMALS AND PETS 58

V.   INTEGRATING HEARING IMPAIRED CHILDREN INTO
     REGULAR SCHOOLS 62

Part II
LANGUAGE TOPICS FOR HEARING IMPAIRED CHILDREN
AGED THREE TO SEVENTEEN YEARS

VI.   LANGUAGE TOPICS FOR CHILDREN AGED FOUR TO
      SEVEN YEARS 75

VII. LANGUAGE TOPICS FOR CHILDREN AGED EIGHT TO
      TWELVE YEARS 115

VIII. LANGUAGE TOPICS FOR CHILDREN AGED THIRTEEN TO
      SEVENTEEN YEARS 161

Bibliography 240

Appendices 245

LANGUAGE DEVELOPMENT

IN DEAF AND

PARTIALLY HEARING

CHILDREN

PART I

LANGUAGE DEVELOPMENT

I DEVELOPING LANGUAGE IN DEAF CHILDREN

LANGUAGE CAN BE DEFINED as any means whereby ideas are communicated using an artificially structured set of symbols. Words are thus not necessarily involved. Gesture and mime are extremely effective methods of communicating basic ideas, and deaf children and adults often employ these extensively. The communication of ideas can effectively be achieved through the plastic arts and through music.

Language here, however, means the comprehensive use of words, spoken or written, in the communication of ideas. It is not proposed to discuss the relationship between thought and language, except to say that numerous studies have shown that despite a much reduced vocabulary, the distribution of intelligence among deaf children, when nonverbal tests are used, approximates the normal. Thinking can take place without language, but verbal reasoning, of course, cannot. Many deaf children who are able to obtain mental ages of say fifteen years, may, if incorrectly taught, have reading vocabulary ages of only eight or nine years and their oral English is frequently not as syntactically correct as that of the average four-year-old child with normal hearing. Such low reading attainment is the direct result of the child's inadequate language development. At five, many normally hearing children have an average vocabulary of some 2,000 words. Some may have as many as 6,000 words and by four and a half are using all the complex sentence forms required in everyday language. If children who are born profoundly deaf have acquired 250 words by the time they are five this has usually been regarded as splendid progress. Many of these words are used in isolation rather than in conventional phrases.

3

Despite this language deprivation, deaf children are able to comprehend new concepts fairly adequately, provided these are skilfully taught. It usually takes much longer, of course, to establish the language form or precise concept with deaf children than it does with children whose hearing is not impaired. It is quite common for deaf children (and a number of deaf adults) to make vague guesses from illustrations, gestures, and the occasional word. This of course can not, as a rule, be considered as comprehension in the normal sense.

Because nouns are relatively easy to teach, there is a tendency for parents and teachers to emphasize the naming of things to the exclusion of other vocabulary. There is also a need for deaf children to acquire acceptable syntactical rules. If parents allow the child's interests to dictate the language, and use natural language themselves, the parts of speech and the syntactical forms frequently look after themselves and teaching sessions are likely to be more interesting to the children. Phrases will begin to be acquired, and these can be followed up at home and at school.

The phrase or sentence is the true thought unit, and learning large numbers of words in isolation has been found to inhibit rather than promote the use of language by normally hearing children (Ginsberg, 1960). One six-year-old deaf child tried to illustrate "the girl pushed the pram," by first drawing a picture of a girl, next another picture of a girl in the act of pushing, and finally, another of a pram. Another deaf boy illustrated "a green tree" with a patch of green and beside it an outline of a tree.

Everyday phrases which develop quite naturally in normally hearing children must usually be specifically taught to deaf ones. So must proverbs, idioms, nursery rhymes, jingles, and songs. Much attention is given to the correct use of question forms in meaningful situations. Innumerable stories which involve direct speech should be told to the children and read by them to give experience of these vitally important language forms. Above all, however, time must be devoted to "conversations" with each child. The Ewings (1971) emphasize this when they stress the importance of 'practical situations that encourage two-way talk'. (p. 58) At first these will consist of gestures from the child and speech from the parent or teacher, but gradually, as words develop in the child, he will need to gesture less. The more intelligible the speech is, the more rapidly will language develop, since nothing is more encouraging to a child's linguistic progress than seeing words begin to work for him. It can be seen, however, that deaf children must work as few normally hearing children do, if they wish to achieve reasonable educational standards. At the same time, it should be remembered, that they should have plenty of exercise, fun, games and, of course, rest. Careful planning by parents, houseparents and teachers is essential.

Lenneberg and others have shown that language acquisition (and a general high level of cognitive operation through the manipulation of arbitrary symbols) is common to all humans. It has been our experience that deaf children, despite a distorted input pattern, if exposed to rich language in appropriate everyday situations, can observe and remember regularities, abstract rules which become increasingly accurate through experiment, correction, improving cognitive capacity and increasing experience. As Tizard has indicated below, (1964) it is a diversity of language experience (both receptive and expressive) which is of such critical importance in developing the child's linguistic skills.

In considering how best to present a basic language subject to a deaf child, one is conscious of innumerable factors: the age, intelligence, (Ewing, 1957) hearing loss, (Dale, 1971) social and emotional adjustment, (Rutter, 1970) previous education and above all the prevailing interests of the child, (Gardner, 1956) his home background and social milieu, (Bernstein, 1971) the curriculum and syllabus of the school, the number and abilities of other members of the class, the personal qualities and skills of the teacher, the teaching methods adopted, evaluative techniques applied and teaching aids available. When one realizes that each of these factors could be further subdivided into ten or twenty subheadings, one begins to appreciate the complexity of a teacher's task.

It is not possible to bear all these considerations in mind in the classroom situation each day, but awareness of them can influence the management of each child and the priorities and emphases given to planning. As much teaching of deaf children on an individual basis as can possibly be arranged, and the importance of thoughtful preparation of work, are clearly indicated. Chapman-Taylor in his survey of language teaching mentioned above, found a small minority of teachers so convinced of the need to work from the children's own interests that they felt it practically impossible to decide what they would do until they entered the classroom each day. "The results in every case" he said, "seemed poor."

Few schools today prescribe in advance exactly what a child shall be taught in language during his school career, but neither do they recommend improvising daily what is to be taught. Language teaching in a child-centred curriculum by an unskilled or insensitive teacher can become chaotic, leaving large gaps in a child's knowledge. Experience does help, of course, in predicting what might represent both interesting and useful language topics for deaf children of various ages. Teachers have found, for example, that six and seven-year-old deaf children are very interested in learning language concerning the foods they eat. It is sensible that this should be mentioned in an outline for less experienced colleagues. This principle of what is of interest to children pervades the whole of this book. No topics have been included that have not been found by at least one, and usually a number of teachers, to be of real interest to deaf children of a certain age, ability and aptitude. Most of the topics presented in Chapters VI, VII and VIII have another feature in common—several lessons or sessions can usefully be spent on each of them. Such topics (or units) enable a teacher to consolidate and extend the language presented in a more natural and meaningful way than is possible with a series of single lessons. Parents and houseparents can also more easily become involved in these situations.

Acquiring a vocabulary and beginning to use it is a highly personal accomplishment. Tizard in *Community Services for the Mentally Handicapped* states:

> The limits to a young child's intellectual development are likewise set at the level of maturation of the central nervous system; providing that the environment in which he lives gives him the opportunity to practice his growing intellectual skills. The need to practice cease-

lessly his linguistic skills, for example, arises from within the child; children talk because they cannot stop, not because adults make them talk. If the interests and needs of young children are carefully observed, they will be found to be themselves the best judges of what is good for them. It is a diversity of experience rather than mere repetition that makes for useful learning.

SOME METHODS OF PRESENTING LANGUAGE

The Auditory Method

It is clear that the easiest way to learn a language is to hear it spoken in meaningful situations and be given opportunities to practice it. Despite, in many cases, a much reduced auditory input, using whatever hearing a child does possess, is of paramount importance in enabling him to comprehend and use speech. Some workers have recommended that all early training of deaf children should be given auditorally (Wedenberg, 1951). In this way, they believe the children become auditorally minded rather than visually so. With profoundly deaf children, however, using only the minute amount of hearing available seems to be inadvisable, and a combination of listening plus watching, with regular and frequent opportunities for listening alone, appears to be much the safest course.

The Listening Reading Speaking Method (LRS)

An important method of language presentation is one which relies heavily on reading as a means of directing the children's attention at the beginning of a session, and frequently throughout, emphasizes the use of the children's hearing. As each lesson develops much oral discussion is also involved and visual aids, damatisation, writing, and drawing all play their usual useful roles.

This approach has been described more fully elsewhere, (Dale, 1971) but in short it may be said often to involve the following steps:

1. The teacher presents a passage of natural language which she knows is appropriate to the reading level of an individual child or the majority of the class if a group lesson is being taken.
2. Speaking close to the microphone, she reads the passage

through at a near normal rate, pointing to each syllable on the page, blackboard or wall sheet as it is read.

3. The child/children copy her phrase by phrase.

4. The meaning of each phrase and the paragraph as a whole is then discussed orally and supplemented with visual aids, dramatisation, etc. as required.

5. Phrases and words are next read while the teacher covers her lips to prevent the child/children from lipreading. These listening games can often be performed by very deaf children (100 db) after they have had regular practice.

6. Written work, involving questions and further reading, is then begun at school and taken home or to the hostel.

Parents have found this LRS technique extremely valuable during the daily reading session.

Mother's Method

A technique for developing language in hearing impaired children which has proved successful is sometimes referred to as *mother's method* because it is based on the *natural method* by which normally hearing children learn to speak in their own homes (Ewing 1958). Essentially it consists of requiring all who come in contact with the deaf child to speak carefully to him about the things that seem of interest to him at a particular time. With profoundly deaf children, as suggested above, speakers must first be sure that the child is watching their lips before they begin to speak. Excellent opportunities for providing this language experience are afforded during the daily routines at home and at school. When getting up and going to bed, at meal times, bath times, when changing clothes or going on a daily walk, splendid opportunities occur for meaningful and interesting language presentation. Giving a wealth of experience of words and phrases in these everyday situations, requires energy, forethought and tact as well as a keen appreciation of what has interested the child. It is important to remember that even quite dull deaf children can learn to comprehend and use speech using natural language methods, but they cannot when formal methods are employed.

After a period of perhaps six months, there is usually definite evidence that the child understands a word or phrase. Some weeks later the child spontaneously attempts to say his first word. These early months—with such effort for so little immediate return—can disturb, disappoint and exhaust parents. Regular sessions with experienced teachers (and parents) can do much to ease these early tensions. The parents need guidance but they also need encouragement and to be listened to—just as the children do.

A Developmental Language Method

Quite exceptional linguistic (and social) development of deaf children was observed at the Peninsula Oral School, near San Francisco, when it was visited in April 1973. Five main factors seemed to be contributing to this:

1. The initiative, sense of purpose and sensitivity of the head teach (Mrs. Leah Grammatico).

2. The quality and positive dedication of the teachers employed.

3. The careful assessment of each child's ability to hear and the full exploitation of this following the prescription of the most suitable hearing aids.

4. The use of a dynamic developmental language programme based on many of the principles enunciated by Piaget.

5. The degree of parental involvement that had been achieved.

Additional factors which contributed to the success of the school included the enthusiasm of supporting staff and student teacher trainees; the fact that there were not a disproportionate number of dually and multiply handicapped deaf children enrolled; class sizes were small by many schools' standards (4–6 children in most classes) ; each child had up to one half hour's individual teaching and auditory training each day; the fact that the aim of the school was to get as many children as possible out into their own schools for normally hearing children by the age of 6 years supported by daily visits from a teacher of the deaf (this meant that parents and children did not have to look forward to 10, 12 or even 14 years' attendance at one special school as is still the case in many schools) ; the classrooms were large, carpeted and attractively decorated, and every child went home at night.

The six response curves given to hearing aids tended to amplify low frequencies rather more than is usual. The majority of the children in this school were severely or profoundly deaf, and seemed, from demonstrations given, to profit markedly from such amplification.

Apart from the activity-centred learning periods to be described below, a feature of the language programme throughout this school seemed to be the teachers' conviction that language should be presented to the children with little regard for their deafness. They talked to them in what would seem to most teachers of the deaf to be a most sophisticated manner. For example, one 5 year old boy had a new pair of red, white and blue sandals. His teacher said, "Oh, you've got very patriotic sandals this morning, haven't you?" "Why are they patriotic? Well, because they're red, white and blue." Another teacher when a six year old child picked up a lemon from the floor, said to her, "Did you know, that's a marvelous source of Vitamin C." The teachers seemed to be continually "stretching" the children's vocabularies in these ways and doubtless parents had been encouraged (and shown how) to do the same. The result was that when the children reached the age of 7 and 8 years, one began to wonder, in many cases, whether they were deaf at all.

Where children have not been exposed to this type of programme, however, such large scale vocabulary expansion is much more difficult—particularly where the out-of-school lives of the children provide little stimulation. Indeed, I can foresee the examples given above of the "patriotic shoes" and "Vitamin C." serving as little more than a source of mild staff room amusement, after the names of some of the least able children in a school have been mentioned. Perhaps, however, they may stimulate many of us to be rather more adventurous in our use of language with the deaf children we teach.

Another feature of the language programme observed was the use of quite lengthy group oral/aural Piagetian sessions which contained much questioning, answering and discussion. One such period with six 5 and 6-year-old children involved the use of 10 carefully made cardboard rabbits of diminishing size. These were placed in order along the bottom of the blackboard. The teacher asked the children what they could say about the largest rabbit. Replies included "He's biggest," "He's the tallest," "He's oldest," "He's fattest" and Mrs. Grammatico intervened to say "He's probably the strongest."

The teacher next asked "How are these rabbits alike?" "They all have ears," "They all hop, they have fluffy tails," "They're all brown" etc.

"Now, what's different about them?" "Some are tallest," "Some are small," "Some are heavy," etc.

The largest, the smallest and one of the middle sized rabbits were then put up on a smaller board and discussed.

Teacher: "This is Flopsy (large one) Mopsy (middle sized one) and Cotton Tail. What can we say about Flopsy?"

Children: "He tall, he's fat. He bigger than Mopsy or Cotton Tail."

Teacher: "How about Mopsy?"

Children: "She's smaller than Flopsy and bigger than Cotton Tail" etc.

This session lasted 45 minutes, whereupon the teacher picked up her bass ukelele and played a little song. The children joined in

Time to plan our work today

Tell me where you want to play.

Work tasks were arranged around the room in such a way that a child could select one or other activity and get on with it without a great deal of supervision—except, of course, for the very necessary interest by the teacher to encourage and give guidance where this was needed. It was a deliberate and important part of the policy of this school that the children should become independent workers as soon as possible. To promote this, thus aiding them when they went to the larger classes in the regular schools, teachers drew heavily on a text by *Mary B. Lorton* entitled *"Workjobs" (Addison-Wesley Publishing Co.— 1972)*. This excellent teacher's manual contains clear illustrations and suggestions for over 100 developmental (Piaget-type) activities for young normally hearing children. Most are directly applicable to deaf children and I believe should be available to all teachers of the deaf dealing with children up to the age of 9 or 10 years. For each lesson, clear guidance is given on the concepts to be developed or the skill to be achieved; the activity involved; how to get started; ideas for follow up and discussion and the materials required. Clear photographs accompany each activity.

To conclude, I should mention another memorable experience on what was a most memorable day. The children had made a short 8 millimetre film of a series of comical activities, e.g. a lady being offered pairs of shoes in a shoe shop, and turning them all down disdainfully until in despair the "salesman" brought her a huge pair of hobnailed boots which she seized delightedly. The children (7–8 year olds) had made tickets to sell to staff and parents, two acted as ushers into the darkened classroom, others were selling 5 cent bags of popcorn. One of the fathers outside was asked if he and his wife worked tremendously hard at home with their girl and he replied "We did, but not now—not any more." The father who would take time off from work to see his daughter's film show, was clearly still doing a great deal at home. One is inclined to think that what this father was indicating was that the worry, fear and despair felt by so many parents of deaf children in the early days, had lifted and given way to a feeling of confidence and peace brought about by the realisation that this first rate school and home had, in four short years, got the handicap of deafness well in hand.

Cued Speech—a complement to oral/aural methods

Cued Speech was developed by R. Orin Cornett at Gallaudet College, Washington, D.C., in 1966 (Cornett, 1972). The rationale behind this method is that by using hand "cues," the visible appearance of all the sounds of spoken language can be made clearly different from each other. The hypothesis is that a child born profoundly deaf will be able to acquire spoken language in much the same way as does a normally hearing one, but through vision rather than hearing.

A valuable feature of Cued Speech is that lipreading of all sounds is essential, i.e. the hand cues accompanying each sound, are not sufficient in themselves. Each hand position and configuration, tells that the sound being said is one of a group of perhaps three sounds—but just which of the three must be determined from the speaker's lips.

A further significant feature which teachers of deaf children have observed when using Cued Speech, is that one is able to speak as one would to a normally hearing child without choosing 'lipreadable' vocabulary. One often says to a deaf child when not using Cued Speech for example, that something is 'beautiful' but not that it is 'gorgeous.' Brother McGrath at St. Gabriel's School for Deaf Boys near Sydney, Australia has observed such 'unlipreadable' words coming into the deaf children's active vocabularies.* He mentioned asking a boy in the sick bay one morning how he was feeling and receiving the reply "So, so."

The use of the 7 hand configurations in 5 positions, enable a speaker to say any word at all. This is a definite advantage over sign languages where each word has a sign and there are over 3,000 words which can be signed—each with a different configuration.

For the above reasons, Cued Speech has been considered seriously by a number of teachers and parents who cannot accept manual methods that do not depend at all on the use of spoken language.

Dr. Cornett is at present investigating the possibility of developing instruments capable of vibrating different points on the skin, or activating tiny lights set into the lenses of spectacles, in response to the presentation of the sounds of speech. The hand positions of Cued Speech would thus not be necessary. The development of such instruments would represent a major breakthrough in the vexing field of speech reception and speech production of deaf people.

Fingerspelling

Fingerspelling involves spelling words by placing the fingers in different configurations which represent the required letters

---

* Personal communication from Brother McGrath.

of the alphabet (Jones, 1968). Deaf or normally hearing people who use fingerspelling in the British Isles, use the two handed alphabet. In most other countries, however, the one handed alphabet is preferred. Many people become very proficient in both sending and receiving fingerspelt words—in some cases, at near the normal rate for oral speech (Scouten, 1969).

Some people use fingerspelling to supplement those aspects of oral speech which are difficult or impossible to lipread e.g. place names, names of people and words like sausages, azalias, or conscientious. Others just fingerspell the initial letter of such words.

Van Uden, and others, however, feel that where such difficulties occur, the spelling should be given by printing the letters in the air—rather than using fingerspelling. This gives the children the sort of experience which they might expect to receive from the general public.

Sign Languages

Sign languages have usually grown out of natural gestures. In consequence, signs for many words in most countries are so similar that at international gatherings deaf people from all nations seem able to converse—at a fairly basic level at least—by using them.

"Signs are the thing" a deaf graduate at Gallaudet College said to me recently, and it is easy to appreciate why signs are so attractive to both deaf children and adults. They represent a clear and rapid means of communicating ideas between two or more people who are familiar with the signs. Unfortunately, the grammatical syntax (if one can call it that) of signed language, is such, that if used consistently out of school hours, it does indeed inhibit the development of conventional language (Dale, 1971).

In the deaf schools in which I have lived, the children used some 250 signs and these were sufficient to meet their basic everyday needs. No signs existed for such words as 'is' 'as' 'of' 'because' or 'until', since these had not been found necessary to communicate ideas. A sentence such as "As I was coming to school this morning, I saw a red bus with a flat tyre," might be signed "Bus, —tyre (or wheel) —flat! —saw."

A few evenings on duty with the children (aided by one or two partially hearing interpreters), were sufficient to learn 200 or so of the signs and it was then quite fun to experiment with their use. It was also a relief to realise that at last one could communicate more freely with those children whose speech was unintelligible. It is important to recognise, however, that if one does nothing more than use this limited signed vocabulary, one is letting the children down badly. As Irene Ewing has said "signs and gestures are the little deaf child's mental salvation, but the greatest threat to his future mental life."

In the American sign language, and an interesting English development, the Gorman-Paget sign language, (Gorman, 1969) there are between 3,000 and 4,000 signs. Even where a far greater number of signs are known, it is tempting, for the sake of speed, to use just the bare essentials, e.g. to say "Shop—me," rather than "I am going up to the shop." Such "shorthand" use of English does nothing, of course, to aid the children's development of syntactical language and can undoubtedly inhibit it. In a number of schools, (particularly the larger residential ones), such abbreviated use of signed language is common between children and hostel staff and vice versa. It is to be regretted.

The Simultaneous Method

. . . means simply the simultaneous use of speech, lipreading, hearing aids, fingerspelling and the language of signs in communicating with the deaf.

This form of communication (albeit with little emphasis on hearing aids) has been practised with university level students at Gallaudet College for many years and is felt there, to be effective.

The Total Approach

The Total Approach is currently receiving much attention in the United States. It appears to be similar to the Simultaneous Method mentioned above, except that integration into ordinary schools is an additional feature in a few programmes. Holcomb has commented favourably on the ability of many of the severely deaf children to integrate into ordinary school classes: "There are usually several hearing children in any class who know the language of signs fluently."

There is already evidence, however, that the lipreading ability and the speech intelligibility of deaf children from oral and regular schools, drop markedly within 3 months of being exposed to Total Communication. It is not surprising to hear reports that enthusiasm for the approach is waning fairly fast.

Consolidation

It should be remembered that children must be given regular and frequent opportunities to practise the language forms presented to them. For this reason, great emphasis is placed on teachers keeping parents and houseparents informed of the work covered at school each day and vice versa. It is then possible to revise and extend the material presented on frequent occasions in meaningful situations. If either parents or houseparents are unable to participate in teaching and revising language, more of this must be done in the school. Agnes Lack suggests:

> The teacher who can think up the happiest ways of practising the same thing, who has many different ways of presenting the same lesson, is the one who will get results in all subjects and whose class will be alive and happy.

In the splendid notes at the end of each lesson, Miss Lack has given innumerable examples of how she would present and consolidate language.

Dr. van Uden, in his book, *A World of Language for Deaf Children,* emphasizes what he calls the *seizing method.* This applies to all deaf children and involves listening to what the child says or attempts to say, seizing and extending this and asking the child to repeat the improved version. It can be very effective. If, for example, a child says "Ball," his mother might say "Yes, it's a lovely ball" "It's a big blue ball isn't it?" "Can you say 'It's a lovely ball'?" or if he seems to want to play, "Can you roll the ball to Mummy?" "You roll it." In this way, one word from the child initiates several phrases from the parent. The more nearly the parent's amplification of the child's utterance approximates what the child was trying to communicate, the more encouraging it is for the child's language development.

It is interesting to compare van Uden's *seizing method* with the *imitation and expansion process* of Bellugi and Brown (1964). In Lenneberg, E. H. (Ed.) *New Directions in the Study of English Language* M.I.T. Press. Parents of young normally learning children expand their children's utterances (30% of the time) into conventional syntactic forms, but they do *not* ask the children to repeat these expansions as parents and teachers of deaf children are recommended to do.

Activity Methods

When parents or houseparents use the daily routines for developing language, as suggested above, they are using similar techniques to those used by teachers in activity lessons. The aim in both situations is to place a deaf child in a meaningful activity situation where language is clearly needed. Virtually all the language topics suggested in Chapters VI, VII and VIII, may be considered for presentation in activity lessons. The idea should precede the language, i.e. the cognitive aspect of the activity should be within the child's or children's experience.

Mrs. Leah Grammatico in a personal communication has written:

> When I first began teaching children of nursery school age, I followed the standard procedure of taking the children singly or in small groups and presenting them with small toys. I would hold up a ball, say ball, and attempt to get it back verbally from the child. When I had run through a number of objects in this fashion, I would play the standard lipreading game of "Give me the ball. Can you find the boat, the baby, etc.?" I was not pleased with the results from this type of teaching because the children became bored easily. I did not feel they made any attempt to lipread any word in the sentences I used except ball, boat, baby, etc. and this seemed to me to be too rigid a way for little children to acquire a lipreading and speaking vocabulary. So I changed my teaching methods. Even though the young deaf child has been surrounded with language since the day he was born, this means little to him. This means that the teacher must utilize meaningful experiences from the child's life at school to give him a solid language foundation. Our playhouse provided material for innumerable language experiences. Calling the nursery school chil-

dren to me I would say "Our baby is dirty. Let us give her a bath. Bobby will you go to the playhouse and get the baby for us? This is the baby (holding her up to my face). Look how dirty she is. What do we need for her bath?" The children will show you with gestures that you need soap, water, pan to bathe her in, towel, washcloth, powder, a clean dress, panties, shoes and socks. Then we bathe the baby. This is a meaningful experience and play for the children. This type of teaching takes a great deal of planning for the teacher, but the results are worth the effort expended. Each day provides many meaningful situations for giving the young child his lipreading speech foundations. The teacher must guide, the children will follow as long as the material is meaningful and fun. "It's time to play outside. Now we must walk quietly down the hall. Go get your coats and hats. Eddie, will you get the ball?" After finger painting. "Look at your hands. I've never seen red hands. Will you go wash your hands?" After awhile you'll have the child holding up his hands and saying "Dirty? Wash?" then "All dirty. Wash hands?," etc.

Each child should be given an individual speech lesson with amplification but this material for this lesson should come from the child's experiences too. For example: If you have been bathing the baby, work on the sounds in baby, soap, coat.

The teacher teaches the children to share by sharing things she has brought from home with them. When a child brings something you would say, "Karen brought her kitty to school. Feel how soft he is. Do you know what he says? Me-ow." Let the children touch your face as you say Me-ow. "Who will share his milk with the kitty? On the library table there is a story about three little kittens. Steve, would you get if for me?" At first you get blank stares, then gestures, then speech, and then language.

I do not mean to exclude drill from the curriculum. Some drill is necessary at any level. I think it should be used much less frequently than it is, however.

Further suggestions for conducting activity lessons are given in *Deaf Children at Home and at School* (Chapter 7). Points to watch include choosing topics that are of interest to the children; making frequent use of objects, pictures, etc.; keeping apparatus out of sight until it is required in the activity; dramatising certain parts to assist in clarifying meanings; using an animated style of presentation; having fun in the lessons; asking questions of the whole class to begin with and, after all have thought about it, to ask one to answer; encouraging the remainder of the class to watch the child who answers; asking the class if the answer was correct; improving the grammar of the answers, rather than accepting single words or signs; revising lessons in pairs or threes and sending to the children's homes or hostels summaries of major points for revision that evening and in everyday situations thereafter.

Individual Methods

We still teach most of the language subjects by traditional class methods, with the children sitting in horseshoe formation around the teacher. Some very good academic results have been achieved employing this technique throughout almost the whole of the children's schooling but more common is quite serious underachievement. We do realise, however, that children differ widely in their interests and capacities to learn, and in consequence, are becoming increasingly interested in the possibilities of arranging individual tutoring sessions in speech, language and auditory training throughout the whole period of the children's education rather than just during their early years. This is discussed further in Chapters V and VI. Most authorities seem to agree that daily individual tutoring sessions are valuable to deaf children from about the mental age of 2½ years. The Ewings (1971), Mrs. Spencer Tracy (1970) and Mildred Groht (1958), give much practical guidance in this regard. Two or three such sessions each day rather than one lengthy period are best if this is possible.

During such periods, topics in which the child has already shown an interest can be used. Van Uden's seizing method is very effective, or as Mildred Groht has said, "The children lead and we follow." The language used should be natural—as demanded by the situation—and not too simple.

> One should give ample opportunity to (express) the emotional content of the language, the exclamations, uncertainties, doubts, wishes, personal standpoints, questions, etc. (van Uden, 1970).

Do not restrict oneself to brief descriptions and statements—The dog is sitting, The girl is walking, This is a car, etc. Most children do not have sufficient interest in them and they are of very little practical use.

Conversation Methods

Britton, (Barnes, et al., 1969) in *Language, the Learner and the School,* after considering a transcript of a tape-recorded discussion on education by four dull fifteen-year-old boys, concludes, "Argument seems to have a limited value for boys and girls whose powers of talk are at the stages of those we have been considering. Mutually supportive joint exploration seems to be more productive."

Teachers of deaf children of this age have frequently experienced the dissatisfaction of trying to have meaningful discussions, except perhaps with those who are very intelligent. The result is that most teachers do not try to use small group discussion as a means of assisting the children's language and thinking. Perhaps the commonest way of overcoming our uneasiness that "I'm doing all the work and they're just sitting there," is to use questions as skilfully as possible and to consider it a failure if we have to tell them anything. We are still the focus of the oral session, however, and the children must as a rule, try out their ideas on us rather than on one another. Many of the lessons described in this book are of this type, but one feels the need to try to contrive more situations in which the children can learn how to discuss problems, often with us, but also amongst themselves. Language thus becomes a more personal and exciting experience.

In the Instituut voor Doven at St. Michielsgestel, in Holland, conversation methods *are* used from the children's earliest years and are considered a major component in their very successful language programmes throughout the school (van Uden 1970). Reading and language development are closely related, of course, and van Uden gives due emphasis to conversation in an outline of his reading scheme. The first step, using conversations, is to seize words, or gestures offered by the child and write up a significant sample, taking care to use colloquial conversational language, "Don't tease him Peter!" "Oops! Where's he gone now?" etc. The second stage, van Uden describes as "receptive reading" where the child is able to grasp new ideas through reading—first through guessing the meaning from the context and later (about aged 9–10 years) to read for information as slightly younger normally hearing children do.

Van Uden criticises reading material which is simply a series of logical statements in a rigid, nonconversational form. An interesting example which he cites (van Uden, 1968) is a story about a cat which jumped on to a table and knocked over a bottle of milk. "Naughty cat" the story and lesson concluded. Van Uden says he would have used more interesting material than this, but if asked to use this particular story, would have said to the children "I do not think the cat was naughty at all," and from this developed a conversation.

With dull deaf children or those not familiar with conversational methods, Britton's mutually supportive joint exploration is indicated. Examples of techniques to promote conversation and discussion are given in Chapters 7 and 8.

Story Telling

Deaf children love stories that are skilfully told. They should have a story every day up to the age of six. Telling and reading stories to them is an art, and suggestions for acquiring this are included in *Deaf Children at Home and at School*. Lady Ethel Ewing, a brilliant teacher of young deaf children, used the story approach in a great deal of her language teaching. Suggestions when using the story method include:

1. Have plenty of material on hand, such as clothes, hats, a walking stick, an umbrella, etc.

2. Plan the story in terms of action.

3. Try to present situations in problem form with the children suggesting the solution.

4. Use dramatization several times during the lesson.

5. Stories stimulate imaginative thinking and the children should be able to identify with the characters and so develop an emotional congruity with them and the story as a whole. This is phychologically and educationally sound. All the children should, of course, have a chance to play a part.

6. Use pictures and blackboard illustrations as well as speech and props, particularly for the main points. This helps children who lipread badly and those who have missed the point.

Ask the children to put the pictures in the correct sequence. This they can do with training even before they can read.

7. Repetition of sentences is invaluable. The children should be encouraged by the teacher and her assistant, to join in all the repetitions. This gets them into the habit of talking and to enjoy speaking because the language has become more and more familiar and meaningful to them. Opportunities should thus be taken to teach correct speech by reinforcing what is good with approval. The story lessons may go on for several months with the sentences becoming more complex with each retelling. These lessons with six and seven-year-olds usually last about half an hour. Keep the sentences natural and not too long.

8. Let the children talk to one another using the teacher's microphone. (This applies to all group language lessons, not only in story ones.) Moral values can be well illustrated in story lessons and followed up in real-life situations.

9. Finally, older children can draw their own pictures after key words have been written up for them, and can then try to write their own story underneath.

Class Or Group Stories

Another useful way to encourage the children and give them confidence to begin writing, is to produce stories collaboratively. At least once a week one class of six and seven-year-old partially hearing children made a class story in the following manner.

Put on headphones. Switch on overhead projector. Draw a grid on the cellophane, or on the blackboard if no overhead projector is available, to show the number of incidents in this story.

Earlier in the year there would be just four squares.

1. Teacher: What are you going to write about? (Several children want to start.) You start, Tim.

Tim: The big dog licked me. He jumped up.

(It may take a few repetitions to get this or any other sentence clear. There may be questions. This is omitted from the remainder of this description, but teachers will

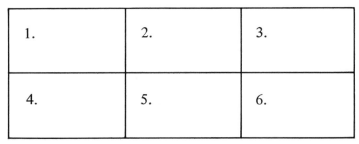

| 1. | 2. | 3. |
| 4. | 5. | 6. |

Figure 1. Grid for displaying group stories.

know how necessary it is and how much time it can take up.)

Teacher sketches the picture into the first square as Tim talks and eventually writes "A big dog licked Tim's face" below it.

2. Teacher: What happened next?

Noel: Tim fell over.

Tim: I'm strong.

Teacher: (Responding to Tim's protest) Yes, we know, but this is only a story.

Sally: And the dog fell over, too. Tim called out, "Mummy."

Teacher draws while the children repeat their sentences. He writes appropriate ones.

3. Teacher: What next?

Many suggestions come.

Pat: The dog ran away.

Teacher: What about Tim's mummy?

Noel: Tim's mummy said "Stop, stop!"

Teacher draws and writes.

Teacher: Let's all read it over.

They read with great energy.

4. Teacher: What next? Sarah?

This lesson was very much enjoyed and produced imaginative effort and excitement. Sarah contributed an idea for the first time. Later each child might draw a picture and write part of the story while the teacher prepares a spirit duplicated copy for each child to take home. The children's pages are pasted on to a concertina book. The older children can complete a story themselves if the first picture is provided. This same technique can be used for language, e.g. helping mother or father, cleaning the car, having a bath, or using previously prepared drawings of a story.

Using Reference Books

Due to the children's low reading comprehension, using dictionaries and books of reference in language projects or assignments is often extremely difficult. Careful preparation and active encouragement is needed, and even then it is a slow process.

In three classes for both deaf and partially hearing children which are attached to an ordinary school, the use of both dictionaries and reference books by the children has been achieved with considerable success. The children are aged from six to eleven years. Dictionaries are introduced to six and seven-year-olds in the following way:

A book of pictures is made containing, for example, a window, buttons, a lock, a drum, etc. The teacher goes through this with the child. When he can tell her the name of an object she asks him, "Can you write it?" If he says he can, she says, "Let us look for it in our dictionary." She finds the page and says, "It is somewhere on this page." The child finds the word. Together they read the entry and compare the spelling. If a child says he cannot write it, the teacher finds it for him if it is an important word. If not, she goes on until they find a picture with a name he can spell. Later the class has competitions finding words.

The teacher and children also work on alphabetical order, saying the alphabet and singing it; parents help the children by asking them to repeat the alphabet and to say which letter comes after another. Occasionally an alphabet sorting tray is used or alphabet games such as Spell Master.

The Junior Writing Dictionary is used to help children correct their own use of plurals, tenses, and adjectival and adverbial forms. As they come to need more difficult words, they use the *Kingsway Dictionary* and make their own alphabetical word lists for use in writing.

Books of reference are best introduced to the children in

meaningful situations, rather than as formal exercises. The teacher may be telling the children a story about a runaway train which went over a bridge and instead of saying, "I have a picture of a train . . ." and then showing it, she would say, "There is a picture of a train on a bridge in one of those blue 'Finding Out' books on the shelf. Who thinks he can find it?"

Reference books should be arranged on a shelf according to subject. In the beginning the children can only identify books by their pictures. Soon, however, they also learn to use the names on the books, and must be told to replace the books carefully after use. One girl is made librarian and she insists that borrowers return reference books to the right place. A little spelling is done every day and the title words of books are included in spelling lessons. This helps the children to find the books they want.

Longman's *My Home* series and *As We Were* are the first books used for reference. As the children master these they begin to make use of the *Read About It* series both at home and in spare moments at school. A step harder are the Ladybird reference books, first used as a source of illustration, later for fact-finding, with or without the teacher's help. Finally they begin to consult Black's *Children's Encyclopaedia* and similar reference books in the school library.

The use of the table of contents and of the index is taught incidentally. Sometimes these are made for books of stories and other collections that the children have written for themselves, and this helps them to understand their function.

Being introduced to the system of using reference books as described, most of the deaf and partially hearing children of average ability, by the age of ten to eleven have become fairly independent readers and fact finders.

Out-Of-Class Activities

If we can measure the success of a method by the zest with which children throw themselves into it, then the most successful work by far is that undertaken out of doors. A survey of school visits conducted in 1966 by Sevante (1966) involved questioning 147 class teachers in 39 of the 69 schools for deaf and partially hearing children in Great Britain. All but 2 of these teachers agreed that educational visits were important. For day-school children it was observed that a few days away from home, e.g. youth hostelling, were particularly valuable. Other comments made by a number of teachers included the benefit of taking photographs on visits and of having at least two staff members for ten children so that talking, observing the pupils' interests, and explaining, could be done effectively during the visit. Many children need encouragement to comment and pass opinions, which helps them retain many more details.

It was further observed that the almost complete deprivation of general knowledge creates a lack of spontaneous interest in many things outside the deaf child's experience, e.g. a visit to an historical site. This underlines the critical importance of careful preparation.

Nearly half of the teachers stated that they would have liked to have taken more visits, if it were not for difficulties involved with transportation, the school schedule, expense, staff shortage, the syllabus, and, in seven cases, county regulations.

Places visited by all groups are listed below in rank order within each group. (Figures in brackets are number of visits made in one year.)

SHOPS: Confectioner (69) grocer (51) vegetable market (48) toy shop (46) baker, pet shop (37) department store (35) bookshop (32) butcher (25) dry goods store (22) hardware store (6) supermarket (6)

COMMERCIAL PREMISES: post office (80) bank (14) office (5) machinery company (4) local government office (2)

INDUSTRIAL: consumer-goods factories (47) food-preparation factories (33) airports (17) docks (14) light engineering factories (13) market and railway works (5) laundries and gasworks (2) heavy industry (2) lumber yard, waterworks, newspaper press, paper mill, sewage works, mine, quarry, tannery, film studio, carpentry shop (1)

AGRICULTURE: dairy, sheep, and poultry farms (34) agricultural shows (14) flower shows (11) dairy/creamery (10) truck farm (4) nursery (4) ploughing competition, cheese factory, strawberry farm, orchard, veterinary quarantine station, parks and cemeteries department, cattle market, egg-packing station (1)

HISTORICAL, NATURAL FEATURES ETC.: beauty spots (49) historic sites (30) historic towns (30) churches (29) cathedrals (25) caves (16) ruins (19) stately homes (19) monuments (13) famous sailing ships (1) windmill (1)

ENTERTAINMENT, SOCIAL, RECREATIONAL: sports matches (71) museums (67) movies (52) circus (28) art exhibition (23) ballet (13) river trip (9) opera (3) orchestral concerts (2)

MISCELLANEOUS VISITS: nature study rambles (62) window shopping (49) railway stations (12) map work (25) carnivals (13) field study (8) processions (7) traffic census centre (4)

One of the most frequent comments made by the 147 teachers was that the behaviour of the deaf children on visits was "usually better than that of normally hearing children."

Successful teaching of language and of class trips in particular, usually requires careful preparation. It involves thinking well ahead, so that while the study of say, the life of boys and girls in Japan is getting under way, arrangements for the preliminary visit to the farm or the post office are being made, and film and filmstrips on camping are ordered for the project to begin three months hence.

One very important effect of thorough preparation is on the attitude of the teacher to that particular piece of work. Half an hour spent in the museum with a pad and pencil a day or so before a visit enables a teacher, not only to interest the class much more in what they will see, but also really to look forward to taking the children there.

One farmer who has frequent requests from schools for classes of city children to visit him, agrees very readily on the one condition that the teachers involved make a preliminary visit. Teachers are realizing more and more, the value of educating children outside the classroom. This is a primary reason for the current emphasis on home training by parents. The interest which is generated when children observe and use real things in real situations is far greater than when working only in the more contrived situations of the schoolroom.

A Check List for Teachers

Before the visit

Plan the trip with hearing children if possible.

Preview the trip before going with class.

Seek authority's permission.

Consider timing. Will children return in time? Will they become over-tired?

Arrange transport.

Notify parents and hostel staff well in advance of the visit. The children should help in writing to their parents and/or house parents.

Details of the group should be sent to the people visited, e.g. how many, what age.

Acquaint oneself with any rules and regulations of the place to be visited.

Keep parents, etc. posted on previsit activities and preparations and language being introduced.

Motivate and prepare the children by using pictures, photographs, stories, films, maps and models. Encourage the use of research techniques.

Should parents or volunteers come?

Consider the possibility of another teacher with special knowledge taking a lesson on the topic with your class.

Make a chart dealing with the most exciting aspects of the visit, but do not labour the subject either before or after to such an extent that children become bored.

Stress the importance of people wherever possible: their work, interests, and general lives.

Briefly discuss, demonstrate, and dramatize good behaviour and safety rules on buses and throughout the visit. Mention litter.

Encourage self discipline and responsibility to make the trip happy and not too regimented.

Will special clothing be required? Discuss with class what clothing would be appropriate.

In case of emergencies, is there enough additional food? additional money? first aid equipment?

Are toilet facilities and rest stops available?

Plastic bags, boxes, plastic (rather than glass) jars for specimens.

Name tags for little children?

Insurance for long field trips?

Any children unable to go must be provided for.

Older children may need notebooks for recording interesting points, answering questions and for communicating with the hearing children.

Help children prepare questions to ask when on the visit.

On the day of the visit

Check dress.

Check hearing aids.

Take photographs.

Arrange deaf children on bus and on the visit so that they can converse with hearing children and adults.

Use card strips for jotting down vocabulary during the trip. Some of these could be prepared beforehand.

Collect specimens, samples, curiosities, literature, etc.

If there is a guide ask her to face the children and speak slowly.

Try to keep the pace reasonably slow and supplement information given by the guide.

Encourage children to observe carefully all that is to be seen.

Emphasize to children that you are thanking the guide and other people before leaving and encourage them to join you.

Have fun. On a whole day trip, for example, children cannot be expected to spend all the time on the bus, at the place, and on the way home, doing scheduled work.

Follow up

Letters of thanks written by children and by teacher.

Praise good behaviour.

A group story and, depending on the children's ability, individual ones. Encourage related research. Models, murals, and books might be made.

Home/school notebooks filled in and parents and hostel staff notified of highlights or difficulties. A copy of the group story and other folders or pamphlets obtained might well be sent home. Some related activities might be suggested to the parents. Encourage children to tell visitors about the visit.

II PARENTS AND HOUSEPARENTS

IF WE HAVE NOT OVERRATED the contribution of schools, most of of us have certainly underrated that of parents and house-parents. There is tremendous potential in what sociologist Strodtbeck has called "the hidden curriculum of the middle-class home." Virtually all homes and hostels can assist a deaf child educationally but, one hastens to add, some need a great deal more practical guidance and assistance than others (Dale, 1969). The following notes were written for parents but they should also be helpful to supervisors and houseparents in residential schools and cottage homes.

Love and Understanding

Give lots of love, smiles and hugs; but when in doubt, err on the firm side rather than the permissive. Put time in on the child. Success is never achieved unless the effort is made. In the long run deaf children repay all the time that is spent on them. In adolescence, children still require much warmth, praise, and encouragement. With older children particularly, it is advisable to ignore slight misdemeanors, and the mention several at once rather than to be continually correcting them.

Hearing Aids

Be sure your child has the most suitable aid or aids. It is important that they are worn comfortably and inconspicuously. Check the aid's performance twice each day. Switch the aid off when conditions are noisy, e.g. on a long car ride; but don't take it off. The child's attention should often be drawn to every-day sounds, such as people's voices, music, doors closing, wa-ter running, dishes clattering when they are being washed, a dog barking. Picking out words and phrases in a book is also excellent practice. Teach the child early, to look after his aid, e.g. to switch it off when not in use, and to clean the ear piece whenever it is dirty. The child should always wear his aid when he is being read to and at these times speak within six inches of the microphones.

Fathers of Deaf Children

As well as noting all the other points made here, fathers can also help in these ways: By talking carefully and playing intelligently and often with the child and showing interest in what he has been doing each day. By listening when the mother talks about the child! By seeing that both the child and the mother have regular outings to places of interest and the child has good places to play. Arranging that the mother has at least one day each month (and preferably some time each week), completely free of the responsibility of the child, so that she can come back to work with him rested and refreshed.

Lipreading

Some people are twice as easy to lipread as are others. The latter, of course, make things unnecessarily difficult for the deaf child and for themselves. Speaking without voice in front of a mirror is a good way to test if you are giving a good pattern to lipread. Adult deaf people are usually pleased to be asked to advise parents (or teachers) on the matter of producing a clear speech pattern.

Language Development

Make the very most of daily routines for introducing, reinforcing and extending language. Speak carefully to your child in correct phrases and sentences, e.g. "Did you like the party this afternoon?" and not "Party good?" Encourage him to say phrases and sentences even though he doesn't know the meaning of every word he says. Remember to commend him when he does express himself properly. When giving objects to a child, always do the talking before the giving (Fig. 2a).

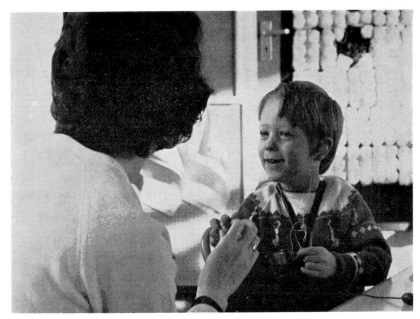

Figure 2a. Teacher does the talking before the giving.

Figure 2b. Making a Christmas decoration.

Keep Your Deaf Child Busy

Have plenty of interesting things to do (Fig. 2b). Make your child part of everything: let him share in housework, in play, in trips, etc., just as other children do. Be sure he has appropriate things to play with. He needs plenty of exercise. Try to make him the finest physical specimen you possibly can.

Pictures and Photos

Use snapshots much more than the average parent usually does. Talk about them and make books using them for illustrations. Some parents buy a home photo-developing kit. Wall maps of the world, your country, and of your town or district, are invaluable.

Speech

Encourage good speech rather than be continually correcting faults. Ask the teacher for advice. Keep a record of words and phrases your child says clearly and ask him to repeat them from time to time.

Liaison With the School

Send your child to school regularly and punctually. Each new school year arrange with your child's teacher that you go and see the class being taught. Attend meetings at the school, and at all times encourage teachers by letting them know that you appreciate what they are doing. Each time your child changes class, invite his teacher to pay a visit to your home.

Home-school notebooks (see below) should be filled in daily, and work given by the teacher gone over carefully each night.

Reading

Always have two or three books by the child's bedside. Get a library card and ask the teacher for advice on books and dictionaries to select. A blackboard in the kitchen can be an excellent help and some parents keep a pad and pencil in every room in the house for jotting down words and phrases and making sketches for their deaf child.

A Family Diary. If well kept is perhaps the best aid to reading for a deaf child (Fig. 3a and b). To begin with, this looks more like a scrap book than a dairy since it contains mostly pictures and drawings of things that have interested the child, with just a word or two underneath them. As the months and years go by, pictures, drawings, and photographs are used less and less, and

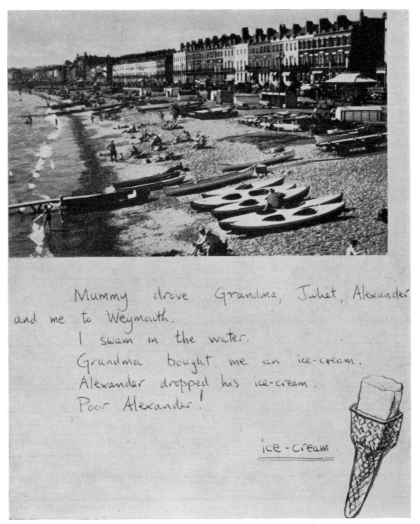

Mummy drove Grandma, Juliet, Alexander and me to Weymouth.
I swam in the water.
Grandma bought me an ice-cream.
Alexander dropped his ice-cream.
Poor Alexander!

ice - cream

Figure 3a. Family diaries are perhaps the best possible reading material for deaf children.

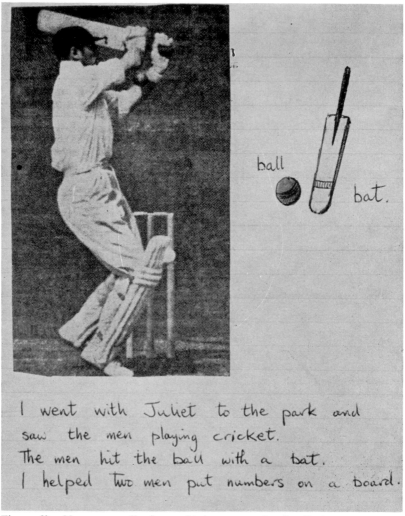

ball

bat.

I went with Juliet to the park and
saw the men playing cricket.
The men hit the ball with a bat.
I helped two men put numbers on a board.

Figure 3b. Newspaper clippings add interest to family diaries.

more and more phrases and sentences are included. The drawings need not be too elaborate. One can use stick figures for people and so on. Coloured pencils should be used to make the sketches more attractive.

This is an extract from a diary kept by the mother of an eight-year-old profoundly deaf girl:

Sunday 1st July. This morning we all had breakfast and got

ready for church. Jennifer got worried and said "We'd better hurry up or we'll be late."

After lunch Dad said "Would you like to go to Shelley Bay?" The girls said "Oh yes! That's a good idea." While they were away, Mum did the dishes and tidied the house.

We thought we would go for a drive in the evening to see Alan and Judith, but when we got there they were away, so Mum said "Never mind we'll just leave a note under the door."

At 8:00 p.m. the girls went off to bed, sleepy but happy.

Sometimes, a point can be made more forcefully to deaf children in writing than by merely telling them. An entry might be: Dad said to Mary "I'm thrilled with your school report about your social studies project. You must be trying very hard," or Mummy said "Mary if you don't come home earlier you won't be allowed to go to Jennifer's to play after school." Whenever possible, direct speech (conversations) should be used to describe the day's happenings.

The words and sentences from the family diary can be excellent for lipreading games and auditory training.

One of the best ways of learning something is to read it just before going to sleep. If possible, therefore, notebooks should be written up in the evening and read with the child when he or she is going to bed. Parents are in a unique position to help their children's reading by keeping these diaries, and every effort should be made to do so.

The Listening-Reading-Speaking Method. This can be very useful indeed with any suitable reading material. The parent reads a phrase and points to each syllable as it is said, with the child watching the page and not the lips of the parent. The parent speaks quietly while holding the microphone of the hearing aid about six inches away. The child is then asked to repeat the same phrase with the hearing aid placed within six inches of his lips while the parent again points to each word.

When the sentences have all been read like this, the parent can often go back and pick some phrases at random and the child can point them out by listening alone. If the child is very deaf, he needs to lip read as well as listen for this last part.

Music

Most deaf children can hear the melody of music. They should be encouraged to listen to music and to learn to tap out rhythms (Croker, 1967). Words of popular songs can often act as good reading practice as well as being another social skill that the children can share with normally hearing children.

Integration

Try to ensure that your child mixes regularly and happily whenever he can with children who speak and hear normally.

An excellent programme which actively involved parents and provided intensive individual tuition was observed in Minnesota recently. The teacher of the deaf, four four-year-old children and their mothers all sat around a circular table. Similar to Fig. 8a.

The lesson was on icing a Ginger Bread Man. The teacher began by taking a mixing bowl from her basket and putting it on her head! The children laughed.

Teacher: Is that right? No! Tell me—No! Come on mothers.

Mothers: (To their own child) No! Tell me—No!

Children responded as best they could two or three times.

Teacher: No, we don't put a bowl on our head do we?
It's a bowl not a hat. Mothers please.

Mothers: It's a bowl not a hat.

Children again repeated and were given the pattern perhaps five or six times. The teacher reminded one mother to speak more loudly and another to keep repeating the phrase several times. The activity continued for 25 minutes in this manner, with each step reinforced by the mothers.

The mothers were urged at the conclusion, to take some similar activity at home and so revise the language presented.

The children attended with their mothers for three mornings each week, and on Saturday mornings, it was not uncommon for similar sessions to be held for fathers.

A technique such as this could be valuable for older deaf children and in addition to mothers and fathers, hostel staff and school visitors could well be asked to act as helpers.

Guidance is needed by parents, but a great deal of understanding and appreciation of their difficulties is also required. Their special knowledge and ability to contribute to their child's educational and social well-being is usually very great. To live happily in a family with a deaf child, and to see him reasonably well-adjusted in the local community and finally to launch the child satisfactorily into life after school requires a great deal of skill, thought, patience, energy and courage. Many parents possess these qualities in full measure and have thus built up a tremendous amount of information about their children which is of inestimable value to teachers. Evidence of some of the pressures and worries placed upon parents by a deaf child, the need for teachers to listen very carefully to them, and the amount of encouragement and assistance required is easy to obtain.

Eight working-class parents of teenaged deaf children during one home visit to each were asked the following questions by a student teacher (Davies-1966).

What were your first reactions on realising that .... was deaf?

(a) Within myself I felt heartbroken. Her father died when Thelma was barely five-years-old. I could not keep it from him that Thelma was deaf. What with the worry and exhaustion through looking after him, my asthma that kept recurring, and now Thelma—her deafness came as a cruel final blow. To help him in his last years, I had to support his theory that she could be made to hear after she was older, although I knew there was no hope short of a miracle. At that time my feelings were numb; I had no time for self-pity and really, it is only latterly that I seem to feel sorry for myself and wonder why some people go through life without any major catastrophe and others, like myself, have an unfair share of worry and sorrow. But I pull myself together and think that perhaps it's not so bad after all. I have remarried and Thelma adores her stepfather who couldn't be kinder to her, and he is helping and supporting me in seeing Thelma grow up into an attractive young woman. I do have a lot to be thankful for.

(b) I had got used to the idea that Ernie was not quite normal, so my family doctor examined him, tested his hearing with bells, drums and whistles and confirmed our suspicion that Ernie was indeed very deaf. In a way, when I was told by the doctor, I felt a sense of relief; it was the worrying, thinking that something was wrong with the baby, yet finding the courage to face up to it and having him medically examined and being given the verdict, that was the worst part of the business.

(c) My husband came from a very narrow, religious background and they firmly believed that it was God's wish that Harry should be deaf and that we must keep him in the background away from life's turmoil. In their eyes it was wrong of me to subject Harry to the rigours of a hearing world and it was our duty to protect him in almost complete isolation. I was very angry that the hospital and doctors did not diagnose his deafness earlier.

(d) My natural concern was that Maureen should live; I didn't want her to die from TB meningitis—any handicap she might be left with was only secondary in my mind. She being only a baby and in the hospital for so long made me condition myself to the fact that she would never be normal. Despite this, on being told by the doctors that she was completely deaf, we still felt very shocked and grieved. In the war, I had worked alongside deaf girls and I got used to communicating with them. This experience gave me encouragement and I felt I could cope with Maureen's problems.

In what situation do you feel most for your child?

(a) I feel most sorry for Charlie when he is in a room full of hearing people. It is obvious he wants to participate in their conversation, and I know that he feels his inability to do so very much.

(b) Well, speech is the obvious worry for me. I hate to see Beatrice struggling with words when she meets strangers. She is basically very friendly and while the rest of the family is chattering away,—although we try not to leave her out of things,—obviously she misses a great deal and gets upset. I worry a lot about this. In every other way, Beatrice is a normal teenager. She's fortunate in having her sister Doreen.

(c) When Thelma is trying to talk with hearing people and she looks to me for help. I try to make her realise that she won't always have me to speak for her, and that it is better to try for herself. I often get upset by this.

(d) Harry is a normal youth in so many ways and loves sport passionately. I think I feel most sorry for him when I see him playing as a member of a hearing cricket team. The others are very kind and so often too helpful and it becomes embarrassing for Harry. When the captain shouts orders to the players and Harry doesn't quite understand and his teammates come to his aid, I think I feel more embarrassed than Harry. I know he hates situations like this. However, I don't believe in helping him too much, and I tell him so.

What period of his/her life would you say was the most difficult for you as his/her mother?

Five mothers replied that adolescence was the most difficult time, and two others stated that when their children started school caused them most anxiety.

Can you pinpoint an example of a situation when your child has made you feel very proud or has given you extreme joy or satisfaction?

(a) Charles was brilliant at sports. He was the perfect athlete and I felt wonderfully proud on many occasions when he has won competitions and been presented with cups and prizes. Another time I felt very happy was when he chanted "Happy Birthday" to me on my birthday. His brother and sister had taught him to say it perfectly. I cried.

(b) I get elated when I know Beatrice has done well at school. She comes home absolutely on top of the world if things have gone well for her. Needlework she does at school and cakes she makes and brings home. She's so happy and never dreams of keeping things for herself. She always gives me little presents—really rubbish most of the time—but knowing that she's unselfish is wonderful. I think I've more happiness from Beatrice than probably any of my other three children—only I wouldn't tell them this!

(c) When we see Ernie struggling with a word he wants to say and he can get a stranger to understand him. We know what a mental and physical battle it has been for him to master the word, and his sense of achievement affects us much more, I am sure, than it does him.

(d) There have been many incidents. Harry is so sensible and uses his initiative quite unexpectedly. When he was eight years old, he travelled daily by himself on the subway to and from school. He had self-confidence at a very early age, and this is so important to the deaf person. I am happy when he brings home hearing friends. To watch him enjoy himself at the hearing club never fails to make me happy. He is academically dull, but this doesn't worry me. I think he has the personality to get through life successfully, once he has realised his full potential.

From what source would you say you have received the most help in bringing up ....?

Speech therapists, friends, members of the family, specialists, visiting teachers of the deaf and teachers were mentioned. It is disconcerting that four of these eight parents did not make any reference to teachers of deaf children in replying to this question.

RESIDENTIAL SCHOOL MANAGEMENT

Factors which can mitigate against educating deaf children for real life situations when they live in residential schools include the strict adherence to timetable routines, lack of opportunity to practice the use of initiative in social situations, isolation from the normally hearing community, and the acceptance of standards of academic attainment and speech which are too low for outside use. Such factors can and do exist in day schools for deaf children, or in units in ordinary schools, but residential schools are more prone to them.

When children live away from home, every effort should be made to maintain a family atmosphere where there is a maximum amount of conversational language. In one such school in England where eighty-five children are in residence, they are divided into small groups each closely supervised by an adult who looks after personal problems, pocket money, letter writing, etc., much as a parent might. There is no assembly or ringing of bells. There is a degree of order; but it is obtained by everyone knowing what to do, everyone being approachable and feeling responsible. The organization is a deliberately loose one. The head teacher, for example, can be approached by any child in his study or at meal times just as any good and kindly father might be, without fuss or formality; and adults are not necessarily given priority or children shut out because a visitor has come.

All the children go out every day on walks, for shopping, or for some other purpose. They do have to ask permission so that the staff know where they are; but permission is readily given and those looking after the children would be concerned if a child did not want to go out. The children, as soon as they can cope, are expected to do their own shopping and to travel within the town by themselves.

Use is regularly made of other educational institutions. For example, some groups of girls go out to a hearing school for homecraft; some boys go to the local college of art to do cabinet making; and some of the children attend evening classes in judo, dressmaking and motor mechanics.

The children also share in the sports activities of the community with children from hearing schools, and many of the latter are invited to term parties. Local visits, short journeys within Britain in the school's minibus, and a long journey to another country are a part of the curriculum. A group of parents and other friends of the school help to raise funds for these journeys and often accompany the children.

Most children go home at weekends.

In another residential school, training of the girls in the attitudes and skills they will need in adult life, such as sharing a room with a hearing girl, living alone in an efficiency apartment, or running their own home and family, begins from the moment they enter school and provide excellent opportunities to develop useful language. Even the youngest are trained to put their own shoes away. The very youngest residential children are encouraged to help make their own beds.

Later (from about age seven to ten) in a dormitory of nine children, the girls, in pairs, are taught under supervision to look after their room.

Two of the girls care for the dormitory for a week. The school nurse supervises, encouraging them and showing them how to sweep or mop properly, perhaps reminding them to empty the wastepaper basket and asking them if there is anything else they might do. The girls are invited, quite voluntarily, to help clean, and take a pride in their own bathrooms.

By this stage they are all responsible for changing bed linen and personal clothing and for their small laundry.

As beds become available and children become mature enough, they move into smaller rooms of up to four beds. Here they receive no direct supervision.

In addition to this, the senior girls take turns in setting the tables for meals, which the headmistress requires to be done well. The junior girls serve at table and take turns, after breakfast only, in learning how to wash and dry dishes and cutlery. Before they leave the school the children also learn how to use a washing machine and gas and electric stoves.

Housekeeping and personal hygiene are a part of their lives, but there are also complementary lessons on these subjects in the classrooms.

Another example of a democratic society in action is contained in an interesting account by the headmistress of life at another school for deaf children.

> For some years we had formal meetings of the whole school (forty to fifty children aged ten to sixteen years) about once a month to discuss the running of the school, the children's problems, teachers' problems, or whatever else might come up. The children took turns as chairman—looking forward to holding this office as they grew older.
>
> Children had to ask the chairman if they could speak, and one teacher kept minutes of any decisions made. At the next meeting these had to be read and confirmed. At all these meetings the children could raise any topic, make any proposals or complaints, and there was never any suggestion of repercussions. They might suggest that they wanted some food they liked at home, or that they should write the menus out, or make a change in "lights out" time, or going for walks unaccompanied, swimming, movies, and so on.

New Parents Living In

One small day and residential school has begun to ask two mothers of children about to enter the school to bring their children and stay with them for a week before the child enters full time. They take part in all the work of the school. Each mother looks after her own child as regards washing, dressing, putting to bed, etc.; but the children sleep in the little dormitory with other children, and the two mothers share a room.

Such a scheme allows the mothers to get to know both the resident and nonresident staff fairly well, to become familiar with the normal day-to-day matters and methods used in the school, to get further insight into teaching techniques and language development, to meet each other and share their common problems, and to tell the staff and teachers some of the important things they have found in their management of the child. It also allows the child to be more sure and confident that his mother knows the school and personnel.

The teacher who visits the homes reported the parents as saying that they learned more in that week at the school than in the previous two years. The school staff is extremely pleased with the scheme.

SOME REFERENCES FOR PARENTS AND HOUSEPARENTS

Ashley, Jack (1973) *Journey Into Silence* Bodley Head

Bloom, Mrs Freddy: *Our Deaf Children.* London, Heinemann, 1962.

Burmeister, Eva (1967) *The Professional Houseparent* Columbia Univ. Press.

Dale, D.M.C.: *Applied Audiology for Children.* Springfield, Thomas, 1969. Esp. Chapts, 3 & 8.

————: *Deaf Children at Home and at School.* London, U London Pr, 1968.

Ewing, Lady Irene and Sir Alexander: *New Opportunities for Deaf Children,* 2nd Ed. London, U London Pr, 1961.

Ewing, Lady Ethel, and Sir Alexander: *Hearing Impaired Children Under Five.* University of Manchester Press, 1971.

————: *Your Child's Hearing,* 3rd Ed. National Deaf Children's Society, 1961.

Groht, Mildred A.: *Natural Language for Deaf Children.* Washington, Alexander Graham Bell Association for the Deaf, 1958, Chapts. 1–6.

Illinois Annual School for Mothers of Deaf Children: *If You Have A Deaf Child.* Urbana, U Illinois Pr, 1959.

Lorton, Mary B. (1972) *Workjobs* Addison Wesley Publishing Co.

Morkovin, B.: *Through the Barriers of Deafness and Isolation.* London, MacMillan, 1960.

Newton, Marg G.: *An Annotated Bibliography of Books for Deaf Children.* Volta Bureau, 1962.

Silverman S.R. and Davis, Hallowell: *Hearing and Deafness.* New York, HREW 1970, Chapts 3, 10–18, 20–22.

Spock, Benjamin: *Baby and Child Care.* New York, Pocket Books, 1957.

Talk: The magazine of the National Deaf Children's Society, 31 Gloucester Place, London, W.1. England.

The Volta Review: An American parents' and teachers' magazine, Washington D.C., Official publication of the Alexander Graham Bell Association for the Deaf, Inc.

Van Uden, A.: *A World of Language for Deaf Children.* St. Michiels Gestel, 1969.

John Tracy Clinic, 806 West Adams Blvd., Los Angeles 9007, California, U.S.A., sends out many excellent suggestions for parents of young deaf children in their Correspondence Course.

III VISUAL AIDS

THERE ARE SOUND psychological reasons why a child's visual sense should be exploited to the fullest while he is being taught. It is well known that of the five senses, sight is by far the most important in learning for most people. In the case of children with serious hearing deficiencies, the use of visual aids is clearly of critical importance, yet they are often not fully used. Research in the East German Ministry of Education Visual Aids Department, has shown that where lecturers use visual aids imaginatively in their training courses, student teachers, when qualified, do likewise.

Blackboard

The most frequently used visual aid, by far, is still the blackboard or chalkboard. It is recommended that all work be neatly and tidily presented and unwanted material erased. It is often useful to use two boards, one for the written summary of the lesson and the other for illustrations and explanations. The lines of written material should be spaced fairly wide apart so that sketches and definitions can be written above unfamiliar words and concepts as the lesson proceeds. Firm, clear lines and uncomplicated sketches and maps have been found to make the most impact. Practice makes perfect, which is encouraging for the nonartistic. So, too, is the fact that very simple figure sketches can be readily understood by children (Fig. 4).

Key words and definitions have more significance if they are printed at the same time as they are being said into the microphone of the hearing aid. They should be printed rather than written and boxed in to make them stand out from the

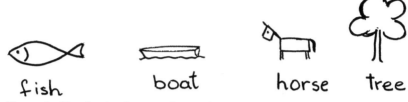

fish   boat   horse   tree

Figure 4. Simple sketches can be readily understood.

rest of the material. Some teachers make chisel pointed chalk for producing wide and narrow straight lines.

The use of proportional squares to aid accurate copying can be helpful if the material is not too complicated. The diagram or map to be copied is ruled up into squares. The blackboard is marked up into a proportionately larger grid and the teacher then copies one square at a time. This can be done quickly with practice.

Seymour, in 1937, found that a light coloured board with dark lettering was more efficient than the conventional white chalk on a blackboard; and both children and adults read dark blue letters on a pale yellow board some 15 percent faster than white chalk letters on a black board. This is possibly one reason for the current popularity of the overhead projector.

Adhesive Boards

There are three main types of these: flannelgraphs, plasti-graphs, and magnetic boards, and all have certain features in common. They provide a means of presenting information quickly, clearly, interestingly, and with considerably more impact than when using blackboard alone. Adhesive boards have been found particularly effective for use with young deaf children and slow-learning older ones. Preparation of items takes time, but these can be used on numerous occasions.

Due to the amount of participation afforded children working with adhesive boards, a class can be kept highly motivated for several sessions. Handling the objects and placing them correctly on the boards adds depth to the learning process. Words and phrases can be revised one whole syllable at a time. This helps the children to learn the words more quickly and to spell and pronounce them more accurately. Adhesive boards are excellent for emphasizing correct word order, and sentences can be built up after each child has been given a word or phrase.

When using this medium, objects to be stuck on the board should be placed in a handy position and in the correct order. Because of the need for earlier preparation, lessons become less flexible and teachers must guard against this. "The class seems fascinated by the guinea pig's sides going in and out as it breathes; but I shan't dwell on it too long, because it's not in my pile of stick-on-phrases." For this reason, adhesive boards should rarely be used in isolation from the blackboard.

One useful technique is to print the bulk of the written material on one blackboard (or on paper if it is to be used again) and to use the adhesive board for building a summary of salient points. A second blackboard can be used for incidental vocabulary.

Stories and incidents can unfold quickly and graphically when adhesive boards are used in much the same way as is possible when telling a story from a good book.

Flannelgraphs are the cheapest and most easily made adhesive boards, and are the most frequently used. In addition to flannel, felt, cheesecloth, or a piece of an old blanket may be secured to a piece of board about three feet wide by two feet high. A hinge in the middle makes it easier to carry about, if this is necessary. The surface of the flannel should be brushed with a clothes brush in an upwards direction to maintain its adhesive properties and the board is best placed on the shelf of a small easel so that it slants slightly backwards.

The figures, objects and phrases to be stuck on should be backed with flannel material before they are cut out and should be perfectly flat. Glass paper can be used for backing, but should be stapled to the figures rather than pasted to prevent them from curling up. If they are kept in a fold of paper in large envelopes they tend not to warp or become damaged and can be easily removed. In this way they are also more easily and safely stored. Cutouts should be drawn on fairly stiff paper. Blotting paper will adhere to flannelboard without preparation. Words and sentences can easily be written on strips of coloured blotting paper with felt-tipped pens. Pictures cut from magazines, old books and comics can be backed. Blotting paper map outlines are very effective; and pieces backed with flannel can include towns, mountains, crops and vegetation. Rivers and routes of explorers or characters in a story are well shown with brightly coloured thick wool and arrows cut from blotting paper. Allowing the children to place the various items accurately often arouses great interest.

Plastigraphs are similar to flannelgraphs except that a plastic sheet is secured to the board and figures are cut from coloured plastic sheeting. Plastigraphs are excellent for bulletin boards where the lettering is not frequently removed. They are somewhat "fiddly" for classroom use as cutouts tend to stick together, and the presence of any dust ruins their adhesive quality. The letters and figures can be cut very clearly and accurately, however; and plastic has a contemporary appeal.

Magnetic Boards consist of sheets of iron. The tin plate used in the canning industry is very suitable. They are often painted with blackboard paint. Objects can be fixed on to them with small magnets (pieces of magnetized metal $3/4$ inch long and $1/8$ inch thick). Magnets should be kept on a piece of metal when not in use so as to retain their force. The magnetic symbols are more costly and time-consuming to make, but are excellent for showing moving objects, since the pieces can be slid along the surface.

Pictures and Photographs

Pictures should have a special place when considering visual aids for children who have a serious communication problem. There is an enormous variety of them on every subject, and they are generally accessible and inexpensive; meanings can often be made clear with a well chosen picture when words alone can help deaf children very little. They are invaluable to teachers and parents of slow learning deaf children. Pictures can easily be taken along on field trips and local visits.

Schools, teachers, parents, and houseparents are well advised to build up first-rate sets of pictures. These can be accumulated gradually, taking care to reject any that are superseded by better ones. Local scouts, girl guides and church groups are often pleased to assist in collecting pictures; and local libraries and museums are also useful sources, particularly for historical pictures. To begin with, pictures may be filed alphabetically. Later, a library-type of cataloguing has been found to be better. Large envelopes are often the best place to store sets of pictures. Reference can also be made in the file to books containing good pictures and illustrations.

A series of lessons given successfully by one teacher of seven-year-olds was based largely on three splendid newspaper photographs of a mother polar bear encouraging her reluctant baby to take his first swim (Fig. 5a,b,c). The children were interested in the story; and when they went to the zoo to see their hero, he obliged by swimming a few strokes for them. They were overjoyed. Unforgettable experiences like these frequently lead to unforgettable words and phrases.

In selecting pictures, teachers and parents should look for those that are as realistic as possible and of good artistic quality. Pictures should be uncluttered and show clearly what is meant,

Figure 5a. Mother polar bear takes her three month old baby ("Pipaluk") to the pond for a swim.

Figure 5b. Pipaluk looks at the water but is too frightened to go in. (Photographs a and b courtesy "London Evening News.")

Figure 5c. Next day, Pipaluk jumps in and swims to the ball.

especially those to be used with young and backward children. If all one needs is a picture of a fish swimming in a river, that of a fish being caught by a fisherman may well divert rather than direct the children's attention.

Snapshots have an air of authenticity about them which seems to have a direct appeal to deaf children. Either by using a Polaroid camera or (for economy), developing film themselves, teachers are frequently able to use snapshots very soon after they are taken; and these become the basis of first-rate reading material.

Pictures and photographs can be mounted on cards leaving wide margins to protect the picture and to show it off well. Portfolios (two large sheets of cardboard hinged at one side) are useful when carrying pictures out of doors. Coloured pictures and photographs have rather more impact than do black and white ones.

As a general rule, reading, listening, and lipreading should be done *before* each picture is shown. If the topic is a difficult one, then less talking would, of course, precede the first presentation of the picture.

A few well-chosen pictures are often more effective in teaching than are a large number of less relevant ones. Children should be allowed to look at a picture in a general way for a minute or so, and their attention should then be drawn to the specific points to be emphasized. When using illustrations, teachers of deaf children should be animated in their presentation and focus clearly on the essential details.

Frequently newspaper and magazine cartoons communicate ideas more succinctly than is possible in words. The children usually enjoy copying them. A classic cartoon in the United States in 1896 was Tillman's allegory prepared for Bryan's campaign. In it a cow stands on a map of the United States. It is being fed by farmers in the West and milked by a Wall Street banker.

PROJECTED VISUAL AIDS, especially when in colour, have a "shock tactic" effect which should never be underrated both for securing attention and imparting information.

Movie Films and Filmstrips seemed, in Chapman-Taylor's survey, to be used rather more sparingly than one might expect, in classes for deaf and partially-hearing children. Both media were being used effectively, however, in some of the schools surveyed especially, it seemed, by some of the younger women teachers. The fact that children from the age of about seven years can help to handle the filmstrip projector is a point in its favour. So too is the interesting reading contained on many strips, and the fact that each picture can be held for as long as the teacher feels is necessary, or can be returned to if required. The report showed that no large schools had enough filmstrip projectors for convenient frequent use. The equipment should be easily and quickly available when wanted. The tape recorder is certainly worthwhile with classes of partially hearing children, and with a suitable amplification system incorporated, with classes of "deaf" children also. Experimentation using carefully prepared tapes, e.g. with the children listening to songs sung by a bass voice accompanied by organ music, while they watch the teacher point to the words, has proved beneficial even with very deaf children. Multiple choice exercises using three or four colloquial phrases have also proved very popular provided these children have time to practise regularly over several weeks.

Before a teacher uses a filmstrip effectively, he must be adept at teaching with ordinary pictures. Lessons can be spoiled by over-illustrating them—eight frames for a forty-minute lesson is recommended for normally hearing children. If a teacher of deaf children has great difficulty in communicating with her class, she might increase this number, but it is often preferable to use other activities between frames, such as dramatization, sketches, etc. When frames are to be left out, the teacher or child projectionist need only place his hand in front of the lens—in this way the pictures to be used in a subsequent lesson will not lose impact.

A recent publication by R. R. Bowker Company lists all sources in the United States which produce or distribute films, filmstrips, slides, film loops, tapes, transparencies, maps and globes. In England a nonprofit making service to teachers, the Educational Foundation for Visual Aids, has been established which inspects audio-visual materials and advises schools and other institutions regarding their suitability.

Filmstrips on a wide variety of topics in language subjects are now available. Many of these are excellent, but a large proportion of them are disappointing: some because they are older and in black and white cannot compare, for example, with the illustrations in many modern books, and others are less suitable because they have not been made with teachers' needs in mind. If it is not possible to obtain filmstrips on approval, it would seem wise to preview them at the distributors.

The slide projector and camera enable teachers and children to make their own records, and therefore are especially useful for journeys or for the study of growing things. A point on photography: close-ups including some of the children stir the memory and rouse interest much more than do distant shots. It takes determination to keep close enough to the subject on occasions, but this does seem to be one instance where half a loaf is better than a whole one.

Television: Educational Programmes

~ In Chapman-Taylor's survey of language—teaching methods mentioned earlier, a particularly successful form was based on the use of television programmes. Here, of course, there are the advantages of long and careful planning of the programmes themselves. The makers can choose the facts that will support their ideas, present the whole visually to make clear their purposes in the booklets for teachers, and reinforce their teaching in booklets for the children. An increasing number of teachers of deaf children are taking advantage of these and carefully preparing the children for each programme (See Chapter VIII).

Video-tape recorders have begun to show real possibilities for teachers of deaf and partially hearing children. Television programmes and "home made" movie films can now be recorded, re-played as often as one wishes and erased when the film is needed for more useful material. Video-tape recordings can also be made to provide lipreading practice and for research projects. Mosley (1974), for example, in a small study, made video-tape recordings of 14 sentences containing 100 test words. Six teachers were shown these recordings 12 times and a quite rapid improvement in early lipreading scores occurred. (Mean first viewings 23% and fifth viewings 69%). Only 10% further improvement occurred, however, on the subsequent 7 viewings. Marked variations were found between individual subjects—5% and 48% correct on first viewings and 54% and 94% respectively on the twelfth.

Audio-Visual Aids

One enterprising teacher of deaf children in Nova Scotia asked the local radio station if they would let her have a copy of some meaningful sounds if she supplied the reel of tape. Her recording of forty-four sounds included the following: ocean liner whistle blast; jet taking off; diesel engine, long train; racing cars; large crowd applause; large crowd laughter; door opening, closing, slamming; thunder; heartbeats; surf; lions roaring; dogs barking; glass breaking; firecrackers; phone dial tone, dialing and busy signal; phone dial tone, dialing and ringing; phone ringing; air hammer and compressor; and fire engine.

Presentation of these to the children with appropriate language and pictures, met with great success.

Language Masters

These are easily portable, recording and playback machines (Figure 8b). They contain a built in microphone and speaker. Recordings are made on twin track tape, mounted on cards—either 8 inches or 4 inches long and $3\frac{1}{2}$ inches wide. Teachers, parents, family members and friends can all record speech material which can be used for language development, auditory training, reading comprehension and, for the less deaf, speech improvement. To gain maximum benefit, the child must be as actively involved as possible. Even five-year-olds can place the cards in the instrument, and children can soon learn to record their own voices. Extracts of music and songs can be recorded to make interesting listening and reading practice. Questions and answers in language work or mathematics can be placed on one card. By cutting out half an inch of the tape after a question has been asked, the language master automatically stops and can be set in motion by pushing the card again when the answer is required.

Language Masters have been found to fit well into schools where the integrated day is practised. Children can work individually at their own pace and level at a time of their own choosing. When children require repetition, the machines, of course, have infinite patience!

Headphones can be attached which enable a child to listen at approximately 100 db above normal threshold of detectability. Where greater amplification is required, a speech training hearing aid can be attached.

IV ANIMALS AND PETS

M OST ANIMALS HAVE immediate interest for children and this fact is of primary importance. To care for pets is felt to be good for children psychologically and morally as well as educationally. Many of the animals' needs are similar to those of humans, so that while caring for them, or studying them, everyday language can be revised and consolidated in a meaningful and pleasant manner. "The rabbit likes lettuce but he doesn't like bread." "The puppy yawned just now." Pets may be used in number work. They can be counted, weighed and measured and calculations of cost of keeping and feeding can be made. In addition to the real-life observations of animals and their behaviour there are, of course, a host of delightful stories about animals. The Beatrix Potter type books are helpful in a rather special way since they introduce animals as people, with speech and personalities identical to those of human beings. The pictures of animals dressed in human clothes and driving cars and flying aeroplanes, etc., intrigue many deaf children and often give them their first taste of fantasy.

For a boarder, having one of his pets at school can often provide a real link with his home in a more tangible form than toys, clothes or photographs of members of the family—important though these things are, of course.

Keeping pets undoubtedly presents some difficulties. There are, however, a large number of animals that are relatively easy to manage; and with careful preparation of facilities (and staff), children should be able to bring some of their pets to school. One point is most important. The adult who takes the final responsibility for the pets, be he caretaker, teacher, housemaster or the school nurse, should be fond of animals and prepared to learn more about caring for them. Unless this is so, one should be careful about launching too ambitious a programme in a boarding school. Feeding and cleaning problems can occur at weekends and during holidays, but often children love to take turns at taking the animals home at such times. One teacher overcame the holidays responsibility by *borrowing* an animal each term from the local pet shop. If it was required by the shop-keeper it was returned. The children understood this 'fostering' arrangement, and very often, one of the children bought the pet before the end of the term.

Ultimately, as suggested above, the success of a children's pets programme depends on interest on the part of the staff or parents if the children are at home. This applies whether the children are deaf or not. If the educational value and pleasure which pets can be to the children is made clear to both staff and parents and an indication that some of the problems (such as housing, feeding, and care on the weekends and during school holidays) are appreciated, all are likely to accept the additional responsibility more cheerfully. The children can quickly become attached to little creatures if care is taken to foster the right attitudes.

Pets include mammals, birds, reptiles, amphibians and fish. Mammals have dispositions more responsive to handling and caressing than most other animals—on the other hand, they usually can bite, and keeping their cages and pens clean can be a problem. They are generally more delicate than other animals and comparatively shorter lived. On the other hand they breed more freely in captivity than do other creatures (if this is an advantage!).

Cage and aviary birds, being brighter, cleaner, and more harmless than the mammals and more lively and interesting than the cold-blooded creatures, have always been favourites as pets—budgerigars, canaries, mynah birds are popular. A bird table in the garden can be of interest. Feeding and watching the birds encourage language use. Later, the children can collect bird pictures, nests and feathers, and refer to books about birds.

Cold-blooded animals like lizards, tortoises and frogs, although having the drawbacks mentioned above, have advantages of their own. As a rule they require much less attention, are easily kept clean and are often able to do with comparatively occasional meals. Their very unfamiliarity as pets renders them extremely interesting to observe. Tortoises are hatched from eggs, while some lizards are born as perfect little reptiles. Frogs, of course, are hatched as tadpoles and only gradually become amphibious. Caterpillars, stick insects, ants and worms can all be kept without undue trouble or expense.

Finally, fish are particularly suitable for indoor pets. Their beauty cannot be fully appreciated or their actions studied in the wild state. They do need particular care, however, as the water in which they are kept is their medium for respiration and in consequence they can suffer more from neglect than any other animals.

In both day and residential schools hamsters, rabbits, mice, baby tortoises, hedgehogs, fish, goats, sheep, guinea pigs, squirrels, canaries, budgerigars, pigeons, bantams and chickens, ducks, geese and goslings have all been kept. Pleasurable experiences with pets at school can lead to life long hobbies and interests.

Kittens do not seem robust enough to stand up to large groups of children. Where there are only three or four children a cat and kittens can be splendid. A dog or puppy, too, may be quite happy in small groups, but can become over-excited and bite when twenty or thirty children all try to play with him at once.

Both mice and hamsters need cages sufficiently large to allow reasonable space for exercise. Rabbits and guinea pigs also need space. Commercial cages are often too small. Exercise wheels, cotton reels, etc. can be placed in cages and the animals will play with them.

A nature table in the classroom or hallway can be used to display fish and insects. Labels and information cards as well as seasonal flora make the table attractive. Interest can also be added by providing a magnifying glass. Simple suggestions are often useful in directing the children's attention and these can lead to further study and discussion, e.g. a notice saying "Watch the goldfish's eyes," helps the children notice that goldfish have no eyelids. The eyes are always open and hence the need for shaded corners and plants becomes clear.

Siting of the pets' homes is important. They ought to be kept where they are safe from rats and foxes and do not become damp and smelly. At the same time they need to be accessible. If teachers have to take their classes across a muddy expanse before they can see the new ducklings, for example, some of their enthusiasm for the project is bound to wane.

A teacher in London has kept a hamster in her classroom in a large flat box for the past three years. As well as learning about him, the children feed him daily and give him water. He is occasionally offered a piece of birthday cake and sweets, and the children even show him their paintings, toys and books. One boy likes to read to him!

A teacher from South India writes:

> In my school we had a dog, a goat and a cow, but because of the head teacher's pressure we had to dispose of them. I closely observed our children's affections to these animals. Marvellous! I think animals can express their sympathetic love to these poor speechless children, better than to us.

Observations by another teacher from Kuala Lumpur included:

> I grew up caring for animals so I like the children to have animals to watch and study but also to love, cuddle and care for. I have taught children to use bird books and binoculars; how to turn up stones and put them down carefully; not to catch butterflies or touch birds' nests.

> One very shy girl surprised us all with her interest in spiders and although I had had a horror of spiders we kept some very happily and spent a lot of time identifying them and building them a proper habitat. Greta became for the first time a focus of attention—it was lovely to see how animated and talkative she became. When she learnt about my (irrational) fear of spiders she warmed to me and showed much sympathy.

References: Public libraries, pet shops, zoos and Societies for the Prevention of Cruelty to Animals all have useful literature.

V INTEGRATING HEARING IMPAIRED CHILDREN INTO REGULAR SCHOOLS

"THE MODERN TREND for all the handicapped," Townsend (1960) has said, "is to try to keep them in their own homes and districts rather than segregate them in institutions. There are big dangers of handicapped people especially, becoming stereotyped and losing some of their personality and drive through congregating in big groups, where it is necessary to impose restrictions such as bells for meal times, bed times and getting up. Their life generally can be much more barren and lacks the variation that one receives in a normal home and street and district."

Tizard (1968) has asked:

Is it *ever* possible to give handicapped children who spend most of their young lives in special schools, where they mix mainly with children who have similar handicaps, the range of experience which will enable them, both as children and later as adults, to live satisfying lives in the ordinary world? Or, to put the question the other way: is it possible to provide in ordinary schools the specialized services that handicapped children require while at the same time ensuring that they mix socially and in school with the ordinary children from their neighborhood.

During recent years, in nearly all countries, more and more interest has been shown in the extent to which children with defective hearing can be taught in ordinary schools.

Director of Lexington School for Deaf Children, New York, Dr. Leo Connor, has stated (Connor, 1971):

I predict that one of the next large-scale movements in the education of the deaf in this country will be an increased emphasis placed on meaningful and effective regular school programmes for deaf children. . . . The concomitant task of organising regular schools for the advent of deaf children and providing the best educational services possible should be the major task of parents groups everywhere.

The manner in which children with impaired hearing are integrated into ordinary schools varies considerably, depending on such factors as the hearing loss of the child, his intelligence, home background, personality, the size of the class in the ordinary school, the ability and aptitude of the teacher of the ordinary class, and the amount and quality of special services available to him. The present situation provides various categories of arrangements for these children.

1. Full-time attendance in a regular class with no additional help except the use of an individual hearing aid and occasional visits from an itinerant teacher of deaf children.
2. Attendance as in 1 but with additional assistance from a visiting teacher of deaf children, or a speech therapist, or a remedial teacher once or twice each week.
3. Daily or twice daily assistance from a teacher of deaf children attached to the staff of the ordinary school in a small room or clinic provided for this purpose.
4. Attendance in a unit class for most of each day but integration in a regular class for subjects such as physical education, art and crafts, aspects of general science, and for technical subjects such as woodwork, typing, technical drawing, etc.
5. Attendance in a special class for approximately half of every day and integration in ordinary class for the other half, but accompanied almost all of the time by the teacher of the deaf, i.e. the special teacher and the ordinary teacher sharing the classroom for activity periods, reading activities, dramatic work, some aspects of mathematics, and art and crafts, etc. The two groups also combine for visits and outings (Figs. 6 and 7).

In the United Kingdom, Australia, New Zealand, and parts of the United States, over half the school-aged children who wear hearing-aids are able to cope in ordinary schools without a special unit attached, i.e. in categories 1 and 2 as described above. In the United Kingdom in 1968, 50 percent of the remainder were attending units in ordinary schools of types 3 and

Figure 6a. The moon (held by a hearing child) orbiting the earth (held by a deaf one).

Figure 6b. Deaf and hearing children can do science experiments together.

Figure 7. Severely and profoundly deaf children use their new group hearing aid for language work in an ordinary school.

4 above; and the remainder were being educated in special schools for deaf and partially hearing children. Twelve years earlier, however, only 4 percent of those requiring daily special educational treatment were receiving it in units and 96 percent were in schools for deaf and partially hearing children.

A number of considerations regarding the establishment of units in ordinary schools and other matters relating to integrated programmes, have been discussed in *Deaf Children at Home and at School.*

The most common times used for hearing impaired children to integrate, are art and physical education. These, of course, are subjects which require a minimum of communication. For more verbal subjects much more support is necessary—either with adult accompaniment to interpret necessary points and for pertinent revision of the material presented, or with carefully written materials and activities. One useful period for integrating is during free creative activity sessions where children are encouraged to talk. Normally hearing children, due to their extensive language development, are often more imaginative in their play than are the deaf ones at first. The latter group, however, aided by the special teacher or helper who should always accompany them, can derive great stimulation from observing what the normally hearing children are doing. One group of five and six-year-old children, for example, visited the beach. On returning to school one normally hearing boy took a crab's carapace and added some eyes and a piece of plasticine as a tail to make it into a stingray. A berry from some seaweed was placed in one corner of his 'island' so that the stingray could "practise his stinging." Another boy made a serpent from driftwood with sheep's wool beard, a ray gun from a volute shell, and some silver paper 'treasure.' This boy said that the serpent lived in a church in the sea, but he was a 'baddy.'

For materials, one teacher said she used virtually anything—cardboard boxes, cake papers, scraps of material, string, cardboard rolls, egg cartons, etc. Natural materials included seaweed, sea shells, feathers, drift wood, cones of various sorts and sizes, acorns and cups, the seeds and pods of various plants, stones, and pebbles. Supplementary material was used such as macaroni in various shapes, crepe paper, wool, cotton, coloured cellophane paper, toothpicks, pipe cleaners, cotton wool, paints, and glue.

It is significant that parents commented on the way these young children subsequently used scrap materials at home for such creative play. One mother said, "My girls used to follow me around, especially on wet days, asking what they could do. But not now."

Language possibilities in an Individual Integration Programme

In September 1970 a research was begun by Miss Iona Hemmings and the writer in which a study was made of 126 severely deaf children—64 in unit classes in 9 schools for normally hearing children and 62 in 2 day schools for deaf children. Due to a variety of psychological, social and pedagogical variables, it was not possible to compare the educational attainments and social adjustment of the two groups. Consideration was given to the results obtained for all the children, however, and these gave no cause for complacency—average reading vocabulary ages (Hamp, 1970) of under 8.6 years for the 22 senior children whose chronological ages averaged 13.5 years and speech virtually unintelligible in many of these 22 cases (Dale, 1971) (consonants 53.2% intelligible on average, and vowels 33.6%). Results such as these are similar to those obtained in earlier and much wider studies (Gentile, 1969; Dept. of Ed., 1962).

One factor which has a depressing effect on the educational attainments of the majority of deaf children is that most lessons must be taken with the whole class. This is largely due to their paucity of language and consequent inability to become independent readers. Class teaching, however, can readily be criticised on the grounds that it implies that all children will be interested in the same topic and will absorb information at approximately the same rate. It is easy to show, however, that deaf children who speak, say 3 times in a 15 minute class lesson, will often speak 25 times in only 5 minutes when worked with individually.

Although teachers reported that all 64 deaf children mentioned above were happy at school and had been accepted quite casually by the other children, only 3 had made *close* friendships with normally hearing children and in these cases, their homes were so far apart that no contact was possible after school hours.

Above, then, are some of the reasons why our interest is currently turning towards the possibility of enabling more and more hearing impaired children to attend their own local schools for normally hearing children, while we make careful special educational and social provision for them there. At the University of London Institute of Education, we are currently engaged in such a research. In short, 6 hearing impaired children aged 9 and 10 years of age have been transferred from a partially hearing unit to their own local schools. Each child is being supported by an itinerant teacher of the deaf who supervises their overall programme and gives individual speech and language tuition for up to 45 minutes each day. In addition, each child has another teacher for half of each day (responsible

Figure 8a. Parent guidance and individual language presentation achieved simultaneously.

Figure 8b. Learning to use a language master for individual reading and auditory training.

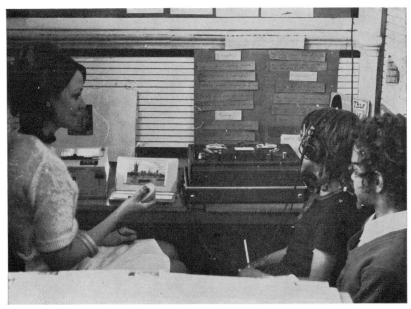

Figure 8c. A cine loop being used for individual language development and lipreading practice.

Figure 8d. Slides (and film strips) and a language master can be used for individual reading, language and listening practice.

Figure 8e. Individual integration programmes often provide opportunities for friendships to develop.

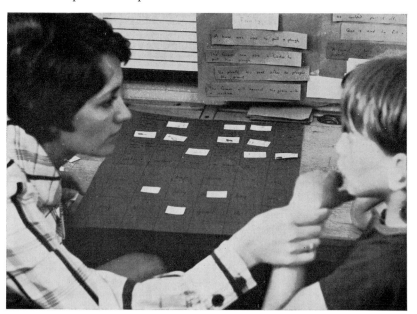

Figure 8f. Speech sessions are conducted daily.

to the teacher of the deaf), to help the child interpret what is happening in class and around the school; to administer reading, lipreading and auditory training sessions using a cineloop, a tape recorder and a language master and to send full reports home to the parents of each day's activities. The velocity of these children's educational progress (Dale, 1973) and social adjustment ratings (Rutter, 1970) (Appendices 5 and 6) have been recorded during 20 months in the unit situation and measures for comparative purposes are being documented during their present placements.

Results to date are most encouraging and a modified form of the experiment is to be extended to two other Local Education Authorities with a further 24 children carefully selected from a unit and a school for deaf children. The cost will be almost halved by including some children who will require less individual attention than has been provided above. For example, 2 visits from a teacher of the deaf each week might be made and 2 or 3 half days from the assistant teacher will enable the ratio of children to teacher to be increased considerably.

It is interesting that in one area of Sweden,* a somewhat similar scheme to the above, is being conducted, except that women who are not teachers are being employed full-time to assist each hearing impaired child in school.

---

* Discussion with Dr. T. Jauhianen and E. Nässtrom.

PART II

LANGUAGE TOPICS FOR HEARING IMPAIRED CHILDREN AGED THREE TO SEVENTEEN YEARS

So that teachers can select topics which seem to be of particular interest to the children they are teaching, the language outline has deliberately been made wide. There are, for example, far more topics in each section than any child could be expected to cover in any depth during a four or five year period. Although some repetition of topics from year to year is not necessarily bad, it is quite useful to regard outlines such as these as check lists, with topics presented ticked off at the end of each term, to ensure that a reasonable sample of centres of interest has been presented.

VI LANGUAGE TOPICS FOR CHILDREN AGED FOUR TO SEVEN YEARS

The following is an outline of different topics and occasions which can be introduced to children in the four to seven year age group. These will help provide them with a working vocabulary based on their immediate needs and interests regarding their surroundings and activities.

1. Current Events

At this level current events means any events that might interest the children: birthdays, arrival of new children, a visitor, a baby animal, etc.

News sessions— (use home/school notebooks)
Activities of prominent people
Dramatic and television items
Sports events
Fairs and Festivals
Newspaper pictures of animals and special events such as space and air travel, ocean liners
Seasonal activities—autumn leaves, snowmen, spring bulbs, fun in the sun
Seasonal events—Christmas, Easter, Halloween, vacation
The weather—Fine, sunny, cloudy, rainy, cold, windy, hot, snowing, hail, thunder, lightning

2. Our Homes and Families

Topics should usually be introduced in activity lessons or in stories so that the meanings are clear and everyday language is used in a natural and interesting way.

Teachers should consider how best they can collaborate

each day with parents and houseparents in using both home and school activities to develop social skills and language.

Cooking activities may be given more meaning after the first occasion, if the children make the cakes, etc. for their own tea party, a class booth in a school bazaar, or some such event.

Making sandwiches
Making toast
Making instant pudding
Making cocoa
Making jelly
Making muffins
Making ice cream
Making cakes
Making fruit salad
Making lettuce salad
Washing a doll
Dressing a doll
Making a bed
Dusting
Sweeping
Making a doll's house and its furniture
Packing a suitcase
Washing dishes
Washing clothes
Cleaning shoes
Cleaning teeth
Dressing oneself
Setting the table
Going to bed
Telling the time
Days of the week
Months of the year
Our near relations
The work our fathers and mothers do
Our pets
Making calendars or cards as presents for parents etc.
Our bathroom
Our bedroom and other rooms
Our home garden

3. Our Class and Our School

Our full names and shortened versions of Christian names
Good health—mentioning parts of the body
How we come to school
Foods—snacks, lunch
Sick children—visits, cards, etc.
Birthdays
Nursery rhymes
Good Manners
Dinner activities—table behaviour, waiting on others
New children
Children who have left us—letters
Keeping our room tidy
Visitors
Our pets and our nature table
Animals—zoo and farm
Our toys—indoor and outdoor
Visiting other classes
Exchanging pictures with other classes
Exploring the school—the office and the typewriter, the janitor's room, the classroom, the staff room, the heating system, the playground, trees, etc.
Making a book of photographs of the staff, with their names and occupations
Letters to members of staff
Thank-you letters to mothers for gifts, etc.
Games we play at school

4. Exploring Our District

Our street and village or town
Going shopping: using different kinds of shops, e.g. the fruit shop to check on names of fruits and countries of origin.
Rules of the road
Beginning map reading and making: making picture maps of walks, looking at a large-scale local map and "walking along it"
Things on the road: the post box and the post van (linked

with writing home, etc.) kinds of vehicles, learner drivers, water hydrants, etc.

Workmen we have seen: people who help us

Two of our local factories, firms or shops: visits with normally hearing children if possible

Normally hearing children in school and at home: visits together

Nature rambles in the park: collecting leaves, flowers, rocks, etc.

The post office: mailing letters, buying stamps

The zoo or circus: a crocodile, a whale—measure length in corridor or playground, a camel, noises of animals and birds.

Nearby places of interest and some of the people who work there: the docks, the airport, the railway station, the police station, the fire station, a farm, the seaside, other schools and other units.

Making Models

Using a basic map shape cut out of a sheet of soft board to sail model boats around; or show roads, air routes, towns, hills.

Our Daily Bread Project

(7 year olds)

Butter and Cheese Making

(7 year olds)

SOME LESSONS AND TEACHING POINTS

The Weather

Mildred Groht (Groht, 1958) criticises teachers who give a daily session on the weather almost as a ritual. She considers that events of significance, such as the first fall of snow, or a hail storm, should be dealt with, but believes that children are not especially interested in daily weather. Teachers who do not have more interesting material planned will often spend far too much time on the subject. It is, however, a very common topic of conversation among adults, and for this reason children should be familiar with brief phrases used to describe the weather: "It's a lovely day." "It's a cold wind." "It's raining very hard out there." "There'll be a frost tonight." "It's too hot."

One way of drawing little children's attention quickly to this language is to place simple phrases and pictures of typical forms of weather—sunny, windy, rainy, cloudy, etc.—on segments of a circular card about two feet in diameter (Fig. 9a). Attached to this by a rivet is a second disc of the same dimensions but with a segment cut out of it just large enough to reveal one of the types of weather shown on the disc beneath. (This is similar to Mildred Groht's "Functional Reading Chart.") The top disc can be turned around by one of the children to show the appropriate picture and phrase for the weather that day. Teacher asks the class, "Is Joan right?"

Children: Yes.

Teacher: Yes, it's cold and windy today. (Repeat.) You'll have to wear warm clothes when you go outside, won't you?

This takes only a minute or so, and more interesting items of news can then be considered.

Another way is to use a combined calendar and weather chart. A large calendar is made, preferably with a picture at the top of each page suggesting weather that might be typical of that month. A series of picture discs illustrating types of weather are made and placed on a separate board (Fig. 9b). Each morning, the previous day's weather disc is removed and the date is crossed out with heavy felt-pen strokes. The children then decide which disc is appropriate for that day. This large calendar is also useful for mentioning coming events and referring to past ones.

The weather can give rise to a number of new language sessions. A teacher might wait for a wet day, for example, and take the children to the door to watch the rain falling. They might put their hands out and be told, "The *rain* makes us *wet*." A few items such as plastic toys could be put out one by one into the rain. "The *rain* has made the *car wet*," "The *rain* makes the *truck wet*," etc. The teacher then asks, "Will I stand out in the rain?"

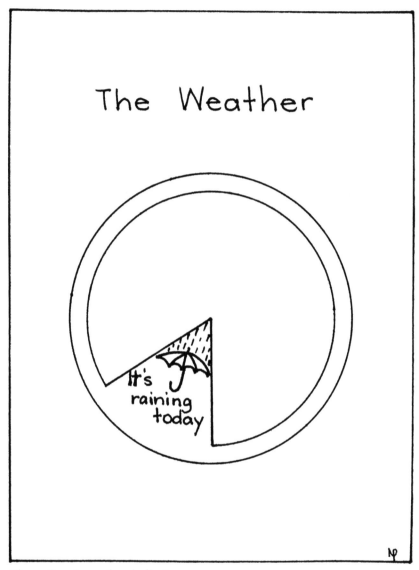

Figure 9a. A weather indicator.

Figure 9b. A weather chart for 4 to 6 year old children.

Children:　No!

Teacher:　No, because I should get wet. But if I have an *umbrella,* I shall *not* get *wet.* (Demonstrate.) Now, Linda, you hold the umbrella and stand in the rain. Is the rain making *Linda wet?*

Children:　No.

Teacher:　No, Linda is dry.

Point out the rain on roof tops nearby and if possible on grass and trees. When everyone returns to class, the teacher would introduce the following poem (the experience having preceded the language). Simple sketches should be used to make the meanings as clear as possible (Figure 10).

> RAIN
>
> Rain on the green grass,
> Rain on the tree,
> Rain on the roof top,
> But not on me!

Assemblies

School or department assemblies should be interesting, informative, encouraging and fun for staff and children alike.

In a nursery and infant school for deaf children with 28 boarders and seven day pupils, assembly is used to make announcements, to promote language, and for social training. The head teacher says, "Good morning everybody," and all the children are encouraged to respond. Next she talks about the weather, "Look outside and tell me, what sort of weather we have today?"

They look and say, "Lovely sunshine," or "Horrible weather," "Foggy," etc. The words to describe the weather may have to be taught, e.g. "Did you have to drive slowly to school, Miss Brown?" Miss Brown plays up to the cue: Yes, I had to be very careful. I couldn't see properly." Other staff members are asked; and the idea of fog is developed.

On a cold day the children may be asked, "Is it cold?" Resident children may say they don't know, so a couple are sent out to see. They report back. A blackboard is used for writing certain words and phrases and for little sketches.

Rain on the green grass
Rain on the tree
Rain on the roof-top

But not on me!

Figure 10. Sketches illustrating a poem on rain.

Next there is mail to distribute. "This letter is for a boy. He is in Mrs. Penhale's class. Who can guess who it is for?" They guess, and the letter is given out. The same is done with mail for the staff.

If someone has been to the dentist, or has cut himself, or if a girl has a new dress, that child steps forward and there is discussion. Thus some little personal item is talked about every day.

On Mondays at this school a point is made of mentioning everyone who has been good and has come back wearing his or her hearing aid. By praising these children the others are encouraged to use their hearing aids at home and return to school wearing them.

Some weeks, a little game is played. The headmistress, not looking at the children, says into the microphone, "John Smith, where are you?" He should be looking and listening; and he pops up and says, "Here I am." This is done with perhaps a dozen more. They all enjoy it.

The children are then told any news of what is going to happen during the week, such as a trip being planned. On a Friday, mention is always made that the children are going home to Mummy. What are they going to do—go shopping, etc? Answers are forthcoming from perhaps six or seven children. This does more than teach language, for it reminds the children of the need for good behaviour, of helping in the home, of friendship, and so on.

Birthdays are another feature of the assemblies. "You are *three* today." "No, *five*," says the child. There is a little fun, a little teasing, a little give and take. The staff often does some measuring and counts the years. Cards and presents are given to the child. Then, "Will you all please ask Mrs. Wiltshire to play the piano?" The older ones do this and everyone tries to sing "Happy Birthday."

Assembly usually takes about fifteen minutes, but it varies from day to day. All members of staff may take part, not only the teachers. For example, once the gardener came in to demonstrate how to plant bulbs (a teacher did the talking). The cook, the secretary, and the house mothers all participate from

OUR WEEKLY NEWSPAPER

This week we are learning about — ROAD SAFETY

Cross where it is safe.

Play where it is safe.

Bike where it is safe.

Keep safe in a bus.

Figure 11. Our weekly newspaper (6 year-old children).

time to time. The overall effect is a feeling of community, the beginning of a sense of responsibility for what goes on in the community, an interest in other people, and an appreciation of their needs and feelings.

Birthdays

The teacher should know the birth date of each child in the class. It is also important to know the brothers' and sisters' birth dates and perhaps those of each child's parents. The children's ages and birthdays are very important to them socially and emotionally as well as contributing to their language and speech development. Sending and receiving invitations, making birthday cards, talking about the party and at the party, all offer meaningful opportunities. The children should also, for example, progress from "I'm seven years old" to more accurate and interesting replies to the question "How old are you?" They can soon learn to say "I'm nearly eight," "I'm just seven," or "I'm seven and a half." In this context meanings of difficult words, such as nearly and just, become more clear in a natural way.

An interesting follow-up activity on one child's birthday in one school was another party to celebrate Baby Bear's Birthday. It illustrated that five year old deaf children (several of whom were virtually wordless) could enjoy and enter into imaginative play when it was presented in connection with a familiar occasion.

Another way of treating birthday activities is used by a teacher in Nova Scotia with slightly older children.

Three days before someone's birthday the class begins to talk about how old they all are. The teacher would then say: "Yes, Murray is five now but he's nearly six. On Friday (pointing to the calendar) Murray will be six. We shall all have a lovely party for him. On Friday, we shall have ice cream and cake." One child points out the picture of ice cream on a wall chart. On the large wall calendar a birthday cake with six candles on it is drawn. During news sessions on Thursday and Friday, the birthday is mentioned again.

In the afternoon, all the children were seated around a small table with the teacher. She briefly referred back to the morning's talk about whose birthday it was and got one of the class to point to the large wall calendar and the date. She then brought forth (from her little bag of goodies!) a box of cake mix.

From here the teacher began with questions to elicit many of the words needed when making a cake. "How will we make t..e cake?" (Opening the box she pretended to pour contents on to the table. Someone shrieked in dismay.) A couple of children made a gesture in the shape of a bowl. To the question "Yes, that's right, but what is that Oliver is saying?" no one could say bowl, so she said, "Yes, we do need a *bowl*. Can you find a bowl—a yellow bowl—in my bag, Oliver?"

The teacher next asked one of the youngsters to pour the mix into the bowl. "What do we need for stirring the cake?" Again someone came up with an answer, either by gesturing or trying to say *spoon*, and it was treated in a similar manner to *bowl*.

The teacher then put an egg on the table and said that they had to put the egg into the bowl, too. (She pretended to drop the whole egg in and they all cried No!) "Oh, yes, what must we do to the egg?" Gestures. "Yes, we must *break* the egg." "Here, Carne, you *break* the egg in the bowl." The she asked, "Will you *stir* the cake, Jackie?"

While Jackie stirred, the teacher watched with a puzzled look on her face. "What is the matter with the cake? It is too thick." Sarah said, "water"; and she produced a measuring cup of water and added it to the cake mix. As each step was completed, the teacher put the phrases and sentences on the flannelgraph easel and read them to the children. Finally the parents and houseparents were informed in the home/school notebooks of the new work covered.

A Nativity Play

One school decided to present the birth of Jesus with readings, mimes and tableaus. The ten children from the partially hearing unit (aged six to eight) shared in this by representing children of different countries coming to worship at the crib.

Preparatory Work: The teacher told them the story; and they drew it and acted it out in their own room beginning from the children's own experience. During the year they had celebrated many birthdays. With Christmas coming up, the teacher said: "It is Christmas Day on December 25th. Whose birthday is that?"

Peter: Mummy.

Sally: Mrs. Woosterman. (A teacher).

Tom (characteristically):   I don't know.

The teacher began to tell the story, "A long, long time ago . . ." and gave the simplest possible outline. She showed a picture of the stable and the Holy Family at Bethlehem. Every day for two weeks they gradually extended the story. The teacher showed more pictures and introduced new details of the shepherds and the wise men. On the second Wednesday the teacher used a filmstrip of the story. The class drew pictures; they wrote and mimed parts. As the children began to grasp the words and understand the story the teacher began to make suggestions for the Christmas play. They would be children coming from different countries to see baby Jesus. What would they look like? The class looked at pictures of children in national dress to find out.

Sally, whose mother comes from the West Indies, and Neville, a Pakistani boy, would represent those countries, and their parents were asked to help with their national costumes. Other costumes came from among the dress-up clothes. Tom became an Arab because that costume fitted him, and the others became a Scot, an Austrian, a Pole, a Welsh girl, a Dutch boy, and a German boy. If they didn't have the right hat they made one out of coloured paper, and they borrowed other articles where they could.

The children talked a lot about all this. They enjoyed the pictures and filmstrip, and of course they loved dressing up. In the classroom they practised going to kneel at the crib.

The Performance: On the night, the children walked from the back of the hall to the front and knelt at the crib just before the final carol.

Results:

1. The children enjoyed the whole project immensely.
2. The class felt more a part of the school than ever before.

3. There wasn't much understanding of other peoples or lands; but the children did achieve an awareness of differences in clothing and they did develop a friendly interest in children of other lands and races. It was a beginning.

The House

A lesson for five and six-year-old deaf children using unimaginative language.

Purpose: To reinforce in a story the names of parts of a house given the previous week and to introduce *the front door, the back door, Johnny* and *Jennifer.*

Material: Large picture of house, flash cards of names of parts of the house, large card "Johnny and Jennifer live in this house," pins, cardboard.

On blackboard: Johnny and Jennifer live in this house.

The roof is red and the curtains are blue.

The television aerial is on the chimney.

Can you see the letter box?

It is on the front door.

Can you see the back door?

It is a green door.

To call the summary of cards built up at the blackboard a story was stretching things somewhat. It was more a straight description of the house. If it had been made into a story—perhaps of Daddy painting the house; coming home in the car, putting it in the garage, climbing on to the roof to paint the television aerial, etc.—the same language would have been introduced in a more natural manner. For some excitement at the end, father could perhaps have stepped backwards into the pot of paint and/or fallen off the ladder.

Making Flowers for Mother

(Six year old deaf children)

Tell the children they are going to make some flowers to take home to Mother. Give each child a piece of crepe paper, whichever colour they prefer, and ask them to say which colour they have chosen. Then show them how to make the flowers, using flash cards with the instructions as well as speech to reinforce the language of previous lessons.

Fold the paper in half—this is done three times.
Cut the paper on the line.
Twist the paper.
Stick the flower into a paper doily.
Repeat steps three times. Turn the doily over. Hold it in the
centre and twist it. Cut tin foil and make a stem with it.

Author's criticism of lesson

This was a good topic for small children and 'all-in' activity
lessons are usually interesting. The teacher did not, however,
make the most of the situation to stimulate interest in language
by conveying the excitement of making a present for Mother.
Although she told them at the beginning, they did not grasp
that they were going to make something for Mother nor even
that it was going to be a flower. Reference to the set of family
photos on the wall, to one of the flowers at the back of the
room, and to one of the paper flowers already made, could have
made this a more meaningful and enjoyable activity for the
children.

Common Courtesies

With young normally hearing children, good manners are
much better caught than taught. One thinks of some schools
for normally hearing children where there are elaborate manners, but very little actual good feeling. Children, for example,
who would snatch away a plate from a child who forgot to say
"Thank you," and who wouldn't dream of passing in front of
an adult without saying "Excuse me," but would giggle about
the same adult behind her back. Unfortunately, deafness pre-
vents little children from acquiring verbal social skills without
their being taught. Apart from the ethical reasons of showing
appreciation for services rendered and awareness of other people's feelings, it is very important to each deaf child's social
acceptability that he has really good manners.

Saying *Please* and *Thank you* are best introduced in real
life situations as the need for them occurs. To teach *Thank you,*
a common practice is for the teacher (or parent or houseparent)
simply to hold the object given until the child looks at her face

and then to say, "Thank you." If this is done regularly over a period, it fairly soon becomes established. There is frequently the stage when the child seems to think *Thank you* is what we say when an object changes hands, ie. that he should say it whether he gives or receives. He brings the teacher a note from his mother; and when teacher says, "Thank you, John," he says, "Thank you." The teacher then puts a finger over the child's lips and says, "No. You gave me this note, so I say 'Thank you,' not you. You could say, 'It's all right,' or 'Fine,' or 'You're welcome.'" Little plays can be helpful to reinforce this.

The same technique works equally well with *please*—practised first at the meal table, when food is deliberately placed out of reach of the child. To begin with, one is delighted to have him ask for anything. "Butter," "Bread," "Peanut butter," etc.; but before long he must be taught to say "Butter, please," "Bread, please," and later still, "Pass the butter, please."

As with most other things in language development, one must not expect immediate success and must patiently persevere while keeping the activity as pleasant as possible.

Learning to keep quiet in quiet places; not to run too much indoors; not to shout in buses and to wait their turn; can all be taught through little dramatised incidents after earlier experiences in real-life situations. Stories and plays about children and animals are invaluable for teaching common courtesies in an impersonal way. Parents and houseparents should be informed of the lessons and stories in home/school notebooks and by giving the children little flash cards of the phrases used to take home.

Consideration for Others

This was a new partially hearing unit with four to eleven year-old children. The younger children, especially, were immature and lacking in self-discipline. They had to learn to accept one another, that each had rights but also had to think about others, and so on. Efforts, therefore, were concentrated as follows:

Giving each older child the responsibility of accompanying a younger child to the taxi each day.

Teaching the children not to barge in on others' conversations. Helping them to share their playthings and to see that each had a turn.

The teacher also wanted to develop ideas not only of how people should behave, but also why. This was often accomplished with dramatic stories.

This is one story the four to six-year-old children enjoyed and acted out again and again. Peter went out with his dog. Peter fell down. His friends saw him and picked him up. They took him back to his mother. His mother washed Peter. She thanked them and Peter thanked them.

The class made up many similar little stories about the sorts of things that might happen to children, e.g. squeezing a finger in a door, getting lost in the snow, running into trouble in a boat.

The presentation can vary, but one form is:

1. The teacher tells the story, sometimes using the children's own names (especially at first), sometimes the names of people in their reading books, and sometimes the names of other children in the school.

2. She tells the story again, this time writing down key sentences with little drawings—even for the under fives (this is part of learning to read).

3. The class discusses the incident. They may ask questions. The teacher may reply herself, but if possible she asks the group to answer. "What do you think Mummy would do?" etc. Or she may ask questions if it is necessary to start the discussion. In the early stages—with the under fives, for example—the exchange takes place mainly between the teacher and the group. As they make progress, however, they begin to answer each other, after beginning with some derisive remark such as, "No, that's rubbish!"

4. In any case, with each story, the children act the incidents. The teacher says, "Who would like to be Peter?" "Peter, where's your house?" As each character is selected, the child immediately assumes that character, e.g. Peter's dog goes down on all fours.

In the early stages, the teacher prompts them, displaying key sentences; and then they act it out sentence by sentence. She does not simply read out the sentences. She asks: "What did Peter do?" "Did he swim?" "No." "Did he fly?" "No." "What did he do?" "He walked." "All right, Peter, you walk" and so it goes on.

Later the children are able to act the story with little or no help—and they often put in additional pieces of their own, which the teacher always welcomes, because it shows they are thinking for themselves and have really understood the incident.

For the little-boy-lost-in-the-snow story, the teacher lets each child suggest an ending. During a lesson with a group under the age of six, two of them decided that father took the car to look for the boys, a third said the lost boy got someone in a house to telephone his parents, another said the parents went to the police, and the last that the child was told off by his mother for being so silly as to go out when it was snowing.

Another suggestion for teaching consideration for others and helpfulness is when a class has a party, makes a cake, makes a doll's bed, etc. the teacher asks: "Does your mother do this at home? Do you help? If the answer is "No," she then suggests they might do so next time. Parents have commented favourably on this!

Daily Routines

The daily routines in school, such as milk break, tidying up, getting ready to go home, are very useful times for teaching meaningful language. In this example, Monty, a bright very deaf four-year-old, has just woken up after the half-hour rest period from 1:00 p.m. to 1:30 p.m. He is lying on his stretcher bed, wearing his vest, underpants and socks.

Teacher: Hello Monty. You can get up now. Bring your clothes.
(Monty begins to look in his bundle of clothes.) Find your jersey. Look, what's this?

Monty: Jersey.

Teacher: Yes. It's your new jersey. Can you say 'It's my jersey'?, etc.

Classroom Walls

All available wall space should be covered with material which is constantly in use. When one enters a classroom in the spring and the autumn-leaves mural is still on the wall, one can be sure that the value of wall space has not been appreciated.

From about the age of seven years, maps of the local district, the country, and the world should always be available, particularly during news and current events sessions.

One experienced teacher who made maximum use of wall space with nine profoundly deaf six and seven-year-old children in a residential deaf school was interviewed and the following is an edited copy of that recording.

Author: Mrs. Jackson, behind this little table of flower plants you have a chart showing measurements. Could you tell us about the flowers and the chart please?

Teacher: Each season I bring flowers from home and we also grow flowers and plants. We have a primula, daffodils, and hyacinths. We have planted the hyacinths; we mentioned that we had put them into the dark cellar and the date and then we brought one out and measured it week by week. To teach measuring, you really have to have some meaning in it. You can't just say twelve inches are a foot; you must teach and show every few days that things are growing and are, for example, one inch high. Other useful language from growing plants includes "The hyacinth died." "I have forsythia here, it is just coming into bud." You have the language of saying that "It's coming into bud," that "It looks dead," "We must remember to water it" and so on.

Author: Some teachers are inclined to call everything "flowers." You seem keen about giving them the proper names.

Teacher: We always believe in giving the right name to whatever thing we are using, no matter how difficult it is. For instance, if you are using a tablespoon, don't call it a big spoon. Give it its right name. It will come back again later on, but if you once establish that it's a big spoon then the child has to unlearn that and start to call it a tablespoon later on. So wherever possible give the right name.

Author: There is one little section on television here, a picture and caption of a chicken just out of the egg. Have you found television a great success with the six and seven year old children, and how much do you use it?

Teacher: I only use the programme called "Finding Out" once a week (10 minutes). It's a good one. It gives activities for the children and also it is simple enough. If they just tell stories, it is an absolute failure for deaf children; they have got to see action. I find that in this programme, even if they are telling a story, they act it.

Author: Next, there is this mass of words here, verbs—all in the past tense. This is different from many schools so can we talk about it?

Teacher: Deaf children have mainly two tenses: the past and the future. In fact if you ever listen to hearing children they are not talking about what they are doing now. They don't swim in the swimming pool saying, "I am swimming," they say "I had a lovely swim yesterday," or "I hope we can go down to the sea and swim tomorrow." That is why I believe that the past tenses and the future tenses are more important than having labels like "I am walking," or "I am playing." We don't use them.

Author: Some of the verbs you have here, e.g. *smelt, swung* and *wrote* are quite unusual for little deaf children. I imagine this is the same principle as you were mentioning earlier, that you give the appropriate word for the occasion.

Teacher: I quite often find that although it sounds unusual, I will need a word like *smelt*. For instance, the other day we blew the candles out on the birthday cake, somebody put his hand to his nose, grimaced and said, "Funny smell— awful." We immediately wrote up *nasty* and *smell* and later on they pointed back to it. "We smelt the candles."

Author: A word about the presentation of new vocabulary. As a new word is needed, do you say it, the children try to say it, and then you write it on the board for them—at the side of the main blackboard?

Teacher: Yes, I always write it up. I have what I call a list of new words at the corner of my blackboard. We keep them up for about two weeks, but we also transfer them to our own little class dictionary (an exercise book arranged alphabetically). The children themselves write the words in the dictionary, taking it in turns. They say, "It's my turn this week, your turn next week." We have a record of the word, but we have no picture of it. On my walls, however, I have a lot of labelled pictures and that is one of the main things I use my walls for—a picture dictionary. One can never teach the structure of language through charts—I merely use them as a picture dictionary. To teach the structure of language the children must use the language. They themselves must write the sentences.

Author: I am interested in this picture dictionary. There must be two hundred words up here on the walls and, as you say, many of them are just single words: *apples, raspberries, sauce, scarf, duffle-coat,* but do you believe the little words like *is, as,* and *was* are best introduced from natural situations—the children being given them as they require them in their own writing?

Teacher: Yes. Supposing I simply had a chart on the wall saying "the same as Carol" it doesn't mean anything. Until they actually use it in a real situation it hasn't gone across.

Author: Looking more closely at your charts, I notice the words have been classified—food, toys, clothes and so on.

Teacher: Yes, I think it is important that the children should know all about their surroundings. Often you will find perhaps teachers talking about Australia and Africa—I know that is important, but does the child know what he ate for dinner? Does he know he ate stew? You would be surprised how difficult some of these words concerning foods are for little deaf children. Nobody tells them the words, nobody writes them. The children just perhaps point to the things and eat them. I find it is important that each day they write up either what they had for breakfast, or what they had for dinner, or what they had for tea. In fact, I find that these six and seven year olds take about a month to begin to differentiate between breakfast, dinner and tea. I find they are really beginning to answer questions when I can say, "What did you have for breakfast this morning?" There are several parts to that—it's a real question, it is not just a heading "what colour," "who," "when." I don't consider those are real questions, although you often hear the teacher say that the children answer questions when they can only respond to such simple things as "What colour?" If you are keeping this sort of language chart you find that such a lot of new words come in, *roll and butter, Christmas pudding, holly,* etc. Are you sure that Mother's going to write *holly* when that child sees the Christmas pudding? Very few parents indeed do that.

Author: When a child is asked what he had for breakfast and he doesn't know the name of it, does he run to the wall and point out what he had on your big chart?

Teacher: Yes, again they take it in turns. We say, "Elaine, you tell me this morning what you had for breakfast," and we point it out on the chart. You really have to do it. In fact, when I first started I had to take them to the meal table and say, "That's the sugar, That's the milk, That's a bacon sandwich," until they had really got to understand it. After a few weeks, when you have that sort of communication going, you can quite easily draw it and point to your charts on the wall.

Author: To introduce these various topics like foods, toys, and clothes is there a certain order, or are they all introduced together?

Teacher: The food I do daily. The clothes, no, they come up in perhaps a discussion of new things. The children begin to get interested in their clothes and so we have a doll's cot and also a little case full of doll's clothes, baby clothes and a grown-up doll. We also have all the things connected with the bed: blankets, sheets and mattresses. All these are labelled. They play with them and they see the labels and often I put them all on the floor and say, "Give me the mattress, give me the sheet," etc., and this of course helps in lipreading. We also go upstairs, make their own beds and talk about what we are doing.

Author: In the corner on the big blackboard there is another quite extensive list of words, without pictures, written up in chalk and headed "Our Meals" and "We Drink."

Teacher: I would, of course, put the pictures up, but I simply haven't got room. As the different dishes crop up at meal times, the language is introduced: We have spaghetti, corned beef, pancakes, lemon curd tart or jam tart. It is interesting to see these six-year-olds say, "Oh yes, I had the lemon curd tart," "What did you have?" "Mine was a jam tart."

Author: Would you say you present language first through the written form and then through lipreading, or the other other way round?

Teacher: That is a difficult question—which comes first? If I was there at the meal I would say, "This is a pancake. You are having pancakes for dinner." In fact I often still do go into the dining room just before I go home and say, "What are you having for dinner? Pancakes today, all right, remember and I will write that for you when we go back into school."

Author: Above that list of words there are further lists—"how much," "how long," and I can see from other things on the walls, pictures and actual objects, that you seem to be applying a number of new mathematics principles.

Teacher: I find the maths must be very practical—in fact it's the only way I find I can teach maths. We go to the shop and buy our sweets. In school we often count money. The actual choosing of the sweets is done by the children. At first I have to say "Come to me, and show me which sweets you want. Oh you want something for three pennies." They carry their money in flat tin boxes so that they can see it—a purse is useless, you can't sort coins out of a purse. Can they get three pennies out? Yes, I say, "Look. There's a two penny piece and a penny." Later on they can do that themselves. When they reach age eight I go into the store (Woolworth's I prefer because the prices

are so well labelled) and I say to them "You can buy something for five pence" or "You can spend five pence today."
So at this stage they have got to go around and say "Now
I have brought something for two pence how much have
I got left? I have got three pence left and for that I can
bet a bar of chocolate." They themselves at this stage have
got to begin to work it out. The mothers send them some
money each week. They keep their own account books,
and they write up each time they spend anything. Every
Monday morning they add up what they spent the last
week, add up what they have received and then usually
I have to come in at this point and help them do the sub-
traction. But by the time they are eight and a half they
can manage their books; and in fact, they keep their own
accounts.

In measuring, I find that they like to measure themselves and measure each other, but until you are actually
using it regularly with deaf children it is useless. Two
and two, I know we all have to do it and find it makes four,
but a lot of that is really hopeless with deaf children. They
are quite prepared to take 9 from 12 or 12 from 9 and still
get the same answer—they really don't see it, so that most
of my mathematics consists of practical work.

In measurements we don't go too far ahead. We weigh
only in pounds and ounces; we measure in feet and inches.

Author: There are two charts over here with everyday questions.

Teacher: These little deaf children don't even know their
mother's name. I ask them, "What is your mother's name?"
They will have learned that Mrs. means *mother,* so they
will put "Mrs. Mother" and "Mr. Daddy" and so I have a
list of questions up there: "What is your mother's name?
What is your daddy's name?" and I call it "Questions all
about you." They learn to answer, "What is your name?"
"How old are you?" "What colour is your hair?" "How
many sisters have you?" At the moment they call them
girls at home, you say how many girls are there at home,
then they will know the difference between boys and girls.
I then translate that into, "How many sisters have you?

How many brothers have you?" Supposing they have none, they have got to learn the word *none*. Next I go on to questions like "What is your mother's name? Your daddy's name? When is your birthday? Where do you live?" This last is a very hard question to begin with. Eventually, however, you can get to the stage where you can say, "Write your own address," and by the time they are eight I find most of them can do all that and I can say, "Address your letter to your mummy, or your birthday card is going to your daddy," and they can get on and do it.

Author: Observing you teaching, Mrs. Jackson, I get the impression that it is all a very urgent thing to you. The minutes are precious when you and the children are in the classroom together. Many of the things we have looked at, if they were used by a less energetic and imaginative teacher, might look a bit uninspiring, but at the moment it has all come alive and is very exciting. The whole business of language development does seem to be tremendously interesting and in fact fascinating to the children.

Teacher: I find that there just aren't enough minutes in the day, I get to Friday and I think, "Oh, I didn't do that, I didn't do this; how are we going to manage to put it all into Friday?" The children themselves at this stage are so full of life and they want to know so much.

SOME METHODS OF PLANNING ACTIVITIES AND GAMES

Nature Rambles in the Woods

The general aim is to develop a friendship with the outdoors, not through a show-and-tell method, but through letting each child find his own way to enjoy and become aware of the wonders of nature.

Too often when source materials are replicas, and not the real thing, the emphasis falls on classification and identification. This is necessary; but it is also necessary to provide a varied learning pattern. Through study out-of-doors one Canadian teacher tries to help the young child develop an awareness and a kinship with nature using his ears, eyes, nose, fingers and feet. The children become conscious of woodland objects, both animate and inanimate, and begin to want to ask, "What is ....?" "Why does ....?" "How ....?" as well as to suggest themselves "Let's do ....," "Can we ....?" "Look at ....," "Come and see ...." It is the teacher's task to help them ask these questions in conventional language. This she often does by using a notebook and pencil.

Ideally such an adventure can cover two or three days of living in a camp in the woods, observing such things as sunrise, the falling of dusk, sunset, the moon and the stars. If this is not possible, the teacher must improvise with field trips, supplemented with stories, pictures, films and objects.

Lesson 1

In preparing a class of seven-year-old deaf children for a field trip, I first bring to the classroom a budgie in a cage and a goldfish in a bowl. After observing these, we talk about them as to where they live, what they eat, who cares for them. This leads into a discussion of where we live, what we eat, and who cares for us. Objects in the classroom provide illustrations for this discussion.

The children are told of the forthcoming trip to the woods. They are shown photos taken earlier, pictures, and books, what the woods are, and what they might see there. At this point the children may be eager to tell of any previous experiences they may have had with the woods, either at school or at home. Next a movie of filmstrip dealing with nature in a wooded area is shown. Following this, the children tell what they had seen in the film or strip. Their observations would be a guide to directing them toward discoveries in the woods the next day. Did they notice how big a tree can be? where the tiny spider lives? how quickly fish swim?, etc.

A language story written on Bristol board and illustrated with pictures and map is then presented. The story might be as follows:

We are going to the woods tomorrow.
We will go early in the morning.
We will wear play clothes.

Mrs. Willis (the teacher's helper, or a parent, or one of the dormitory staff who loves the children and is free to come) will come with us.

Mrs. Daniels will drive us in the car.

For dinner we will cook hot dogs. We will have cheese, milk, apples and cookies, too.

It will be lovely, *but* we must be careful.

Don't run away in the woods.

Don't get lost.

This little story can be taught using the listening-reading-speaking method (Chapter I). Practice of lipreading and speech occur incidently as the story is taught. Through the use of a simple map, the children see where we are going to go.

To further illustrate the story and what will take place, the children can act out the story, getting dressed in imaginary play clothes and packing a picnic basket with imitation objects. This brings in the concept of time, and language structures of what, when, and how, although this will not be taught formally at this time.

Individual tablework, such as stencils of the woods and woodland creatures, are prepared for the children to colour.

Notes are previously sent to parents and houseparents telling of the trip and providing them with some information useful for reinforcement and follow up outside the classroom.

Lesson 2

On the day of the trip each child is checked to see that he is properly dressed, and that his hearing-aid is in working order. The teacher takes with her the lunch, a camera, plastic containers for samples, notebook, felt pen and pencil.

As the class is driven to its destination, the route is followed on the map. When the children leave the car, although they must be allowed discovery on their own, it is important that they realise the necessity for staying together and within close range of the teacher.

Help the children to discover.

"Do trees always stand still?" "Close your eyes, turn circles under the trees then look up at the whirl of leaves."

A leaf drops on a child's face. "Trees *do,* do things."
Play tree games. Stretch arms wide for spring, fold them for
winter, bend the tree as the winds blows, flutter fallen
leaves.
A fallen tree covered with fungi. Will they ask, "What is it?
Why?" Play on it like a piano.
Someone finds a spider. Watch its actions and movements.
A bird? Where is its home? Why isn't it in a cage? A rab-
bit. Why doesn't it wait? A fish? How quickly it moves!
And so on as they come upon different treasures.

Six or eight photographs are taken of significant points of
greatest interest to the children. Constant use of the note pad
and pencil helps them name their discoveries and keeps a record for the teacher when back in the classroom. Each child is
given a note of at least one phrase or sentence he has brought
forward spontaneously.

At meal time, gather wood for a fire. Everyone can help in
some way, even if it is just finding his or her own stick on which
to cook a hot dog. Constantly encourage spontaneous conversation. These activities help the children realise the need for
group participation, politeness, and helpfulness, as well as the
need for prudence and fire prevention, following safety rules
and leaving an area clean.

Even the very smell of wood burning will be unknown to
some of the children. Things like this are brought to their attention.

For children of this age, a rest on blankets spread on the
ground is often welcome when lunch is finished. Afterwards
continue with the explorations.

A spider? "It's Daddy Longlegs."
Lie in a spruce bed, smell the needles, look at the sky through
the branches.
Crawl in, up, around, under, over things.
Locate tiny creatures in various hiding places.
Listen to the sounds. "Can you hear ....?" "It's a
................."
Shadows in the morning, at noon, in the afternoon would
be drawn to their attention.

Encourage them to discover, to watch, to feel. The teacher should continually be taking pictures when the child is unaware and is not posing for the shot.

When it comes time to go back, will each child have an appreciation of the wonders of the woods in a way no nature book or film could impart? Hopefully, such adventures will help the child begin to develop a kinship with the woods, an awareness of nature, and a friendship with the outdoors.

Notes are made for parents and houseparents in the home/school notebooks about the points which each child tells the teacher or the helper were most interesting. The less able children, of course, cannot understand what is required of them, and one must write what one has observed them to be interested in, and use a sketch or two to try to help them understand.

Lesson 3

Back in the classroom the next day, pictures and stories help the children to relive the experiences. Once again, the story taken the first day is reviewed, and verbs changed to the past tense. The route taken is located again; and we talk about the distance and the time to go and come back.

In books we find other pictures of what we had seen. The pictures of the class's personal experiences are used to create our story in a storybook album, e.g. a picture of Jimmy with the spider. Under it the caption, "Jimmy found Daddy Long-legs."

Projects such as drawing their own pictures, creating forest creatures from various materials, and simple map work might be started.

We talk again about the house pets and compare them with the animals found in the forest.

The LRS method is used to associate language meaning and understanding of the pictures in the album. Speech practices and drills are referred to often. The storybook album provides a common place for all the class to label, study, and classify, and to talk about time and time again.

COMMENT: It is appreciated that some of the questions

asked in this series of three lessons will be difficult for very deaf children to understand immediately. "Do trees always stand still?" would be beyond many six-year-olds. If just one or two can capture the excitement of the illusion that by making themselves giddy and looking up, they can "Make the tree turn!" however, it helps them enter the world of fantasy and become aware that there are different planes of thought from the purely practical.

Another point which becomes clear is that a great deal of thought, preparation, and energy is required of the teacher. There is no escaping this, if one wishes to obtain the desired results with the children and to derive real satisfaction from teaching them.

Making Butter

This can be good fun for children of any age from about six years upwards. For older children, it can be an excellent preliminary to visiting a dairy factory, as will be seen later. Preparation involves bringing to school a pound or half-pound packet of butter, sufficient thick slices of bread to give each child a quarter of a slice, a half-pint carton of cream which has been out of the refrigerator for at least twenty-four hours, two half-pound jars, one with a screw-type lid, some salt, a jug of water, a small mixing bowl, a plate, a table knife, and a teaspoon.

On the blackboard, overhead projector, or paper turn-over sheet, the teacher of six or seven-year-old children could have written

Making butter

Pour some cream in the jar.
Screw the lid on tightly.
Shake the jar.
Has the cream changed to butter yet?
Shake it for a long time.
Now the cream has changed to butter.
Pour off the buttermilk.
Add half a teaspoon of salt.
Wash the butter twice.
Spread it on some bread and try it.

(With little children who have very limited language, just "Pour the cream in the jar, shake the jar, add salt, and eat the butter" would be sufficient written material.)

All the apparatus needed during the lesson has been carefully concealed on a side table; only the reading sheet is on view at the beginning. The activity lesson runs as follows:

The teacher reads the summary from the reading sheet, at a shade slower than normal speed, tapping each syllable as she says it. The children then read this after her, line by line, as best they can. This is partly to focus their attention a little more accurately on the vocabulary and language forms which are to be considered during the lesson, partly to aid the children who are poor lipreaders, and partly to get the whole class participating orally at an early stage—a sort of "pipe opener." One wants them to think about the sense of the words and the passage as a whole, to say as much as they can, to use plenty of voice, and to derive pleasure from doing so.

Next, go over the passage again, to tease out the meaning as precisely as possible. (The problem of catering to various levels of ability which exist in virtually every class is, as suggested earlier, a real disadvantage in group lessons such as this. One must be careful to remember that largely by skilful questioning, and individual follow-up work, one can often help keep the brightest and the least able children in the class extended and interested.)

During this reading-for-meaning session, the teacher should try never to do anything for the children if they can reasonably be expected to do it themselves, and also to try to tell them as little as possible. This slows lessons down, especially while children are getting used to this approach, but eventually it pays off. In considering the title "Making Butter," the word *making* is too difficult for these little children either to work out for themselves or even to have explained to them. It is better just said, and left. It will come up often in the future, because we are going to be making cakes, making beds, making a doll's house and a host of other things. Gradually its meaning will become apparent, as it did to those of us with normal hearing, and will require a minimum of specific teaching; so too with *is* and *as, of,* etc. The meaning of *butter,* on the other hand, is, of course, of quite critical importance.

Teacher takes a piece of coloured chalk, underlines the word *butter* and asks, "What is butter?" One or two may know and begin to make "spreading" gestures. If not, the teacher might say, "Yes, you do. You know what butter is. At home when you have breakfast, you take some bread and a knife and ....?" If there is still no response, quickly pick up a piece of bread and the knife from the side table and sit at the little table in the middle of the semicircle of children and say, "Here is my bread and my knife. What else do I need?" The spreading gestures are highly likely to appear and the teacher is able to prompt the children and say, "Yes, I want to spread—what?" One or two children may then try to say *butter.* If not, the teacher could assume that although the children knew what was being talked about, they did not know the word and so should be told it two or three times, and then be shown it again in the title, and be asked to try and say it.

"There is some *butter* on my table. Who could bring the *butter* for me?" No response from the class, so teacher repeats question, this time with an indicative glance (but not a gesture with the hands) toward the table as she says it. "All right Jimmy, you go and bring me the *butter* from my table." As he goes, "Jimmy is going to bring some *butter*—you watch." Hopefully, Jimmy will select the butter from the items on the table; but if not, the teacher would say to the rest of the class, "Is that *butter*?" (Holding up the plate Jimmy has brought.) "No. That's not butter," and to save further delay, would go and select the butter herself.

If the class proves to be as difficult to teach as this class has been so far, the teacher might well say to herself at this stage, "I've pitched the work too high for the class, so on this first occasion I shall work along faster, doing, and showing the children more than is desirable, just so that I can maintain their interest; and will depend on the second, third, and fourth revisions of the lesson to get real pupil participation." She would then say to the class "We're going to *make* some *butter*—you watch."

The teacher then puts the cream and the jar on the little table and says, "We've got to *pour cream* in the jar." She indicates this on the written sheet and asks, "Who can *pour* the *cream* in the *jar?*" Although the children cannot lipread this question at all well, they have a fair idea what the action will be. A volunteer stands at the back so that all the children can see what she is doing, and after taking the lid off the cream carton, is told, "Not all of it, Mary, only half." She does not understand and tries to pour the whole amount out. She is stopped halfway and told, "There. That's right, just half." Teacher shows her halfway down the carton and says again, "Not *all* of the *cream* just *half* of it."

Teacher picks up the lid of the jar and asks, "What shall we do now?" The class excitedly begins to gesture twisting the lid and when all have seen what is to happen are told, "Yes. We'll screw the *lid* on tightly. Look at it here" (Pointing to the written summary.) "*Screw* the lid on *tightly.*" "You come and screw the lid on tightly, Peter." "What is he doing?" "Yes, he's screwing the lid on tightly." Peter does not get the lid really tight so the class is asked again, "Is that tight?"—showing them with finger and thumb that it is loose. Teacher tightens the lid and says, "That's *tight.* Now we must *shake* the *jar.* Can you shake the jar, Jennifer?" Jennifer begins to unscrew the lid. "No, don't unscrew it. *Shake* it." This time she tilts the jar from side to side. Teacher, "Yes, but much faster." Turns are taken at shaking the jar until finally the cream breaks and then turns to butter.

The children are given time to wonder at this quite dramatic little event, and reference is then made to the packet of butter and half carton of cream and to the sentence, "The cream has changed to butter."

The buttermilk is poured off and "add half a teaspoon of *salt*" is considered. Salt is understood by three of the class when "salt and pepper" is said. The remainder need no further explanation after a quick sketch of a table containing two salt and pepper containers. Mary is asked to add *half* a teaspoon of salt and she is reminded of half a carton of cream.

"Is the butter finished now?" teacher inquires. "Yes" say

three, "No" says one, and the four others do not understand the question. The child who said the butter was not finished said (in gestures) that we must stir it.

"No," says the teacher. "Look at the page up here." "Wash" says Susan. The teacher agrees and holds out the water jug to Susan. Jennifer is asked to *"shake* the jar" and is able to do so at the first asking this time. The word *twice* is now underlined and teacher explains it means two times and writes this above the word in coloured chalk.

The butter is finally spread on the small pieces of bread and teacher writes *eat* above the word *try* and the children are quick to oblige.

In their home/school notebooks that afternoon the teacher writes: "We made some butter in a jar today. I shall tell you more about it tomorrow."

The following day the children were able to go through the steps of making butter very readily indeed and the teacher was able to concentrate more on asking them to lipread the phrase. and try to identify them by listening alone. Each sentence had been run off on the spirit duplicator and the children took home those which they could say fairly well and could understand.

On the third day, after a brief revision as before, variations were included such as: "What other things do we shake?" "How much water do we use in the jar?" It is seen that it is less than a *half.*

"Small," John says and teacher agrees, saying it is about *one third.* The fraction 1/3 is written and the children are encouraged to see that the amount of water in the jar is about 1/3 of the way up the side and three equal measurements are taken to reach the top. The whole passage is written into the home/school notebooks and at the bottom is added "Tomorrow we shall be making jelly."

A Visit to the Bus Depot
(Seven nine-year-old deaf children)

From some general discussion, the teacher realised that these children had no idea what a bus or a bus driver did all day. He made a preliminary visit to the local bus depot and the project was discussed. Some of the children who came in taxis passed a big bus depot, so the depot was sketched on the board. Those who had passed it knew what it was. The teacher said, "We will go to the bus depot at Milton."

They went straight out to the school minibus and in ten minutes were there. It was a slack moment, and there were many buses in, so they stood at the door and looked in at the journey indicators. Someone recognised our town name, someone else where Auntie lived, etc. Then the drivers began to come out and drive off, so the class got into their bus and followed the one marked "Cotterham." It was a short journey so we were able to follow him along the whole of his route, stopping where he stopped. Just out of Cotterham the conductor turned the indicator back to Milton. We followed him back most of the way, until the children could see that he was going back to where he had come from. They returned to school.

The teacher began to write on the board a detailed account of what they had done, in proper sequence. The children would talk about each point, and he would select useful sentences. Then he erased some of the key words or phrases, and the children copied the account, filling in the gaps; and these were taken home. (Another method the teacher sometimes uses is to let them draw the sequence of events.)

On subsequent days the children reported what they had seen about buses on their journeys to school. They were clearly following up this new interest. From that we discussed:

The people in the bus depot—their different kinds of work and whether they had homes and families—a bus driver and conductor were invited to come and have tea with the class.

The bus timetable—we dramatised people catching and just missing buses and waiting in the cold at a bus stop.

The level crossing—waiting for the train—where the train was going to and from—and that another train had gone over a bridge which we went under. *Why* was that? (They could not say but the feeling of curiosity was stimulated.)

The traffic circle—we went down to see this and noted the pedestrian subway nearby, comparing it with the train bridge.

We followed the whole route on a simple map.

Evaluation

They began to see that there was sense and regularity in transport systems and that buses don't just go here and there at the whim of the driver. The train on its rails emphasised this. They continued to consolidate their appreciation of the function of a map in another real life situation.

Children in Other Lands

(Partially hearing children seven and eight years old)

The teacher had worked in Uganda, so he told the children about a little girl he knew there called Nusamba who became totally deaf at the age of five.

"Once upon a time there was a little girl called Nusamba. She lived in a house in the forest, far away in Uganda." (Africa and Uganda were found on the globe.)

He showed the children Nusamba's painting of her house in the forest. They talked about her home; what it was made of—mud rolls and corrugated iron roof. They talked about the garden. The teacher told them about peanuts and bananas and how Nusamba worked in the garden. Good pictorial material from the Ugandan Embassy and a filmstrip from the National Film Library were a great help.

The children were then told about preparing the evening meal with bananas. How they peeled the bananas, wrapped them up in a banana leaf, and steamed them in a pot. He had a photograph to show this, and the children wrapped four bananas in rhubarb leaves and steamed them.

Next the teacher told them how, when she was five years old, Nusamba was very ill and became deaf. All her friends went to school but she couldn't go. Nusamba was sorry because her friends left her alone. Then a school for deaf children was started and she was one of the first to go there.

The class talked about the schools in Uganda and how Nusamba loved painting (examples were shown) and that eventually she went to an ordinary school where she is using lipreading only and is doing quite well. The teacher brought in many other details, and there were discussions on many points.

This story lasted for four weeks. Usually one stage of the story was written on the overhead projector and shown after the teacher had told it. It was then dealt with using the listening-reading-speaking method.

Sometimes the teacher would lead up to an interesting point; and then the class would guess the ending, they were then asked to read to see what did happen and finally this was discussed to ensure that all had understood.

The children here began to develop an interest in how people live in other countries. They wrote about what they remembered of incidents in the life of Nusamba and took them home to their parents.

SUGGESTED BIBLIOGRAPHY

I. Current Events

Bennett, C. M., and Jackson, C. V.: *Make it Yourself.* London, John Murray, 1960.

Catherall, A., and Holt, P. N.: *Working with the Weather.* London, Bailey Brothers and Swinfen Ltd.

Clarke, Millie: *A Book for Winter.* Weaton of Exeter, 1963.

Gibson, G. H.: *About Our Weather.* London, Frederick Muller Ltd., 1960.

Konkle, Janet: *The Christmas Kitten.* Chicago, Children's, 1953.

Marino, Dorothy: *Goodbye Thunderstorm.* Philadelphia, Lippincott, 1958.

Munch, Theodore W.: *What is a Rocket?* (Collins Pageant of Knowledge Series). London and Glasgow, Collins, Sons and Co. Ltd., 1961.

Prehn, Monika: *Let's Make a Christmas Crib.* London, Boon Ltd., 1966.

Raymond, John: *Men on the Moon.* London, Collins, 1964.

Targett, B. R. H., and Green, M. C.: *Space Age Craft,* George G. Harrap & Co. Ltd., 1967.

II. Our Homes & Families

Bertail, Inez: *Time For Bed.* New York, Doubleday, 1961.

Clark, Kay: *All By Himself: All By Herself.* New York, Plakie Torp Inc., 1950.

Clarke, Mollie: *At School,* (Looking at Words Book No. II). Glasgow, University Press, 1964.

Corbett, J.: *How-do-you-do-Cookery.* Edinburgh and London, Thomas Nelson & Sons.

D'Amato, J., and D'Amato, A.: *Eighty Things to Make in Cardboard.* Middlesex, The Hamlyn Publishing Group Ltd., 1969.

Dark, Irene, and Arnold, E. J.: *The House That Jack Built Series.* Leeds.

1. *A Loaf of Bread*	3. *Eggs for Breakfast*
2. *A Bottle of Milk*	4. *A Scarf to Wear*

Gagg, M. E.: *Telling the Time*, (A Ladybird Learning to Read Book). Loughborough, Wills & Hepworth Ltd., 1962.

Hastings, Howard L.: *Pets*. Chicago, Hampton Publishing Co., 1958.

Hautzig, Esther: *Let's Make Presents*. London, Morrison & Gibb Ltd., 1964.

Holmes, Edward: *All About Pets*. London, Young World Publications Ltd., 1967.

Jenkin, Janet I.: *Let's Make Scones*. London, Longmans, Green & Co. Ltd., 1966.

Kirsch, D., and Kirsch-Korn, J.: *Make Your Own Doll's House*. London, B. T. Batsford Ltd., 1969.

Low, Alice: *Open Up My Suitcase*. New York, Golden Press Inc., 1969.

Osswald, Edith: *Come Play House*. New York, Golden Press Inc., 1948.

Pajot, Anne Marie: *Patrick the Piglet*. Edinburgh & London, Thomas Nelson & Sons, 1966.

Showers, Paul: *How Many Teeth*. A & C Black Ltd., 1967.

Stevenson, Robert Louis: *A Child's Garden of Verses*. Oxford U Pr, 1966.

Set TRG 158-1	*Set TRG 158-2*
1. *In the Bathroom*	1. *Going to School*
2. *Getting Up*	2. *At School*
3. *Dressing*	3. *Dinner Time*
4. *Breakfast*	4. *Helping Mother*

Taverner, Nixie: *Cellograph Work Books*. London, Philograph Publications.

Uttley, Alison: *Little Grey Rabbit's Washing Day*. London, Collins, 1969.

Webster, James: *Making a Doll's House*, (The Ladybird Book of Toys and Games to Make). Loughborough, Wills and Hepworth Ltd.

Widerberg, S.: *Judy at School*. London, Burke Publishing Co., 1968.

III. Our Class and Our School

Alexander, Jean: *Playday—Off to School*. Oxford, Pergamon, 1965.

Bethers, Ray: *How Did We Get Our Names*. London, MacMillan, 1966.

Boyce, E. R.: *In Hospital*. London, MacMillan, 1961.

Buckley, Helen E.: *The Little Boy and the Birthday*. Surrey, The World's Work, 1960.

Haymes, Olive: *The Junior True Book of Health*. Chicago, Children's, 1961.

Hinshaw, Alice: *Your Body and You*. A Junior True Book, Chicago, Children's.

Hunnicutt, C. W., and Crambs, J. D.: *I Play*. New York, Singer, 1957.

Miller, Kate: *Being Ill and Getting Better*. Oxford University Press, 1968.

Ormsby, V. H.: *Twenty One Children*. Philadelphia, Lippincott, 1957.

Sandberg, Inger, and Lasse: *Anna's Mother Has A Birthday*. Buckinghamshire, Richard Sadler & Brown Ltd., 1967.

Schatz, Letta: *When Will My Birthday Be?* Surrey, The World's Work, 1963.

IV. Exploring Our District

Adams, H.: *Postmen and the Post Office*. Blackwell, 1961.
Aulaire, I. M.d', and E.D': *Animals Everywhere*. New York, Doubleday.
Barham, Jeffrey: *Mapping a model village*. *Child Education Quarterly*, 45; 5, April 1968.
Berg, Leila: *Three Men Went to Work*. London, Methuen & Co. Ltd.
Bradune, E. S.: *Everyday Things*. Huddersfield, Schofield & Sims Ltd.
Bruna, Dick: *The Little Bird*. Methuen, London 1969.
Child Education Quarterly: 46; 3, Spring 1969.
Dawson, R. B., and Dawson, R.: *A Walk in the City*. New York, Viking Pr.
Deverson, H. J.: *The Story of Bread*. Middlesex, Penguin Books Ltd., 1964.
Evans Brothers, and Headway Readers: *The Book of the Air*. London, Evans Brothers Ltd.
Evans Headway Readers: *The Book of the Cinema*. London, Evans Brothers Ltd., 1962.
Flack, M., and Wiesse, K.: *The Story About Ping*. London, Picture Puffins, 1968.
Green, Carla: *I Want to be a Zoo Keeper*. Chicago, Children's, 1957.
———: *I Want To Be A Postman*. Edinburgh, and London, W. and R. Chambers Ltd., 1957.
Hutchins, P. *Rosie's Walk* Picture Puffin, Middlesex, England 1972
Lenski, Lois: *The Little Aeroplane*. London, New York, Oxford University Press, 1958.
———: *The Little Fire Engine*. London, Oxford University Press, 1946.
Murray, G., and Golden Pleasure Books Ltd.: *Ring Up The Fire Brigade!* London, New York, Toronto, Sydney, The Hamlyn Publishing Group Ltd., 1968.
Paterson, A. B.: *Weary Will the Wombat*. Melbourne, Handsdowne Press Ltd. 1971
Scarry, Richard: *The Great Pie Robbery*. Collins, 1969.
Slobodkina, Esphyr: *Moving Day for the Middlemans*. London, Toronto, Abelard-Schuman.
Steiner, Charlotte: *Terry Writes a Letter*. New York, Crowell Publishing Co., 1959.
Tolstoy, Alexei: *The Great Big Enormous Turnip*. Heineman 1969.

V. For General Reference

Scarry, Richard: *Storybook Dictionary*. Hamlyn, 1972.
Seuss, Dr., and Eastman, P. D.: *The Cat in the Hat Beginner Book Dictionary*. Collins and Harvell, 1964.
Stevenson, Robert Louis: *A Child's Garden of Verses*. Oxford University Press, 1966.
Suschitzky, W.: *The Giant Golden Book of Animals*. New York, Golden, 1958.

VII LANGUAGE TOPICS FOR CHILDREN AGED EIGHT TO TWELVE YEARS

1. Current Events

DURING THESE YEARS current events may begin by including all that is suggested for four to seven-year-old children, with some additions. Development should be aimed toward greater reference to *newspaper* and *television news,* to more careful selection of events, and a more mature manner of taking part in discussions. Maps should be used regularly.

Awareness of time and the seasons
Seasonal changes. Activities during different vacations.
The sun, moon and stars
Night and day
Weather observations: daily recording on graphs of wind direction, temperature, barometric pressure, cloud formation
The newspaper
Use of class newspaper
Magazines
A class magazine

2. Our Homes and Families

Revision and extension of many of the topics listed for the younger age group.

Electricity—its nature, uses and dangers
Water—how water gets from the sky to our homes, its uses, steam
Heating homes
Safety precautions in the home
Furnishing a house

Language needed at meal times
Helping mother in the home
Helping father in and around the house
Bringing a friend home
Visiting a friend
Other children in the family
Our holidays
Caring for our animals
Where we live (including maps and directions)
How to preserve food, eggs, fruit
Practical cookery for boys and girls
Dressmaking
Painting the house
Our television programmes
Types of living conditions—flat (apartment), hostel, bungalow, tent, house, homes on water, houses on stilts, etc.
How to dress nicely—cleanliness, tidiness, tasteful use of accessories: ties, brooches, etc.
Washing hair
Looking after a bicycle
Pitching a small tent
Taking a photograph
Making toys for other children
Removing stains
Mowing a lawn
Ironing a blouse or shirt
Consideration for others, e.g. when buying Christmas or birthday gifts, what will please the recipient?
The story of myself (an autobiography)

3. Our Class and Our School

Revision and extension, where applicable, of topics listed in Chapter VI, as well as:
Establishing standards and routines
Language for classroom duties and daily routines
Our health—discussing common diseases
keeping records of height and weight
fitness tests

exercise, rest and sleep
planning a balanced diet
School records—educational and audiological records discussed privately and in a friendly way with each child.

4. *Exploring our Neighbourhood and District*
As in Chapter VI plus:
Where to buy different things
How to make up a grocery order
Language used at the hairdresser's
Language used when buying shoes, sweets, etc.
Emergencies—artificial respiration
    danger of power lines
    road accidents
    first-aid procedures
    doctors
    hospitalization
    dentists
    telegrams and the telephone
    fire prevention, behaviour in case of fire and the fire department
Manners—writing and acknowledging invitations
    visiting friends
    entertaining visitors and visiting sports teams
    hospital visiting
    respecting other people's property
    arguing effectively (and politely!)
Being careful about accepting gifts or invitations from strangers
Schools for normally hearing boys and girls
People who work in our neighbourhood: (Visits, preferably in the company of normally hearing boys and girls, should often be arranged in conjunction with the following topics.)
Home builders—an architect
    a bricklayer
    a plumber
    an electrician

a painter and decorator

Building materials—bricks, wood, stone, clay, glass, cement, steel

Food—farms of different types and the people who work on them

the grocer or supermarket worker

the milkman

the butcher—different types of meat

the fishmonger—different types of fish

"Plenty of pure water is the basic need of man and beast."

Clothing—selling children's clothes

the menswear shop

the ladies' clothing shop

the man who sells us shoes

the man who repairs our shoes

dry cleaning clothes

Communication—the news boy and newspaper production

the mailman and the story of a letter

the T.V. repair man

the telephonist

Travel—a bus driver

a taxi driver

an aeroplane pilot

a ship's captain

a train engineer

a bridge builder

transport timetables

buying a ticket

Culture and religion—a local clergyman

an artist

a member of an orchestra

a potter

Sanitation and health—a dustman

a doctor

a dentist

a public health nurse

Security—a policeman

a fireman

a soldier

a sailor

an airman

"The Country Code"

Preservation of wildlife

Map work (Maps should always be made to show something purposeful and be specific and related continuously to current events.)

> how some well-known streets got their names
>
> the making of large picture maps by children
>
> the use of large scale maps of the locality and the countryside visited
>
> maps of our country
>
> the globe and maps of the world

Imaginative work using painting, modelling, mime, stories (This topic overlaps and is basic to work with Sect. 7)

> What was this place like when Mother and Father were children?
>
> What was it like long, long ago? (When the castle was in use, when cave men lived here, etc.)

5. Children and their Families across the Country

Essentially the theme is how families live in each of several other, rather different, parts of the country? For example, London children might study how people live in a mining, farming, fishing, or forestry area in Cornwall, Kent, Wales, Scotland, or the Lake District—taking only two or three examples in a year.

These studies should usually be centred around the life of the people at home, work and school, and when moving about—not just series of facts and statistics to be learned and quickly forgotten.

Map work related to this can often be based on a large map made of soft board. This can be used for the placement of models, routes and shipping. It can be cleared off and used again for new topics.

Cities and major towns, rivers, mountains and lakes, etc. should be referred to frequently in lessons and current events sessions and children taught how to locate them independently.

Entertainments—a day in the life of a sports star
national sport personalities, record holders
card games
party games
dancing, different types
hobbies and games of different kinds
how to arrange flowers
manners, being a good loser and a good winner
patience, waiting one's turn

6. Stories and Studies of Children and their Families in other Countries

This theme aims primarily at developing a friendly, intelligent, interest in other countries and their ways of life. By use of films, film strips, television, pictures, and stories (supported by mime, dramatic play, and all the arts) the children try to imagine what it is to be a boy or girl in some other countries: Lapland/Greenland, China, India, New Guinea, Australia, etc. Two or three per year might be enough for older children. Younger ones could study six or more if materials are available.

Children from other countries who have come to live here: map work will derive from the above studies and should include use of the globe and the atlas. It is more important to have and use a large globe than a large wall map. Wall maps are better to be of equal area projection than the Mercator type.

Most of the following topics are better taken as part of the first topic in this theme, or as part of current events. It is important to consider the lives of the people engaged in these different occupations.

Underground treasure—gold, iron, coal, natural gas, oil, oil rigs, etc.

Where and how commodities grow or are manufactured and the lives of those who produce them—tea, coffee, fruit, cheese, milk, paper, cotton, wool, plastics, rubber, sugar, rice, glass, shoes, television sets, electric ranges, clothes, etc.

Transport—ways of going to school in other countries

Health—hygiene for boys and girls in other countries
diseases: their effect and control

Sport—Olympic Games
  international sportsmen
Music, songs and games enjoyed by children in other countries
Pen pals
Collections—stamps
  pictures of birds, animals, plants and trees
  cars, aeroplanes, ships
  touring sports teams and athletes

7. Children and their Families in other Times

This theme may best be treated as parallel to Section 6 with periods chosen because of their striking differences, and because they illustrate major ideas, such as that of change, or show how people have tried in different ways to meet the same problems of survival and of achieving a good life. Current events can profitably act as the starting point for such studies.

In the United Kingdom (ancient, medieval, 19th century industrial life)
In the United States (Red Indians, pioneers, slaves)
In China (the porcelain and silk makers)
In Australia (Aborigines in the desert)
Child labour—Lord Shaftesbury
The unhappiness of poverty—Oliver Twist, Charles Dickens
Early Men—the cave dwellers

Some other activities that may be related to the foregoing themes, or may simply be part of the social life of the school.

Being a member of a club
Taking part in classwork with hearing children in the same, or another school
Sharing in out-of-class activities and projects with other deaf or hearing children
Making a contribution in the form of services to the school or the community. (Gardening, odd jobs, or messages for people who need help, etc.)
Making a gift to sick or needy people
Being a member of a committee to decide where to go, etc.

Helping to serve food, clear tables, tidy the classroom or dormitory, clean the bathroom, bath the "babies"

Taking part in a play, bazaar, or other project affecting the whole school

Running the assembly

Aspects of World History

Explorers: Columbus, Cortez (Pizarro), Cook, Livingstone

Inventors: G. Stephenson, Wright brothers, von Braun

Famous people: Confucius, Alexander the Great, St. Patrick, St. Francis, Joan of Arc, Michaelangelo, Florence Nightingale, Abraham Lincoln

Famous events and places: the pyramids, Stonehenge, coming of the Normans, Taj Mahal, Plague and Fire of London, How the West was Won (U.S.A.), Kremlin, White House.

Classical Stories (These will differ from country to country and should include other types of traditional literature.)

The Boy who cried "Wolf!"

Bruce and the Spider

Romulus and Remus

Robin Hood

The Pied Piper

David and Goliath

St. Francis of Assisi

Horatius at the Bridge

The Battle of Marathon

Cyclops

The Golden Apples

Dadalus and Icarus

Hercules

The Hare and the Tortoise

Hiawatha

King Canute

Sinbad the Sailor

Ali Baba

Hannibal

The Wooden Horse of Troy

TEACHING TECHNIQUES FOR DIFFERENT ACTIVITIES
News

The following is one method of teaching language through news which one teacher has been using for some time with severely deaf children aged seven to nine years. It is similar to that she used with a class of normally hearing children aged six and seven.

Each morning, as soon as the children come into school and have settled down, I begin individual speech teaching, and the rest continue on their own to write pieces of individual news on the blackboard. Later I call the class together and we read through the various items. I show the children how to correct it and where there are blank spaces, I help them supply the words. After this, I choose the most interesting sentences and write them in an exercise book which we call "Our Reading Book." Similarly, the children choose sentences from the blackboard and copy them into an exercise book which is called their own reading book. At the end of term they take their reading books home and I encourage them to read their books to their parents.

I want to emphasize the children's own books—*their* ideas produced by themselves in written form and only altered by me where necessary to make grammatical sense. They have not copied me. My book, in fact, consists of items copied from them. The books I make are kept along with the usual story books on the shelves and they have proved to be some of the most popular reading books because the children can understand them. They are about experiences in which they have actually participated.

A Class Newspaper

(Eleven and twelve-year-old profoundly deaf girls of good average intelligence)

The class newspaper started almost by accident as part of another study, although the class had always written news in exercise books. The other study was a topic called "Finding Out About Our Village."

The class began by looking at a map of the village and the surrounding countryside and tried to locate their position. They pinpointed the school, and then began, in the children's phrase, "walking along the map." They went out and looked at old houses, and talked about them and how people lived in them. They walked along the old coach road, and visited the coaching inns. They saw a local play about Dick Turpin, and tried to imagine travel in those days. They visited an old church, looked at the birth registers, and talked about how history is written from such documents.

As the class did this they drew pictures and wrote stories about their work, and made books from them.

Next, a closer look was taken at local services. The fire station, police station, a dairy and various shops were visited. The children scanned the local newspaper for items of interest. Several appeared—a sale of Brownies' work, a picture of one girl's sister, etc. So the class visited the newspaper office; and the children were shown the whole process of newspaper production. They were fascinated and asked dozens of questions.

After this, the class decided to make a newspaper of their own. They did this; and pasted their work, both stories and pictures, on a long sheet of paper.

The teacher's method was to edit the children's work and include everyone's contribution. In this way, there was a big effort from the children and they were given help in producing a final version. This (editing, adapting, correcting, etc.), is, of course, what happens in a real newspaper and the children had seen some of this on their visit.

The first newspaper was worked on for four weeks. When interest began to flag the class turned to other work. If done again, the teacher thought she would try appointing two children to be editors each week. Their job would be to read each piece of news, and point out errors to the writers. When they had agreed to a final version, the teacher might look over it. The editors would then paste the various stories and pictures on to a brown paper page about the size of an ordinary newspaper. The pages for one week would be sewn together to make an edition.

St. Patrick's Day

(Eight and nine year old children in a partially hearing unit)

Modified listening-reading-speaking (LRS) lesson on the story of St. Patrick.

St. Patrick lived a long time ago. (c385–461 A.D.)
He was born in Wales.
One day some pirates came from Ireland and *raided* Patrick's father's farm.
Patrick was *captured*. He was sixteen.
He was taken to Ireland and sold as a *slave*. He had to look after pigs and sheep for six years. He was *unhappy* and *prayed to God*.
Later he became a priest and taught the people about God.
The Irish remember St. Patrick and wear a bunch of shamrock in his honour each year on March 17th.

Teacher had a well illustrated book to help explain the more difficult words.

Mother's Day

(Eight year old deaf children)

Teacher: Sunday (referring to calendar) is a very special day. Who knows what day it is?
Children: Mother's Day.
Teacher: Why are most mothers good to us?
Children: They cook our food, wash our clothes, polish the furniture, clean the floors and so on.
(Pictures shown of these activities.)
Teacher: What could we do to help Mummy on Sunday?
Children suggest ideas such as: wash the dishes, set the table, make mother a cup of tea, etc.
Teacher: Today we will make a card for Mummy.
You will take it home, but will you give it too Mummy today?
Children eventually realise that they must keep it until Sunday.
Teacher: What will you do with it?
Children: Hide it.
Different places suggested to hide it.
Ask each child where he or she will hide the card.
Hiding a card without Mummy seeing it is dramatised.
Teacher: I have made a card for Mother's Day. Let's look inside.
Nothing there. What will we write?

Most of the children suggest 'Love from ....'

Teacher: Yes, we will write 'Love from Margaret'; but we will also write a short poem to tell Mummy how much we like her. Blackboard turned and poem read by teacher and then by children, and then all together twice more, as meaning was discussed.

> I have such a good mummy
> I want to say
> Lots of Love
> On Mother's Day

Poem used for speech material twice more during the day.

Accidents at Home

(Nine-year-old partially hearing children.)

This lesson, lasting $1\frac{1}{4}$ hours, was part of a project entitled "Emergencies."

A picture of a kitchen showing the following common causes of accidents in the home was drawn on a large sheet of paper: trailing cord from an electric heater, a frayed electric cord, toys left in the middle of the floor, gas leaks, a pair of scissors or knives left lying round, rucked and frayed carpets, fire with no screen, poisons left out on the table, and saucepans with handles protruding over the edge of the cooker.

The picture was discussed and the children asked to spot the dangers. Each source of danger was discussed in turn and the children asked to relate their experiences. The class were asked to suggest ways in which they could prevent accidents at home. It was pointed out that there are far more accidents in homes than on the roads.

How to deal with all of the possible accidents that could occur in the illustrated kitchen was very briefly discussed. The children spotted all of the sources of danger except the frayed cord and the possibility of escaping gas. The lesson concluded with the children giving written answers to the following questions:

> Should the scissors be on the floor?
> Is the electric heater in a safe place?
> Should the carpet be flat?

Is this a safe home?

Do you live in a safe home?

The children were asked to let their parents see the questions and to tell them about the sources of accidents in the kitchen and finally try to write out the list discussed.

Making Ginger Beer (non-alcoholic)

(Eight to nine-year-old partially hearing children)

Making ginger beer is a fairly lengthy process so it is a good idea first to bring some for the children to taste to stimulate their interest before the series begins.

Lesson 1

Materials: a jar and cork with air-locks

the ingredients

a cup

teaspoon

jug

a chart with labelled drawings of the items used.

The following recipe was written on a turnover paper chart.

How to make Ginger Beer

This is an old recipe to make ginger beer. We use a yeast plant. Keep the yeast plant in a jar in the light but not on a hot, sunny window sill.

Place two ounces of baker's yeast in a jar, add two cups of water, two teaspoons of sugar and two teaspoons of ground ginger. A plant has now been made from which ginger beer can be made as follows:

Feed daily for seven days with one teaspoon of ground ginger and one teaspoon of sugar.

Procedure

After the children had tried the ginger beer, they were asked if they would like to make some. The recipe was read to the children and then reread line by line, with the children repeating it. Meanings of the passages were clarified with regular reference to the recipe. The teacher showed them the original in an old recipe book. The children took turns in carrying out each of the instructions.

The chart was then shown and the children were told to try to memorize the drawings and labels. They were helped to do this by covering up first a word and then a picture. Some of the labels were then covered up and the children asked to write on their note pads. Finally, they made labelled drawings in their books and wrote a few sentences about making ginger beer.

Lesson 2 (8 days later)

Materials: knife, gallon jar, lemon squeezer, funnel, muslin, yeast plant (made in Lesson 1), two flasks of hot water, 1 lb. sugar, 2 lemons.

The following instructions were written on a chart:

Put a *funnel* in a clean jar.

Put *muslin* in the funnel.

Pour the yeast plant into the muslin.

Squeeze the juice from 2 lemons.

Pour the lemon juice into the jar.

Pour very hot water into the jar.

Add 1 lb. sugar to the *liquid.*

Fill the jar with cold water.

Leave the liquid for 8 days.

THE GINGER BEER WILL THEN BE READY TO DRINK

Procedure

The equipment was set on a table near the blackboard. The children sat in a semicircle.

The children were shown the yeast plant in the jar, and asked how it was made. "We fed the plant every day." "A teaspoon of ...."

The chart was shown and the first instruction was read to the class. The children were then asked to repeat it. After discussing the meaning, a child carried out the instruction. The language of each sentence and phrase was worked over actively and thoroughly. "What do you think this word means?" "What does that phrase mean?" The funnel was shown to the class and a sketch was drawn above the word in the text on the blackboard.

Simple definitions of new vocabulary were also written above the words and phrases in coloured chalk. Careful speech was required of the children and brief assistance was given to the class and to individuals as the lesson went along. The children were asked to take a copy of the instructions home to discuss with the family and to bring back the names of ten liquids.

Lesson 3   The Final Step

Materials: 9 wine bottles
    9 corks and bottle tops
    9 labels printed "This ginger beer will be ready to drink on Thursday, 3rd April"
    a funnel
    muslin cloth
    filter papers
    chart showing last week's lesson

The following instructions were written on a third chart:
    Put the funnel in an *empty* bottle
    Fold a filter paper *twice* to make a right angle
    Make a funnel shape with the filter paper
    Put the *filter paper* in the funnel
    Pour some ginger beer into the filter paper
    The *liquid* will go through the filter paper
    The *yeast* will be left in the filter paper
    When the bottle is half-full, either push a *cork* into the bottle or use a bottle top
    Stick a label on the bottle

Procedure and Content

The equipment was set on a table near the blackboard.

The children were shown the large jar of ginger beer. Last week's lesson was reviewed referring to the chart made describing the different steps. The new instructions were worked through in a manner similar to the previous two lessons. By going over them nine times every child had the opportunity of bottling his own ginger beer.

The seven steps in bottling the ginger beer were taken home by the children.

Common Courtesies

(Bright seven and eight-year-old deaf children)

Dramatised activities for consolidating language. First written on a chart and then dramatized in a group:

Teacher: Good morning, ...
Children: Good morning, Miss ....
Teacher: How are you this morning?
Children: Very well, thank you, or I'm fine thank you.
Child: May I borrow your scissors please?
Teacher: Yes. But don't be long, will you?
Child: No, I won't be. Thank you.
Child: May I borrow your pencil, please?
Teacher: No, I'm sorry, I'm using it myself. Could you ask Miss Brown for one?
Child: All right. etc.

Cards were given out containing the questions and answers, and the children practised each activity in pairs before returning to the group to act their piece. They worked for two days; and then duplicated sheets of the words used in the five activities were taken home and to the hostel for practice there.

Picture Maps

(A series of three lessons with a class of seven to nine-year-old children, profoundly deaf and slow learning.)

Lesson 1

The teacher told the children they would be going for a walk, and upon returning would draw where they had walked, so they should look carefully at everything they passed and remember it.

They then all went for a ten-minute walk down the school drive, across the road and along the pavement until reaching the green. They returned the same way.

Going down the drive, the teacher pointed out the lamp post, trees, and the gate to the field. After that she asked the children what they could see. They soon realised what was required and pointed out the caretaker's house, school gates, trees, a car, and the road.

They crossed the road, using it as an opportunity for road drill. On the left they noticed several houses, and on the right only a farm wall. The children pointed out lamp posts, but were puzzled by a telegraph pole. The teacher pointed out the wires to different houses where there were telephones. Charles indicated a manhole cover and suggested that there were wires under the ground. The teacher drew the children's attention to masses of crocuses in some of the gardens. The children indicated the mailbox. The last house had a different fence, and they examined it. At the corner was a traffic diversion sign, and this was discussed. Roadmen could be seen working in the distance. Opposite was a field.

The group returned to school by the same route, repeating the observation of all the things already noticed. The road sign for the school and a "House for Sale" notice were added to the list.

Back in the classroom, the teacher drew an outline of the school on the blackboard and of a child walking away from it, beginning the line of the walk. The children were asked who could continue the line. Three children in turn tried and each drew a straight line. Ronnie corrected it by making the sharp right turn where they had crossed the road.

The teacher then brought a large sheet of paper which was placed on the floor. She drew the school in one corner and copied Ronnie's line of the walk. Next she produced the toy box and asked the children if they could remember what they had seen. The caretaker's house was mentioned. George found a model house; but couldn't place it correctly on the line. After two other children had tried, Jimmy found the correct location. The children recalled and similarly placed lamp posts, more houses, flowers (Feltcraft flowers were used), the telegraph pole (a pencil on end), the cat, the gate, and some cars. They did not remember the field, mailbox, farm, or trees, about which the teacher reminded them.

The children had shown more keenness than the teacher had expected in making this three-dimensional map. She suggested that they drew it for themselves, leaving the big one on the floor for them to copy. As a class, they were not yet adept at copying details correctly; but Charles and Jimmy spent a long time on it, and produced even more correct details than on the original.

The teacher then put away the models, reproduced them pictorially on the large sheet, labelled them, and put this map on the classroom wall, where the children all read the names of the different items, following the line of the route.

Spirit-duplicated descriptions of the walk were given to the children to show the hostel staff and to take home at the weekend.

Lesson 2—(one week later)

The class travelled by school bus to the nearest busy street. The school bus was parked and they walked for ten minutes. They entered a church and looked around inside, crossed the road using the proper drill, looked through the windows of a library, visited the railway station, traversed the crossing, noticed a telephone box, passed a sweet shop, garage, toy shop, grocery shop and bus stop. They then retraced their steps, reinforcing the first impressions.

Back at school, the children were prepared to reproduce the map of their walk as in the previous lesson. The teacher drew the parked school bus and a walking figure on the blackboard. The children were asked to draw the line where they had walked. The first child drew a straight line; but the second child corrected it to a right turn at the corner.

The teacher then copied this line on to a large sheet of paper on the floor. The children were asked what they had seen on the walk. Whoever suggested a building found a model or picture of it and placed it on the map. This time, most objects were correctly placed at the first attempt, including a church, a picture of children crossing the street, a house with a picture of a library interior for the library, a model station, two gates to suggest the crossing, the sweet shop, the toy shop, and some cars for the garage. The bus stop was mentioned. They then discussed what took place in a library. They were also familiar with the church and the railway station, having previously visited these.

The children were eager to draw their own copies of the "map." Ronnie added a school to his, although the others had forgotten that they had passed one. The maps copied were somewhat better than those of the first lesson, though there were some mistakes in location (e.g. the crossing gates were placed on the railway line, but not at the point where the road crossed it). The new vocabulary was written on the blackboard and the children were asked to indicate the names of the objects on their maps. Four out of seven of them were able to fit all the labels correctly to the drawings. Two added "Sunday school" beside the church (although this had not been mentioned) and another wrote "new car" at the garage showrooms and "Jesus Cross" at the churchyard. Ronnie drew a squiggly line for the road where the school bus had been parked, indicating that it was potholed and bumpy. Dorothy drew a child walking up the steps to the library, which was correct; but added a blue sky and a yellow sun at the top of her map. Jimmy drew the chairs in the Sunday school hall. Several children drew the bell rope which they had seen inside the church, as well as the bell they had seen from the outside. Charles drew children waiting at the corner where they had crossed the road.

The objects were then removed from their places on the diagram and the teacher drew them in, labelled them, and pinned the sheet on the wall with the first map, to serve as a reminder of the outing, for vocabulary practice, for the children to show visitors, and to help them with their interpretation of maps. Duplicates were sent to the hostel staff and parents as before.

Lesson 3—(*two weeks later*)

The teacher told the children that they were going to a big pond and that they must observe and remember everything they saw in order to draw a map.

The class travelled by school bus for some miles, parked by the lake, and walked beside it for some distance, returning the same way. This time the teacher did very little pointing out, as the children were very eager to talk about everything they saw.

On returning to the classroom, each child was given a piece of chalk and had the chance to draw the route on the blackboard. This time, the children were expected to include the route taken by the school bus as well as that of the walk. Susan drew a line weaving about all over the board, suggesting that it was "a long way." Dorothy and Beth really had no idea what was required of them. George understood; but his sense of direction was astray. Charles and Jimmy made good attempts and Ronnie showed a much more mature sense of direction and observation. He showed the correct left turn at the end of the school drive and drew the two intersections passed on the route. He further suggested with zig-zag breaks in the roads, that the way should really extend beyond the limits of the board.

As his route was so similar to the true one, it was left drawn on the blackboard; and the class worked with this as a pictorial map instead of using a three-dimensional one with models. All the suggestions were included.

After this, each child coloured the objects he or she had suggested. Incidental discussion included the destination of the lady, what operation the tractor was performing, the purpose of the water tower and how the fisherman could stand in the lake without getting his legs wet.

The children settled down eagerly to copy the map adding the names of each object. There was an all-round improvement in accuracy; but most of the children lost interest before they had copied all the pictures. Only Ronnie showed greater perseverence and completed the whole map correctly.

Conclusions

The teacher was agreeably surprised at the interest and concentration which this series of lessons encouraged. All the children in the group had contributed something, and each had shown progress in some direction. The memory training was clearly good for them and their powers of observation had certainly improved. New vocabulary and language had been introduced, and the children's pertinent questioning showed that new concepts were being formed. The range of new topics and the map work introduced in these lessons provided much material for future work in social studies.

Cooperation through Shopping Activities

(Nine multiply-handicapped profoundly deaf girls, aged 12–15, with low IQ's and from very modest homes)

My first task was to teach the children how to work together in twos and threes because this class was habitually tied to its desks—the children felt guilty if they left them—and there was everlasting senseless quarelling. I secured a room with space, but they thought it was a punishment to be widely separated. Playing shopping was found to be a successful activity to reduce this feeling.

I produced empty cartons with the prices and a lot of cardboard money. We put tables together to make shopping counters. The children themselves did this. They collected paper bags, shopping bags, and things to buy and sell. We had scales, and a coin drawer, and 'The Edmunton Shop' was written up in large letters.

The children decided who was to be shopkeeper—one at a time—for the day. They took it in turns. We ignored the timetable while interest lasted. They went shopping and gave money, but did little about change though occasionally I helped with this.

Experiences relating to shape, size, and weight cropped up all the time. Someone showed me that two packets of one shape equalled one packet of another shape. I would then draw the attention of the rest of the class to this observation. It was a matter of looking for suitable opportunities to teach meaningful language.

As an offshoot of this activity, the children set up a hairdressing department marked:

Shampoo and set	50p
Trim	30p

They would come in, buy something, and one would draw the other's attention to the notice. "Oh yes, we must have a hair-do." All this was done mainly by signing.

We next went on for a manicure. Our row of coloured cupboard doors suggested washing machines and so we had a laundromat. The last facility was a cafe. These all functioned at once.

RESULTS: A much better relationship between the children was established with less quarrelling, better adjustment, some language development, some skill with money and weighing, and some ideas of tidiness (they sorted things into departments, e.g. sweets, pet foods, etc., and everything was put into order at the end of each week).

They learned to work together a little and this showed up elsewhere, in the cookery room, for example. They even began washing up for each other.

Through signs, even though in a simple way, they did begin to carry on some discussions. They considered each other's and my ideas for example, of arranging the shop, making a decision, carrying it out, making a judgment, agreeing to change it, and so on.

In a very limited way they experienced all that a hearing group would have done—and now that we have started, we look forward to finding other ways to encourage further progress.

People Who Help Us

(8 seven to nine-year-old partially hearing children)

During six weeks of one term, one class studied the policeman and the mailman in some detail and also touched on a number of other occupations. Since then, they have studied the fireman in detail, and other people connected with emergency services—such as a nurse, doctor, telephone-operator and ambulance driver—and finally revisited the fireman again. All these were connected up in general discussions and by means of pictures and visits.

The different topics arose from a number of sources: the books they had been reading had accounts of some of the people mentioned; one girl's father was a mailman; someone's grandmother was a nurse; the sight of the fire station which was passed when going swimming; the sight of an ambulance; the fact that some of the children had been in hospital; some collected stamps and the school received from the local post office an excellent set of pictures, diagrams, and books, sufficient for the whole class.

So each study began in a different way.

The Post Office

After school one day I displayed all the material received from the post office on the wall and on tables. The children came in, and at once wanted to go and look because the pictures were so attractive. I let them look at the pictures and talk freely about them for about twenty minutes. During that time they asked me questions about the uniforms and the methods of transport (some of the pictures were historical), pointing out the pictures they liked.

They asked each other questions: "Why did some of the old mail carriers have guns?" and so on. They could not give the answers, and this provided some teaching material for later lessons.

At the first lesson they were so full of comments and questions that I did not attempt other teaching. Instead, I suggested that they might like to draw some of the things they had seen. They enjoyed doing that, and wrote a little about what they had drawn—not by copying, for the captions were rather too difficult for them to read.

Next day I raised the question: What happens to a letter today when we post it?

The children formed a group around me and I held up our reading book on the postman. The children looked at the pictures and began to ask questions to which I usually asked them to provide answers if they could. For example, when looking at pictures of a train delivering or picking up mail automatically they asked "What is the bag for?" And I replied "What do you think?" The children thought it was just another kind of postbox and that the train would stop and a man would take out the letters (most of them had already seen a postbox box being cleared). Automatic collection was a new idea, and so from picture to picture we talked our way towards an understanding of what was happening.

At the end of the lesson, I asked the children to collect old envelopes so we could study them. When a sufficient variety of envelopes had been accumulated, we talked again about sorting and addresses and the children learned some more new words and increased their understanding. They seemed to have assumed that their own addresses were simply to be learned in case they got lost! We decided that we would visit the local post office.

The following morning we prepared a letter and parcel for a child who was in hospital, and discussed the reason for each line of the address. Next we set out to the post office.

On arrival there we had the parcel weighed. The children bought and licked the stamps and put them on. They posted the letter, and as they did so, they read the notices on the different letter drops: "London" "Outside London" and "Abroad," and we discussed these words.

Back at school I asked the children what would happen to our letter and parcel and they were able to explain this step by step.

One day I received some air-letters from Australia and I asked how they had come to England and how my reply would go back. We also discussed surface mail going by ship.

The children had been writing letters to a student teacher who had been at the school, as well as to other friends. In their exercise books they had pasted examples of old letters and stamps, and had written an account of the journey of a letter.

One boy went to Ireland for his holiday and couldn't find the mailboxes because they were painted green! (English mail boxes are red) .

Elizabeth's postman father kindly visited the school one lunch time.

Our final exercise was to play a post office game called "Crazy Capers" which we bought from a shop. Parents were informed daily throughout the course of this topic.

The Emergency Services

As a first step the teacher brought a newspaper picture to the class of a pair of twins who had fallen into a canal. She told the children what had happened: someone fished the twins out, somene else dialled 999 (the emergency number) , and an ambulance arrived on the scene. The twins were taken to the hospital, and later were able to go home. There was a long digression to explain what twins were. The children dramatised the whole story. Each took a rôle—one of the twins, the person who telephoned, the ambulance driver, etc. This lasted about one hour.

The following day, the procedure of telephoning (using a toy phone) was practised and the story of the twins was written down.

The next story, with pictures, was about a fire caused by knocking over an oil heater. This time the children said what had to be done: "Dial 999, give the address, and ask for the fire station." This allowed review of previous work on the postman and addresses.

Another story the teacher told in this context concerned a boy who saw a man trying to break into a house. "What would you have done?" she asked.

Ethel: Go and get the policeman.

Ray: Knock him on the head.

Larry: Dial 999.

Others: Yes, dial 999.

Teacher: Yes, that would be best. Shall we act it?

All: Oh, Yes.

All the boys wanted to be the policeman; but one had to be the robber. The girls were just onlookers.

As a follow up, the next visit was to the telephone exchange. The children were allowed to listen on the operators' earphones. Some could hear a little—the others pretended they could. The operators explained that a red light appeared when a 999 call came through, and so it was always handled immediately.

They were then taken to see the canteen and rest room where the exchange staff eat and the night staff rest. The teacher played their piano, and everyone had soft drinks and crackers. (Thus broadening the study to something beyond "work".) Letters of thanks were subsequently sent to the manager of the telephone exchange after discussion of what it would be apropriate to say.

As a final exercise each child was given a card with a message about an emergency situation, i.e. you have just seen a car accident, a fire, etc. and each had to decide what would be needed before dialing 999 on our internal telephone, giving the location of the accident (they gave their own addresses) and asking for the relevant emergency service, fire brigade, policeman, or an ambulance. The children had been shown how to use a

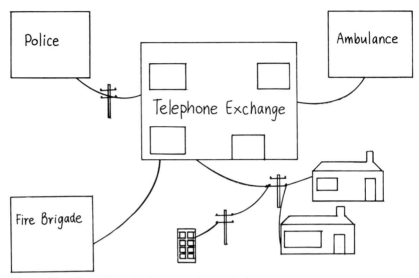

Figure 12. How the telephone exchange helps us.

hearing aid with the telephone. Some could hear but others could not.

It was felt, small as they were, that these children did learn what to do in quite a range of emergencies. Most of them had never used a telephone before; but having done so gave them the confidence to try again.

The Nurse

Lesson given to four children, three aged seven and one eight year old, bright but severely deaf.

"As I am not a trained teacher of deaf children I had a word with Miss Ashley first to see how she tackled the subject. She said that she had brought a nurse's uniform and used the Lady-bird book *The Nurse*."

LESSON: I wrote on the board 'Sometimes we feel sick. We go to bed. The doctor comes and he makes us better.'

The children read it, and Helen started off by saying her mummy had gone to the dentist because she had a pink gum (gum boil). After that I asked if Peter (her brother) was still feeling unwell, and she said he had a cough.

I reminded them that Mrs. James (a teacher) was still at home and Loretta said, 'Bad back.' I asked her to say, 'Mrs. James has a bad back.' I asked the class what else made one feel unwell, and Helen pantomimed bandaging a broken leg. I gave them the language. Then she pantomimed her arm in a sling and again I gave them the words. Helen said, 'Mrs. Bellingham went to hospital—broken leg.; Jane said 'Miss Allen went to hospital—bad stomach.'

I asked who the people were who worked in a hospital. 'The doctor.'

'Who else?' I asked and produced the reading book about nurses. They told me 'the nurse!' and we looked through the book. A picture of a mother and baby produced, 'Mrs. Menzies went to the hospital. Mrs. Menzies had a baby.' We talked about it, and found the words 'ambulance' and 'stretcher' in the text.

DRAMATIZATION: I produced the nurse's uniform. Jane and Helen were nurses, Lorretta the doctor, Alan the patient and I was Mummy. I telephoned for the doctor. He phoned for the ambulance, and Alan was taken to the hospital. The nurses asked him his name and put him to bed, drawing the curtains.

The curtains were drawn back when the doctor came to examine him (using a microphone for the stethoscope and a milk straw for the thermometer). The doctor then gave him medicine.

I visited with a bunch of flowers and asked when he would come home. The nurse said, 'Saturday.'

Helen drew the curtains back and forth several times to denote the passing of time, and I collected Alan and brought him home. There was joy all round.

I wrote on the board who was who and what we did, etc., and the children repeated, wrote, and drew the story and took it home.

Verb Tenses

Difficulties in teaching the tense of verbs to deaf children, are legendary. Useful suggestions are contained in Agnes Lack's *Teaching Language to Deaf Children*.

An experienced teacher of deaf slow-learning seven-year-old children planned her language lessons to introduce a certain amount of formal work on verbs in a natural manner. One term she emphasized three verb tenses: future, present progressive, and past. Simply putting a list of these tenses on the blackboard accomplished nothing. Nor did it work to make an exercise of it and have all the verbs put in the past or in the future. The children may do it, but they won't know what they are doing.

She explained the way she found best.

"We said, 'We shall make a cake,' and we wrote all the things we should do on the blackboard: Go to the shop and buy the various things and what we should do with them. When we had done all these things and the cake was baked, we crossed off the future parts of each verb and changed them into the past tense. The children saw it happen:

shall buy	became	bought
will cost	became	cost
will carry	became	carried
will weigh	became	weighed
will cook	became	cooked

and finally,

will eat	became	ate

"Naturally, we didn't let it rest there. Whenever we were setting off for the shops again, someone wrote the verb in the future and when we came back we crossed it out and put it in the past. We said 'We shall wash the doll's clothes,' and we did. Another day we said, 'We shall go upstairs and make Susan's bed,' and we did."

The Country Code

Many of the social habits and concepts which are learned by normally hearing children have to be taught formally to deaf children. These include cautionary behaviour in the home or crossing roads, an awareness of potential sources of danger, and an understanding of the meaning and need for conservation. A journey in the country is, of course, needed to bring these country code points to life.

1. *Guard against risk of fire*
   Great damage is done every year to crops, plantations, wood-lands, and pasture grasses. A still-lighted match or cigarette thrown away or pipe carelessly knocked out, picnic fires not properly put out or lighted near dry grass or trees can quickly start a blaze.
2. *Fasten all gates*
   If animals get out of a field they stray. As a result, they may do serious damage to crops, suffer injury on the roads, or eat food that is harmful.
3. *Keep dogs under control*
   Animals are easily frightened, even by small playful dogs.
4. *If there are paths, keep to them to cross farmland*
   Crops are damaged by treading; flattened crops are difficult to harvest. Grass is a valuable crop.
5. *Avoid damaging fences, hedges, and walls*
   If these are damaged, gaps will be caused. Where a man or child goes, an animal can usually follow.
6. *Leave no litter*
   Litter is not only unsightly but can be dangerous. Broken glass, particularly, can harm animals and interfere with the working of machinery.
7. *Safeguard water supplies*
   Countrymen often rely on wells and streams for clean water supply. We must be careful not to make them dirty.
8. *Protect wild life, plants, and trees*
   Wild animals should not be disturbed, plants uprooted, nor trees treated roughly.
9. *Go carefully on country roads*
   If there is no footpath, walk facing the oncoming traffic.

Compass Points

(Twelve-year-old deaf children in a residential school)

The children were given magnetic compasses and with these they found various directions from the school. Next, they found the direction of their homes from the school and were able to point in that direction. This was achieved by using two different methods:

1. From a map of New South Wales (Australia). The children discovered the compass direction of their home from Parramatta (a small town near the school). Using a magnetic compass, they could then translate this abstract direction, say northwest, into a real direction that could actually be pointed out.
2. The children correctly orientated a large map of New South Wales by placing north as shown on the map toward the north as shown on a magnetic compass. They could then see their hometown on the map in relation to Parramatta and be able to point in that direction. In doing this, they were of course, finding the direction without using a compass except for the initial orientation.

Latitude and Longitude

It was made clear to the children that lines of latitude and longitude existed on a map, but were not actually marked on the earth's surface. The equator, tropics, and polar circles were shown to be lines of latitude with particular names. The children were then shown how to find a place by using the index in their atlas. This gave them the latitude and longitude in degrees and they could then proceed to find the place on the map. Dividing the world up with these lines has made it much easier for people (especially sailors and flight crews) to find exactly where they are, for example, when sailing or flying over the sea.

Maps

Ragan and McAulay suggest a sequence of development of map skills for normally hearing children. The real map symbols are not introduced to the children until the age of ten. By the time a child is twelve-years-old, the writers consider he should have acquired the following map concepts: direction, scale, the legend or key, topographical features, ability to read facts from a map (why cities have grown, where they are, etc.), latitude and longitude. They should have the ability to use the following map symbols: capital cities, falls, highways, mountains, railways, rivers, airports, coast line, sand or desert, canal, bridge, tunnel, and dam. The authors consider "the globe is the most essential tool for social studies," and certain skills are necessary for its use to demonstrate night and day, the seasons, and how to plot points on it accurately by using latitude and longitude.

Considerable time must, therefore, be devoted to map and globe work; but, if carefully planned and frequently introduced, it can be fairly easily taught and is very practical and enjoyable for deaf children from quite an early age.

Children of Other Lands

(Using films with deaf children ages nine to eleven)

First preview the film and make a list of key words and phrases. The children are told ahead of time what the next film will be about. On the book table have a display of books about the country to be shown. On the wall of the room have a large map of the world, and have a globe handy. Photographs or pictures or books are placed ready for use as needed. Sentences with blanks to be filled in are printed on the spirit duplicator ready for the children's use and for taking home.

First lesson—in the classroom

Key words and phrases are written on the board, e.g. "Switzerland," "gorgeous mountains and lakes," "different kinds of cheese," etc.

1. Using pictures from books, teach the words and phrases. A sequence that can be used fairly often is:

    Say something about the picture.

    Show the picture.

    Ask the children to say a sentence about the picture.

    Repeat the best phrase.

    Ask the class to repeat it. Next, ask them to try to write it on their note pads or on scrap paper. The teacher writes the phrase on a card.

    Show the phrase on the card.

    Say the phrase all together; and then ask each child in

random order, so that he or she is not sure when his or her turn is coming and must watch carefully.

Show the pictures and say the phrases together.

The children are asked to say the phrases or words after the teacher several times, first as a group, and then briskly four or five children at a time.

2. Talk about the pictures: the animals, what the people are doing, etc. Where possible, refer back to other countries, e.g. for the skiing pictures, refer back to the film on Norway shown earlier.

3. "We are going to see a film tomorrow about Switzerland. What do you think we will see?" Questions and answers follow to cover all that the children can be expected to know at this point. "Can you find Switzerland in your atlas and on the globe?" "Have you seen Switzerland on television?"

4. The children copy down the key words and phrases from the cards.

Second lesson—in the film room then the classroom

1. Show the film the first time with the emphasis on enjoyment. The children may turn to their friends or teacher to communicate such things as, "Beautiful mountains." "The cow has a bell around its neck." They may thus miss parts of the film and it should therefore be shown again to ensure that it has been adequately seen.

2. Talk about the film using the key words and phrases where possible. Also listen very carefully to the thoughts and ideas expressed by the children so that these can be followed up carefully in class. Use all the words from the previous day's blackboard.

3. Return to the class room, say the most interesting words and phrases. The children watch the teacher's lips and write the words or phrases as best they can.

4. Exercises—The children fill in the gaps in written sentences, e.g.

In S............... there are many m...................

The houses are made of ....

5. The children may write what they can about Switzerland, while the teacher helps individual children who ask for as-

sistance—rather like van Uden's (van Uden, 1968) diary technique.

Third lesson—in the film room

"We are going to see the film of Switzerland again. What will we see?" (The key words and sentences are available on the board for the children to look at.) "What else shall we look for?"

When ideas have been discussed, show the film.

Look again at some sections.

If possible, we may compare with our pictures or slides.

The children write more sentences about Switzerland.

Fourth lesson—in the classroom

"Where is Switzerland?" Find Switzerland in the children's atlases and on the globe.

"What were the people doing in the film?" Compare with this country and other known countries. After this talk, the children again write. Some may do a comprehension exercise. Others may do a free composition.

Later lessons

The work may be taken further, both in the study of the country and its people, and in the development of language by using a second film, or by dramatising (skiing, mountain climbing, driving the cows, etc.), modelling (a chalet on a mountain) or painting.

By this age, the children's interests are broadening and their horizons widening. Maps, not only of their locality or town, but also of the country they live in and of the world, are becoming more and more interesting. Globes are still extremely useful to remind the children that the earth is a rotating sphere and to consolidate material learned using flat maps. If teachers use maps regularly they can introduce and draw the children's attention incidentally at first to some of the essential terms used in map reading, e.g. north, south, east, and west; the equator and the North and South Poles; keys or legends to maps; latitude and longitude; some indication of scale; contour lines showing the height of different parts of the country; prevailing winds; and how the latitude, height and prevailing winds affect the climate of a place and the lives of the people who live there. Such introductory references should precede formal teaching of map reading skills although formal teaching is necessary, especially with eleven and twelve-year-old children. Children enjoy, and should have regular opportunities to make maps once they have obtained at least some of the above information. Since television and communication satellites, today's children have more need and more incentive to read maps than ever before.

For ten to twelve-year-old children, the cause of days and night can readily be illustrated by means of a slide projector light representing the sun shining on to a globe as it is slowly revolved in a darkened corner of the room. The seasons are better shown out of doors using a large yellow ball as the sun, held on the top of a small child's head, while a second child walks around him on a chalked eliptical orbit (some 30 feet in length) holding the globe (see Fig. 6a). This second child, while spinning the earth slowly in an anticlockwise direction, must be careful to keep the axis of the earth pointing in one direction so that it can be seen that the sun's rays reach the northern hemisphere more directly during one half of the orbit, and the southern hemisphere during the other thus causing summer and winter. The equator can be seen to receive fairly direct rays during daytime, throughout the year, and so people living there do not experience the four seasons.

Practical suggestions for making outline, contour and blackboard maps are given by Ragan and McAulay (1964).

"Waltzing Matilda"

(Nine and ten-year-old deaf and partially hearing children)

Once upon a time in Australia a tramp put up his tent near a pond, and under a tree for the shade. The tramp sang a song as he waited for his "billy" to boil on the campfire. He sang "You'll come A-Waltzing Matilda with Me."

The map of Australia was found in atlases and a picture shown of the swagman by the billabong. The record of the first verse of "Waltzing Matilda" was played twice through the group hearing aid. Words of the song were pointed out on a chart as the song was sung. The full story was told using a flannelgraph. After repetition the following day, the story was written in four stages and taken home to parents.

Our Fruit

(Eight partially hearing children aged eight years)

A straightforward little series of lessons was devised to give the children some basic information on the fruit they eat and where it grows. The partially hearing unit was near to the river Thames where cargo ships could be seen loading and unloading. At the beginning of this series, few of the children seemed to have related this to the food they ate. When asked, "Where do oranges come from? for example; they replied, "The shop."

"Where do they grow?"

One said, "Farm"

"Where are the farms?"

No reply.

"Do they grow in London?"

"No. Far away."

The children had been introduced to a globe and had begun to appreciate that there are other countries around the earth. They had learned that the equatorial regions are mainly hot, the North and South Poles are extremely cold, and in between there is a warmer climate.

A visit was made to the docks when fruit was being unloaded. Some bananas had come from Jamaica; and this was very helpful because one of the girls had come from Jamaica two years before. The children seemed to appreciate fully that the bananas had come an extremely long way in the cargo ship and not just from a mile or so down the river.

The following day this LRS lesson and activity was taken:

This afternoon we will make a cargo ship.

A cargo ship carries *goods,* not *passengers.*

It has a bridge where the captain stands.

The *helmsman steers* the ship with the wheel.

Under the *deck* is the *hold, covered* by a *hatch.*

The lesson series then followed. One fruit was dealt with

each day; and the children were told in advance which would be dealt with on each of the six days. They were asked (through their home/school notebooks) to try to find labels on fruit boxes or wrapping papers, saying where the various fruits had come from. This worked very well, and a fine selection of colourful labels was obtained.

LESSON 1

Materials: Pictures of oranges from Jamaica, the outline map of the world, atlases, pictures and a photo of the ships on the river, four oranges, reference book *Man Grows Fruit* by Kathleen Brooks and Janet Duchesne.

There was a brief discussion of where Harriet comes from and how she and her family came. "What was it like in Jamaica, Harriet?" She was asked to bring some pictures or photos for the next day. The following were shown to the children and treated as an LRS lesson:

Oranges grow on big, leafy trees.

They need a lot of sunshine and plenty of water.

They are brought to us by cargo ship.

"Everyone seems to love oranges" said Miss James.

Oranges don't grow in England.

Where do they come from?

Children can write this in their topic books with an illustration and are asked to find out where oranges and apples come from for tomorrow's lesson.

LESSON 2

Materials: Map outline of world, crayons and children's atlases.

Various advertising matter found at the grocer's on fruits, especially apples.

Picture of a cargo boat at the docks, and an apple orchard.

First, we had a short review of yesterday's activity and marked where oranges grow on the world map, after the children had found the countries in their atlases. Then a reference to the text on the blackboard.

Here are four apples.

Apples are grown in many countries of the world, in gardens or in large orchards.

These have come from South Africa.

Where else do apples come from?

Following a discussion of the information brought from home, areas where apples are grown were marked on the world map after they had been found by the children. The children wrote this in their topic books and illustrated it.

LESSON 3

LRS Method

We are going to have a filmstrip.

One of the places where grapes and apples come from in the United States of America is California.

(Can you find California?)

The fruit needs sunshine and water to grow.

California has lots of sun and irrigation water.

The apples are packed in boxes, and sent to England by cargo boat.

After the children had read and understood the text they had the filmstrip. Phrases were read from the strip as it went along and a spirit-duplicated copy of an edited version of the text was given to the class to stick in their topic books and take home to their parents.

LESSON 4

Materials:

Reference books: "Geest Industries Ltd."; *Man Grows Fruit: Some Fruits; Looking at Everyday Things*

Eight bananas

There was a discussion of where bananas come from, showing what each child had found out about bananas.

LRS

A banana plant is very tall.

The leaves grow at the top.

The plant has one stem.

A bunch of bananas is called a hand.

Each banana is called a finger.

Bananas grow in hot damp countries, like the West Indies, the Canary Islands, Samoa and Africa.

Cutting bananas and boxing them is very hot work.

The children wrote and illustrated this in their books. Afterwards, they had a banana to eat. This language proved too technical to interest these children, and should have related more to people than to the banana plant, and been more conversational than purely descriptive.

Pineapples and grapes were dealt with in a similar manner, except that a flannelgraph was used and this helped bring the lessons to life. The series proved of interest to the children and their parents; and some useful information was learned by the class.

HISTORY AND PEOPLE

The study of original documents is recognized as an exceptionally powerful medium in bringing history to life for students. Few people would fail to be affected when reading from Nelson's *Victory* log book or Captain Scott's dairy (Fig. 13) in the manuscript room of the British Museum. History suddenly comes to life. It is, of course, not feasible to see a great many original documents; but photographs of them are available and these are also extremely valuable for teaching. Jackdaw Publications, 30 Bedford Square, London W.C.1., has compiled over eighty collections of contemporary documents on historical topics. A fairly full account of each event is also included that can readily be adapted by teachers for the language levels of different children. Maps, such as that shown in Figure 14, portraits, and historical sketches have been photographed and are excellent for use with small groups of children. Some of the titles include:

Columbus and the Discovery of America
The Spanish Armada
Shaftesbury and the Working Children
The Mayflower and the Pilgrim Fathers
Young Shakespeare
Joan of Arc
The Slave Trade and its Abolition
The Voyages of Captain Cook
The Indian Mutiny

Winston Churchill
The Russian Revolution
Caxton and the Early Printers
The Development of Writing
The French Revolution
Canadian Jackdaw:
Confederation 1867
The Fur Trade
Briston and the Cabots

French and Social Studies

This teacher is a trained teacher of French language. He takes a group of hearing and partially hearing children from Surrey in England to France or Belgium each year. He teaches French in the Ministry's pilot scheme, to the hearing children, four half-hour periods a week and to the partially hearing four quarter-hour periods weekly. Only partially hearing children ten years and older attempt French.

The pictured objects for the course are drawn on cellophane and used with the overhead projector. The teaching is entirely oral until ten years or older for hearing children and at the teacher's discretion for the partially hearing children. All lessons, including classroom instructions, are conducted entirely in French. English is resorted to only if children are really confused or if a point has failed to get over after several efforts in French.

The high point of the teaching comes when the children go to France and find that their language works. The children learn that French people meet their problems or needs in a variety of ways different from their own, though living in similar physical circumstances. They thus develop, not only tolerance for a different culture, but the ability to think a little more clearly about other people, and to enjoy them and make friends with them.

Details of the method are in the Nuffield French Course 1 (a) and Mary Glasgow's *Bon Voyage*.

When observed, this class was learning to speak French remarkably well. They responded in French to pictures and to French words and questions naturally, in a good accent and with delight. They sang in French with a recorded song as accompaniment. The teacher feels that the work is also justified as an effective form of auditory training and articulation exercises.

Television Programmes related to Practical Studies

(Seven to nine year old partially hearing children)

Last year when the children were looking at a television programme on cave paintings, they said the Stone Age people looked like monkeys and were not very clever.

The teacher decided to help them to form a better judgment. The class collected some flint stones to make tools. The teacher asked, "What weapon would be strong enough to kill an animal for food?" Some said, "An axe."

But the flint was round and smooth until someone dropped one and it broke. He found a sharp flake and thought it would make a little spear. This gave the children the idea of chipping. They decided to make an axe. They wondered how to fasten it to the shaft. They found a stick for a shaft and wanted to use string, but were not permitted. They tried grass—it broke. Then they tried a creeper—this was better. Finally, they decided a piece of animal skin would be much better.

A final discussion on the cavemen produced the ideas that they used the materials they had very well indeed and were really very clever and that we are rather lazy because we go to shops for everything.

Similarly with the Romans, the class made wax tablets and wrote messages on them; and they tried to make a Roman mosaic with stones they found outside by setting them in clay. It was very difficult.

Later the class went to Belham and the children admired the mosaic floor.

In these ways, by trying to do the things themselves, and talking about their success, the children came to appreciate some of the abilities and difficulties of peoples of the past.

It also produced an intense and permanent interest in the subject studied.

The Lives of Stone-Age People

(Eleven to twelve year old children with hearing losses 50-90+ dB)

Lessons were once weekly for one and a quarter hours, with some additional time for art and crafts during the week.

Extensive grounds and a school minibus proved a tremendous asset. The teacher prepared the children for a visit to Radlett Roman Palace to take place in mid-July. A study was made of Southern England before the Roman occupation. Life in the Stone Age would then be compared with life under the Romans.

Four lessons were given, under the following headings:

1. *How do we find out about history?*

Archaeologists were described as "history detectives." A small school dig was started in part of the grounds, to let the children become aware of the methods used by archaeologists. The measuring out of the site was also linked to math lessons.

2. *How people lived in the Middle Stone Age*

The making of fire.

Hunting—types of animals, the weapons used.

The making of dugout canoes.

Food—fruit, bones, berries, meat and fish.

Tools of bone, flint, bark, skin and wood. Flint tools were made from material collected in the school grounds.

Settlement around Radlett.

A large model of a Stone Age village was made. This relief model included houses, dugout canoes, people, and animals. The children spent considerable time making accurate figures to complete the model. The people were dressed in skins and furs and were complete with tools, canoes, etc. Great thought was given by the children to the placement of the individual models, every effort being made to make the model authentic.

3. *The development of primitive agriculture on the chalklands*

Domestication of animals.

The growing of crops.

Stone-Age houses.

The development of pottery and weaving.

Trading between villages led to the making of beaten tracks and footpaths—the beginning of roads.

Fighting led to the building of strong hill forts.

4. *Preparation and visit to the Archaeology Room of Barclay Museum*

This included a wide selection of exhibits of Stone-Age implements of all kinds, skeletons from the Whitehawk Burials and aerial photographs of eight Stone-Age camps sited in Sussex.

A display of relevant library books.

A selection of visual aids.

The museum visit.

Each child had an individual work sheet to complete (App. 3). They took with them sketch books and additional drawing paper. The children were in the museum for about three-quarters of an hour. The work sheet proved to be invaluable and was much enjoyed. The children really had to search for the answers to the questions.

Compiling a book "Our Visit to the Barclay Museum."

The children's work sheets and sketches were included in this.

Stone-Age exhibition

An arrangement was made with the School Loan Department of the Museum to borrow a selection of Stone-Age exhibits for a month.

Imaginative writing about the Stone-Age

The children had to imagine that they lived at Whitehawk Camp and described their family, house, food and work. This was done very well by the brighter group.

A television programme on the Radlett mosaics

Simple mosaic making was described. It was decided to let the children make their own mosaics in the weekly, two-hour art and craft lessons.

A wide variety of materials was used: shells, seeds, wood,

etc. These were set into clay or plaster of Paris. A small exhibition of mosaics was then put up for the rest of the school to see.

This topic proved to be particularly relevant to the children's interests. There were endless opportunities for language development, and all the children seemed to get very involved in the work. The teacher thought this is a very suitable topic for eleven and twelve-year-old partially hearing children and planned to make it six or eight weeks' work rather than four next time.

Reference Books Used

Dickenson, A.: *The First Book of Stone Age Men,* Ward.
Mellursh, H. E.: *Finding Out About Stone Age Britain,* Muller.
Peach, L.: *Stone Age Man in Britain,* Ladybird.
Quennell, M.: *Everyday Life in Prehistoric Times,* Batesford.
Lynch, P.: *From the Cave to the City,* Arnold.
Barker, E.: *Queensway History Book 1,* Evans Brothers.
Hansen, Hans-Ole: *I Built a Stone Age House,* Phoenix House Ltd.

Religious Education

What constitutes essential biblical study material is no longer firmly laid down, but much Old Testament material favoured in the past is less obviously relevant, while the life and teachings of Christ, newly interpreted, are as relevant as ever, and there is much other human thought and experience in the Bible from which wise selection can be made. From the Department of Education and Science publica-itons "Religious Education, Present and Future", H.M.S.O. 1969.

A number of the topics listed in Sections 1 and 11 are dealt with in some of the growing volume of books written for children who wish to learn English as a second language. Often the lessons are not well worded, and need to be adapted to suit particular deaf children. The topics and illustrations and a certain amount of the text, however, are frequently very helpful. Such a series is "Structural Readers—1 and 2" by Kathleen Kruizinga (Federal Publications Ltd, F.A.M. House, Jalan Birch, Kuala Lumpur). The topics for lessons in this series include: a driving lesson, a Saturday Holiday, a meeting of the swimming club, the postman, the new boy, a visit to the hairdresser, a school sports meeting, Sinbad the Sailor, Baby elephant comes home, the commercial traveller, good manners, Ahmed catches the thief.

SUGGESTED BIBLIOGRAPHY

Films and Filmstrips

Catalogue of Captioned Films for the Deaf. Washington, Department of Health, Education and Welfare, 1969.

Project Life—Instructional Material for Primary Language. Washington, Department of Health Education and Welfare, 1966.

Visual Aids, Part I–Part VIII. Educational Foundation for Visual Aids, 33 Queen Anne Street, London, W.1., 1968.

Current Events (See also Chapter VI)

Morrison, Sean, and Freeman, Ira: *Where the Rain Comes From.* Roger Schlesinger, R.H.S. Publications.

McGloskey, Robert: *Time of Wonder.* New York, Viking.

————: *Safety in the Home.* "Working World" Series, Cassell.

Our Homes and Families

Devereux, K.: *Health in the Home* (for girls). Cassell.

Epstein, Beryl, and Epstein, Sam: *Grandpa's Wonderful Glass.* Grosset and Dunlap.

Gagg, M. E:. *Shopping with Mother.* Wills and Hepworth.

————: *Helping at Home.* Wills and Hepworth.

Heilbronner, Joan, and Chalmers, Mary: *The Happy Birthday Present.* World's Work.

Howells, E.: *Health in the Home* (for boys). Cassell.

Hertz, Crete Janus: *Lina and Lisa Have Measles.* London, Burke Books.

Kerr, Judith: *The Tiger who Came to Tea.* Collins.

Sauvain, Philip A.: *Exploring at Home.* Hulton's Environmental Studies.

Sedgewick, Ursula: *My Learn-To-Cook Book.* Paul Hamlyn.

Thwaite, Anne: *Toby Moves House.* Longmans.

————: *Toby Stays with Jane.* Longmans.

————: *Jane and Toby Start School.* Longmans.

Our Class and Our School

Gagg, M. E:. *Going to School.* Wills and Hepworth.

Hinshaw, Alice: *The True Book of Your Body.* Children's.

Podendorf, Illa: *The True Book of More Science Experiments.* Chicago, Children's.

Widenburg: *Judy at School.* Burke Books.

Wood, E.: *Our Friends of the Garden.* Geoffrey Chapman.

Exploring our Neighborhood and District

Brown, Daisy: *Tubby, Tiny and Top.* Lyons and Carnahan.

————: "Reading for Fun" Series.

Buff, Mary, and Buff, Conrad: *Hurry, Scurry and Flurry.* New York, Viking PR.

Dolch, Edward, and Dolch, Marguerite: *Some are Small.* Champaign, Garrard.

————: *Zoo is Home.* Champaign, Garrard.

————: *Monkey Friends.* Champaign, Garrard.

Falk, Ann Mari: *The Ambulance.* Burke Books.

Greene, Carla: *I Want to be a Scientist.* H. Chambers.

————: *I Want to be a Teacher.* H. Chambers.

————: *I Want to be a Carpenter.* H. Chambers.

————: *I Want to be a Farmer.* H. Chambers.

————: *I Want to be a Doctor.* H. Chambers.

————: *I Want to be a Nurse.* H. Chambers.

————: *I Want to be a Policeman.* H. Chambers.

————: *I Want to be a Roadbuilder.* H. Chambers.

————: *I Want to be a Mechanic.* H. Chambers.

————: *I Want to be a Cowboy.* H. Chambers.

Peterson, Hans: *The New Bridge.* Burke Books.

Southgate, V., and Havenhand, J.: *The Fireman.* Wills and Hepworth.

————: *The Policeman.* Wills and Hepworth.

————: *The Nurse.* Wills and Hepworth.

————: *The Fisherman.* Wills and Hepworth.

————: *The Farmer.* Wills and Hepworth.

————: *The Builder.* Wills and Hepworth.

————: *The Miner.* Wills and Hepworth.

————: *The Postman.* Wills and Hepworth.

————: *The Soldier.* Wills and Hepworth.

————: *The Sailor.* Wills and Hepworth.

————: *The Airman.* Wills and Hepworth.

————: *The Roadmakers.* Wills and Hepworth.

————: *The Story of Football.* Wills and Hepworth.

————: *The Story of Railways.* Wills and Hepworth.

————: *The Story of Ships.* Wills and Hepworth.

Children in Other Countries and Other Times

Greekmore, Raymond: *Furvio (a Japanese boy).* Eau Claire, Hale.

Hunt, W. Ben: *Indian Crafts and Lore.* Paul Hanlyn.

Kawaguchi, Sanse: *Taro's Festival Day (a Japanese boy).* Boston, Little.

Parin D'Aulaire, Ingrid, and Parin D'Aulaire, Edgar: *Ola* (a child of Norway). New York, Doubleday.

Politi, Leo: *Juanita* (Mexican life on Olivera St., Los Angeles). New York, Scribner's.

Reid, Barbara: *Carlo's Cricket.* New York, McGraw.

Sasek: "Children Everywhere" series. Methuen.

————: *This is London.* W. H. Allen.

————: *This is Paris.* W. H. Allen.

————: *This is Hong Kong.* W. H. Allen.

————: *This is New York.* W. H. Allen.

————: *This is Greece.* W. H. Allen.

————: *This is Scotland.* W. H. Allen.

————: *Story of Oil.* Wills and Hepworth.

————: *Flight one Australia.* Wills and Hepworth.

————: *Flight two Canada.* Wills and Hepworth.

————: *Flight three U.S.A.* Wills and Hepworth.

————: *Flight four U.S.A.* Wills and Hepworth.

————: *Flight five Africa.* Wills and Hepworth.

————: *Flight six The Holyland.* Wills and Hepworth.

Signobosc, Francoise: *Jeanne-Marie in Gay Paris.* New York, Scribners.

Small, Ernest: *Baba Yaga* (a Russian child). Boston, Houghton Mifflin.

VIII LANGUAGE TOPICS FOR CHILDREN AGED THIRTEEN TO SEVENTEEN YEARS

THE SYLLABUS AT THIS LEVEL should become increasingly orientated to employment and life after school days are over.
This, however, should not be interpreted too narrowly. Opportunities should be made for children to observe a variety of occupations. "Life after school days are over" should not refer only to
local events and activities. Some interest in national and world
affairs is to be expected and encouraged. It is possible that the
most fruitful work in this direction may stem from an interest
in current events and in attempting to understand them.

In addition to illustrated project books prepared on various
topics by the pupils, evaluation of what has been learned can
be by written tests conducted at the end of each topic and/or
at the end of each term and also by five- or ten-minute individual oral examinations by a senior teacher or colleague.

1. *Revision* and extension of pertinent topics listed in the previous two sections
2. *Current Events*
Daily newspapers and periodicals should be diligently used.
Television programmes.
Local and national elections should be studied as they occur.
Out of school activities of day pupils
weekly boarders
full-time boarders
Understanding some of the problems of immigrants
One aim of the work in current events is to help the children
develop an orderly method of study by following up a few
major events, e.g. a war in some part of the world. This method
may be developed from questions following an observation
thus:

There is trouble between Country A and Country B.
What does each side say is the problem?
What sort of solution might be possible?
We must begin by finding out what the situation is and
  has been in these countries and try to understand things
  better.

Sources of information would include books on each country,
newspaper editorials and articles rewritten by the teacher at
the appropriate level for the class, films, filmstrips, and magazines and school publications for use with television programmes
or for class reading.

This kind of work might lead into or replace much of that
suggested in the next section and that outlined on Sub-section 4.

3. Topics from Human Geography

(Most of these topics should begin from current events).
Travel and Transport
  Air—The work of an airport
      Air services available—timetables and air routes
      Plotting and keeping on the correct course
      The largest airliners
      Supersonic airliners
      Space travel and research (the astronauts)
  Sea—Who builds the world's ships today?
      A study of some of the men who build a ship
      Some famous sailors
      Dangers of the sea—storms, fog, icebergs, currents, light-
        houses, rocks, sands, ship's pilots, and rescue work.
  Land—Road haulage
      Our railways today
      The motor car—development and different models, etc.
      Transcontinental roads and railways
      The camel-train driver
      The life of a long distance train or truck driver
      The world's taxis
How climate affects the lives of people and the distribution
  of population.
Natural Regions—Tropical forest: People of Central Africa

Hot and dry: Australian Aborigines, Arab tribesman,
   Death Valley
Mediterranean: Italy, S. France, Spain, Greece
Temperate grasslands: N. America, Br. Isles, Scandinavia,
   Australia, New Zealand (Fig. 15).
Cold and wet: Eskimos
Monsoon: India, Malaysia
Geographical factors which affect these regions: land mass,
   seas, winds, latitude, longitude and altitude.
   How man modifies such regions (Fig. 16).
Droughts
Hurricanes
Volcanoes—Pompei
Major mountain ranges and uplands—their effect on the cli-
   mate and settlement.
   The Rockies

Figure 15. The old and the new. While men with horses and dogs move sheep in the foreground a topdressing aircraft drops fertilizer on the hills beyond. The loading machine on the truck fills the aircraft's hopper within a few seconds of landing. Havelock North, Hawkes Bay, New Zealand. (Photograph by courtesy The High Commissioner for New Zealand.)

Figure 16a. Lake Eucumbene—a storage reservoir in the Snowy Mountains, New South Wales, Australia. The hydro-electric scheme will provide 3,000,000 kilowatts of electricity annually and 2,000,000 acre-feet of water for irrigation. (Australian News and Information Bureau)

    The Andes
    The Eastern and Western Ghats in India
    The Himalayas
    The Caucasus
Important rivers—how they influence the people
    The Amazon
    The Congo
    The Danube
    The Rhine and the Elbe
    The Mississippi and Missouri
    The Volga
    The Nile
    The Ganges and the Indus
Soil erosion—wind, water and ice.

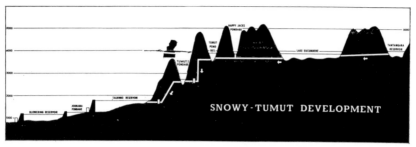

Figure 16b. Water is stored in man-made lakes in the winter and released in the hot summer months.

Figure 16c. Pressure pipelines for Murray II power Station under construction as part of the Snowy Mountains Scheme in the Australian Alps. The scheme includes the building of 17 large dams, about 100 miles of tunnels, nine power stations—some of which are hundreds of feet underground— and over 80 miles of aqueducts. (Australian News and Information Bureau Photograph)

The fifteen largest cities in the world and why they are where they are:
Tokyo, New York, London, Shanghai, Peking, Moscow, Calcutta, Bombay, Sao Paulo, Chicago, Rio de Janiero, Berlin, Paris, Cairo, Sydney.
Map study—interesting geographical features
Mount Everest, Suez Canal, Panama, Canal, Sahara Desert, Pacific Ocean, Atlantic Ocean, Indian Ocean, South Pole (Antarctic) North Pole (Arctic), Great Lakes (N. America), Black Sea, Red Sea, Scandinavia, Mediterranean, Lake Victoria, West Indies, East Indies.
Sightseeing in our own country.
Ref: Travel agencies and public libraries.
Sightseeing throughout the world—imaginary tour.
Supported by films, film strips, slides, books, travel brochures and teachers' and parents' travel experiences, an exciting project in social studies can develop from taking an imaginary tour to some of the world's most interesting places. The following places were recommended by a leading travel agency:
Athens—the Acropolis and other examples of Greek civilisation.
Venice—unique location and artistic wealth, the meeting place of East and West. Once the greatest seaport in Europe.
Florence—where banking and commerce became patrons of the Arts.
Istanbul—gateway to the mystic East and a mixture of modern civilisation and memories of the barbaric past.
Hawaii—the 49th American state, most famous of the Pacific island paradises.
Jerusalem—home of Jewish, Moslem and Christian religions. The ancient and the modern side by side.
Moscow—capital of the communist world. Red Square and the Kremlin, seat of the Soviet Government.
Grand Canyon—one of the natural wonders of the world.
New York—Broadway, Times Square, Central Park, America's largest and most exciting city.

Rio de Janerio—former capital of Brazil, one of the largest of South American cities, famous Sugar Loaf Mountain.

Mount Kilimanjaro—snow in Africa. One of the most impressive mountains in the African continent.

Mexico City—home of the Aztecs. A modern city high above sea level.

The Ganges—holy river of the Hindus where hundreds of thousands make the pilgrimage every year.

Peking—always a mystery to the West, this ancient capital holds all the fascination of the ancient China of the emperor's and Chairman Mao's modern China.

Great Barrier Reef (Australia)—one of the finest examples of coral formation in the world. Viewed through a glass bottomed boat an experience of a lifetime. The reef stretches for about 1,200 miles.

Japan—a country of great natural beauty and modern endeavour.

Cairo—a modern jumping off point to the land of the Pharoahs. A complete civilisation thrived here when most of the World was still primitive.

Greenland—the northern tip of the civilized world. The land of the Eskimo and breathtaking natural beauty.

Cape Town—South Africa's capital. Sun, sea, surf coupled with a thriving city. Famous for its Table Top Mountain.

Bangkok—capital of Thailand—temples, palaces and the famous floating market. From the tourist point of view a unique city.

The Alexander Graham Bell Association for the Deaf has recently arranged with the National Geographic Society and the U.S. Office of Education, to published *World Traveler*. A magazine specifically written for deaf children which has been adapted from the National Geographic's School Bulletin.

HISTORY—World, National and Local

"The driest thing that the mouse could think of when the bedraggled company assembled at the edge of Alice's Pool of Tears, was history." R. J. Unstead suggests that this is the conventional view of history, but asks if this is necessary, and goes on to show clearly that it is not.

Strong, in *History in the Primary School* stresses the need for imaginative selection on the part of the teacher from the vast mass of recorded fact. "No historian, however scholarly, erudite, or versatile, can take the whole field of human endeavour for his province." He suggests that teachers must make a careful selection from the information available; but the danger is that the child may so easily be wrenched from the natural line of his inquisitiveness by having superimposed upon him a course of lessons drawn up on the basis of a purely academic syllabus.

Keeping as much as possible of the material presented related to the lives of the children and to current events, can assist in creating and maintaining interest levels:

He who would understand these things rightly must not confine his observations to palaces and solemn days. He must see ordinary men as they appear in their ordinary business and in their ordinary pleasure (Macaulay, 1848).

Carlyle, too, stressed the importance of seeing social life through the ages as "the aggregate of all the individual men's lives who constitute society."

Watson has emphasized the important point that one value of history over present day environmental studies is that it stimulates the imagination of deaf children. As with geographical studies, current events are usually an excellent means of creating a meaningful lead in to topics. Conversely, the daily news becomes much more interesting as a result of the world history studies. World history also aids the learning of geographical facts. Frequent use of charts, time charts and maps is necessary.

Topics from which a selection may be made

I   Film strips are available on virtually all the topics listed below.

    a) Geographical discoveries (revision of explorers covered in Section II). Jackdaw series—Conquest of Mexico No. 51; Columbus and the Discovery of America, No. 4; Mayflower and the Pilgrim Fathers, No. 8.

b) European colonization in America, Africa and the Far East. Ref. Strong, C. F. The Early Modern World, pp. 154–165, Map p. 163

II *United States of America*

a) Causes and Course of American Revolution (1775–1783) Ref: Strong, C. F. *America Yesterday and Today.*

b) Personalities of American Revolution, e.g., Washington. Ref: Strong, *ibid,* and *Encyclopaedia Britannica.*

c) Constitution of U.S.A. (ref. Strong, *ibid.*) (diagrammatic form and discuss differences with e.g. British Constitution). An American election and how it is run.

d) American Civil War: results, personality of Lincoln, Reconstruction (William, Strong, *ibid,* Case and Hall)

e) Westward Development of U.S.A. (Map) and reasons, methods, highways, relations with Indians, etc. (Ref. Williams, Case and Hall)

f) U.S.A. as a World Power (Ref. Williams)

g) Prohibition; Depression; New Deal (Roosevelt) (Ref.) Williams)

h) Personalities and development in 20th Century Ref. Tull and Bulwer

i) America in World War II

j) "The New Frontier," J. F. Kennedy's work.

k) The Atlantic Alliance.

Note: It is possible to adapt the study of world history for less able children by concentrating less on political events and studying personalities and social life in greater detail. The War of Independence can thus be studied around Washington's career; the Civil War around Lincoln; stories of the Indians in Westward Expansion, the film industry and great film stars, the Depression, space development and the 20th century. These topics appeal more readily to children who are less able to grasp topics such as The American Constitution, America in World War II, etc.

III *Russia*

a) Expansion of Russia 1550–1900 (Strong, *ibid.*) (Map)

b) Peter the Great (Strong, *ibid.*)

c) Catherine the Great (Strong, *ibid.*)
d) 19th Century development in Russia (Case and Hall) conditions of people; Tzardom, etc. (Williams, *ibid.*)
e) Reasons for Revolution of 1917 (Case and Hall, Williams) Jackdaw series No. 42, Tull and Bulwer (*ibid*).
Soviet Russia: Personalities and work of Lenin, Stalin, Khruschev. Technological advance; Communism, Society (Case and Hall; Williams; Tull and Bulwer)

IV   *Africa* (Williams)
a) Exploration: important explorers (e.g. Livingstone); where they went; condition in Africa.
b) Colonisation in the 19th Century: scramble for Africa (Case and Hall).
c) The New Nations: independence in Africa; problems faced by an emergent state, e.g. Ghana (Tull and Bulwer).

V   *The Far East*
A. *China* (Williams)
a) Before opened to West; Chinese society; culture and civilisation; inventions (gunpowder, printing, etc.)
b) European influences (Case and Hall); Revolution under Sun Yat Sen 1911.
c) Communism; 1949 (Tull and Bulwer); Mao Tse Tung; Chiang Kai Shek.
d) Influence of China in South East Asia.

B. *Japan* (Case and Hall; Williams)
a) Before opened to West; Japanese customs and government.
b) European influences.
c) Expansion of Japan to 1945 (Tull and Bulwer)
d) Modern situations in Japanese Life; Industry; Important cities.

VI   *Britain:*
a) *The Middle Ages*
Emphasis on the Norman Invasion, castles, Life on a medieval farm, life in a medieval village, the medieval church and monastery, the Crusades, John and Magna Carta, growth of Parliament to 1500.

b) *Tudor England and the Stuarts*
   Emphasis on the Reformation and Henry VIII, seamen and Armada.
   Charles I and the Civil War. Oliver Cromwell.
   Marlborough, life in Britain in the reign of Queen Anne.

c) *18th Century*
   Life in England in 1750, the Agrarian Revolution, the American War of Independence, a typical 18th century Parliamentary election, William Pitt (younger) and French Wars.

d) *19th Century*
   The Industrial Revolution, need for social reform in factories, mines etc., life of poor in 19th century, reformers, e.g. Shaftesbury, social reforms, life in reign of Queen Victoria (in, say, 1850) comparison with today (e.g. schools, clothes, general behaviour, etc.). growth of British Empire (map work), Gladstone, Disraeli.

e) *20th Century*
   Effect of First World War on Britain, life in Britain during the Second World War; Winston Churchill, the Commonwealth. Life in 1970 and comparison with the previous century, e.g. a day in the life of a family—comparing domestic chores, clothes, communications, shopping, leisure and travel, etc.

References

Case, S. L., and Hall, D. J.: Modern European History through Maps and Diagrams. Elmsford, Pergamon, 1971.
Films and Filmstrips from E.F.V.A., 33 Queen Anne St. London W.
Jackdaw Series; relevant topics. Jackdaw Publications, Jonathan Cape.
Longmans, Richards, D.: *Tudors and Stuarts,* 1967.
Milliken, E. K.: *Norman and Angevin.* George Harrap, 1958.
Philips Atlas of Modern History. G. Philips and Son, 1965.
Richards, D., and Hunt, J. W.: *Modern Britain.* Lohgmans, 1967.
Strong, C. F.: *America, Yesterday and Today.* University of London Press.
————: *History in the Primary School.* University of London Press.
————: *The Early Modern World.* University of London Press.

Tull, A. K., and Bulver, P. M.: *Britain and the World in the 19th Century.* Blandford, 1966.
———: *Britain and the World in the 20th Century.* Blandford, 1967.
Unstead, R. J.: *England, the Medieval Scene.* Black, 1962.
Williams, G.: *Portrait of World History.* Arnold, 1966.

Mapwork

Each child can be given a loose leaf file to contain the following outline maps:

1. *America*
   (a) Western Expansion
   (b) Civil War
   (c) The 50 States of U.S.A.
2. *Russia*
   (a) Expansion of Russia to 1914
   (b) The Communist World post-1945
3. *Africa*
   (a) Exploration
   (b) Africa and the European Powers (in the late 19th/early 20th Century)
   (c) Africa Today
4. *The Far East*
   (a) Japanese Expansion to 1942
   (b) China and European Influence
5. *Great Britain*
   (a) Seamen of Elizabeth—world map to show journeys, etc.
   (b) Britain in 1750 showing population and industry—farming, mining, etc., and land communication.
   (c) Britain in 1950 with some facts for comparison.
   (d) Map of world showing British Empire in 19th century.
   (e) Map of British Commonwealth today.

NOTE: Some of these maps look formidable for children to transfer on to outline, but they make interesting lessons because they introduce geographical factors—extent of land and the influence of a country (e.g. China in South East Asia, Japan in the East). They can also be considerably modified by the teacher to include only the points that it is wished to illustrate, by simplification of facts, and colouring.

ILLUSTRATIONS: These are invaluable for wall charts, etc., and can be obtained from a variety of sources: Newspapers and periodicals, often in supplements: museums (for cultural illustration, e.g. Chinese and Japanese); radio and television pamphlets: every year there are pamphlets covering some part of world history that are up to date and full of interesting material, including photographs and information in chart and diagrammatic form.

Additional Topics in World History

Changes in inter-personal communications—mail.

Changes in mass media—press, radio, television.

Changes in leisure time pursuits.

Humanitarian movements—penal reforms, the abolition of slavery, the Red Cross.

Imbalance of world wealth—the affluent societies
    the underdeveloped countries
    population problems

War—its causes; a basic pattern in a changing setting; social implications; weapons used and geographical location, e.g. pre-20th century—Peloponnesian War (Xerxes), the Hundred Years War (Joan of Arc), the French Revolution, and Napoleonic Wars (Napoleon Bonaparte).

World War I and World War II

The clash of races—19th century—The American Indian
    20th century—Nazi racism
        Arabs and Jews
        Turks and Greeks
        Black and White

Some Religious and Social Institutions; (Ref. Pears Cyclopaedia—Ed. L. Barker)
    Mohammedanism (Islam)
    Buddhism
    Confucianism
    Hinduism
    Christianity
    Judaism

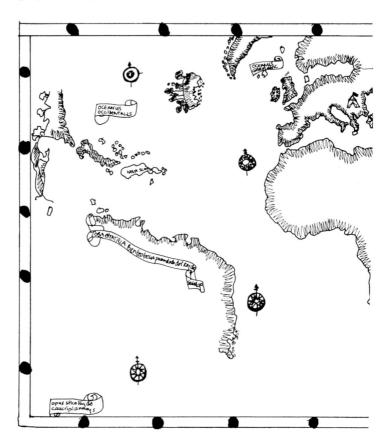

The lives and work of some famous men and women—where these have not been studied in the World History Course above. (Ref: Encyclopaedias and Public Libraries).

Scientists

Taken in sufficient detail to illustrate the application of scientific methods and the propounding of a theory and its testing. Galileo, Newton, Darwin, Rutherford, Einstein, von Braun.

Political Leaders and Personalities

Washington, Lincoln, Napoleon, Lenin, Stalin, Pankhurst, Hitler, Churchill, Roosevelt, Nkrumah, Kennedy, Mao Tse Tung.

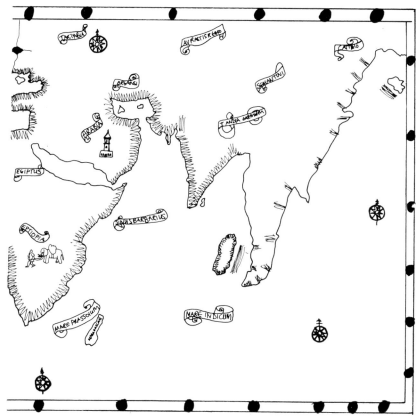

Figure 13. Map of the known world about the time of the death of Christopher Columbus.

Inventors and Engineers
Watt, Davy, Stephenson, De Lesseps, Bell, Edison, Ford, Marconi.

Explorers
Revision of Columbus (See Fig 13), daGama and Magellan; Tasman, Cook, Livingstone, Hudson, Bleriot, Scott (Fig. 14), Shackleton, Hillary and Tenzing, Armstrong, Aldrin, and Collins.

Medical Researchers and Workers
Jenner, Pasteur, Lister, Nightingale, Curie, Fleming, Salk, Barnard.

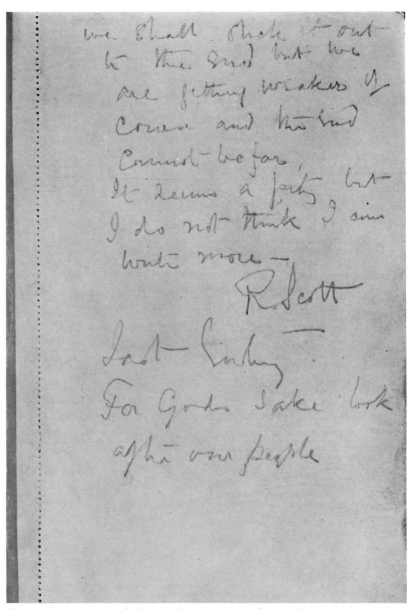

Figure 14. Last page of Captain Robert Scott's diary. (Courtesy British Museum and Sir Peter Scott)

We shall stick it out to the end but we are getting weaker of course and the end cannot be far. It seems a pity but I do not think I can write more. Last Entry. For God's sake look after our people.

R. Scott

B. *NATIONAL HISTORY*

A study of our nation's history in more detail than the outline given above for major countries (except Britain).

Some suggested lines of study:

A general survey of everyday life during the last 200 years.

A day in the life of a rich and a poor family in 1970; 1900; 1850; 1800.

Changes in leisure time pursuits.

Changes in taste and design—architecture, furniture, dress.

Landmarks in the country's history.

C. Just as the study of local government helps children to appreciate national government, so the investigation of local history is an invaluable aid in the teaching of national history. To see the remains of an ancient road, the site of a battle field or the home of a statesman, helps to create a bridge between the classroom and the world outside, as well as to stretch the imagination from the present into the past. The local museum, the record office, the reference library (for old newspapers), the parish church records, an old homestead, or factory, an archaeological site, are all useful for reference or better, for visiting, and helping the history of the district come to life. The history library in the school should contain local histories, survey maps of the area, and books useful for teachers such as Tate's "The Parish Chest" (Cambridge, 1960). To be intelligible to deaf children, much editing of most documentary material is, of course, needed before they can study independently from it.

5. *Home Management*

Most of these topics are best taken in situations where the class simulates the real situation of managing a home. Talks by deaf adults can often be extremely useful.

Budgeting—income and expenses
  choices in buying: influences on our judgment.
  planned buying
  instalment and credit buying
  guarantees, receipts, trade directories
Cost of living

Standards of living
Boarding
Renting a house or apartment
Living with parents—advantages and disadvantages for married and unmarried people
Living in flats (apartments) —sharing costs, duties, etc.
Buying a house or apartment—house agents, advertisements, surveyors, lawyers, mortgages, insurance.
Home maintenance—interior decorating
    plumbing
    electrical appliances
    exterior upkeep
    improvements, e.g. adding a bedroom or bathroom
Rates—payment for community service, e.g. rubbish collection, water supply, roads, parks, etc.
Buying a car
    dealers
    advertisements
    mechanical checking
    instalment buying
Elementary servicing of a car—battery, tyres, petrol, oil, radiator, etc.
Safety in the home—electrical appliances, gas, heating, poisons, inflammable materials and substances, security of the house against burglars and intruders
First Aid
Borrowing money—from friends, from banks, etc.
Saving—banks, building societies
Insurance—life, house, property
Taxes
Home gardening
Food—diets, care in purchasing
Family planning, having babies, infant and child care
Clothing

6. Social Living

Talks and demonstrations by deaf and normally-hearing outsiders should be considered from time to time with many of these topics.

Personal hygiene—good grooming hints

Common courtesies
  in other people's houses
  at meetings
  in discussions
  in humour
  when shopping
  on the roads
  learning to disagree without being disagreeable

Entertaining
  morning coffee
  afternoon tea
  friends to lunch or supper
  parties
  picnics
  invitations to deaf adults and other local friends: as
    guests and as speakers

The rôle of the host and hostess

Looking after an invalid

Our neighbours—the logic of good neighbourliness

The importance of such traits of character as honesty,
  charity, justice, and humility—How these have been shown
  in the lives of certain people

Religion and church going

Courting—dating, petting, engagement, marriage, separa-
  tion, divorce

Family planning

Smoking—the habit and the hazards

Alcohol

Drugs

Respect for people of different race, religion and colour

Games of chance

Movies and the theatre

The Visual Arts (see Appendix 2)—painters, sculptors,
  architects, workers with metal and glass

Planning vacations
Driving Lessons
Adult hobbies, games and sports:

Art	Indoor plants
Baseball	Knitting
Basketball	Motoring
Boat building	Movies
Bowling	Music
Cards	Painting
Carpet bowling	Photography
Chess	Plasticine modelling
Clock repairing	Racing
Cooking	Radio
Crossword puzzles	Reading
Cycling	Religion
Discussion groups	Sewing
Drawing	Skating
Fishing	Skiing
Gardening	Stamp collecting
Golf	Swimming
Football	Table tennis
Handwork	Television
Hockey	Toy making
House maintenance	Woodwork

Letter writing
> Winston Churchill's suggestions to writers of English have relevance; "Broadly speaking, the short words are best and the old words, when short, are best of all."

friendly letters
business letters—writing for holiday brochures, etc.
invitations
accepting or declining invitations
letters of thanks after visits and outings
pen friends in other countries
lettters of sympathy to someone who is ill or to those who have been bereaved

An analysis of a newspaper
  news
  features
  editorials
  advertisements
  announcements
Regular discussions on the topic of meeting and making friends with normally hearing boys and girls. Hearing people have problems in integrating with others too. The importance of possessing a pleasant personality and also speaking as clearly as possible, competence in lipreading as well as the ability to read and write if one wishes to mix more than superficially with normally hearing people. Discuss this statement: "Friendships are fragile things and should be treated as such."

The significance to each child of his educational, audiological and social school records—private discussions.

7. Occupations

Regular visits to see a variety of occupations are necessary. In their study of the jobs undertaken by deaf female school leavers, Connor and Rosenstein (1963) advocate a more serious and active role in the school programme for vocational training. They do not, however, envisage that schools should become trade training centres and suggest that the needs of the children can best be met by a balanced curriculum of academic subjects including reading, writing, social studies, science, and mathematics. They also draw attention to the fact that few schools provide systematic and organized vocational guidance.

Vocational guidance
Work experience
Vocational training and placement
Factory work — historical information, study of factory organization, care of workers in a modern factory
Local industry and employment prospects
Trade unions
Employers' organisations
Further education

evening classes

day release schemes

The social value of various occupations—need for good carpenters, mechanics, etc., as well as good doctors; responsibilities of workers

8. Social and Political Changes

Much of the work under this heading becomes more meaningful if the students are given the opportunity of participating actively in the running of their school.

The development of local government

city, borough

county

organization

function

The growth of political parties

Living and working conditions—now and fifty years ago

The Trade Union Movement

Reforms in health, education and welfare

Some knowledge of leading personalities

The census

Voting

World government—organization and function

9. Social Services

Care of the elderly

Assistance to handicapped people—studies of other handicapped children: blind, crippled, mentally defective, cerebral palsied (Fig. 17)

Crime and the Law—types of crime, alternatives to prison, types of prison.

Marriage guidance councils

Citizen's advice bureaus

Charitable and government social services

Libraries

Parks—municipal gardening

Museums and art galleries

Hospitals

Some practical experience in the field of social service is very desirable. A common fear is that the deaf child offering help may place too great a strain on those he wishes to help. This difficulty is real, but has often been overcome. Some suggestions:

A community help service—Teams of three or four children help to clear up a garden, or paint a wall, or perform a similar job for an elderly person.

Scouts look out for jobs that need doing in the community, obtain permission from the authority, and do them.

Senior girls "adopt" an old age pensioner—perhaps a deaf one.

Help to hospital by an able child, e.g. filing X-ray records.

New babies—knitting and sewing clothes for relatives and for friends of the school.

Recognizing difficulties and unhappiness in others and trying tactfully to help them—perhaps among members of the class.

Saving to buy a guide dog for a blind person—after a visit by a blind person or to a school or class for blind children

Some Additional References

Allison, A.: *Design for Living Series. Running your Home, Food and Entertainment.* Mills and Boon, Ltd., 1969.

Boult, G. V.: *We go to Work.* George Harrap, 1961.

Brennan, W. K.: *Family Finance* (Background to Living 2). E. J. Arnold & Son Ltd., 1966.

Brennan, W. K.: *Money Banks and Banking* (Background to Living 3). E. J. Arnold & Son Ltd., 1966.

Brennan, W. K.: *Shops and Shopping* (Background to Living 3). E. J. Arnold & Son Ltd., 1966.

Brennan, W. K.: *Social Services* (Background to Living 6). E. J. Arnold & Son Ltd., 1966.

Brennan, W. K.: *The Nation's Business,* Background to Living No. 5. E. J. Arnold & Son Ltd., 1966.

Carmichael, P.: *Your safety,* Modern Living Series. Longmans, 1964.

———: *Probe 1—Population and Family Planning.* S.C.M. Press Ltd., 66 Bloomsbury St., W.C.1.

———: *Complete Letterwriter for Ladies and Gentlemen.* Ward, Lock & Co. Ltd., 1968.

Creese, A.: *Cookery—The Young Homemakers First Book*. Mills and Boon, Ltd., 1965.

Creese, A.: *The Young Homemaker Series,* First Book. Mills and Boon, Ltd., 1967.

———: *The Young Homemaker Series. Looking After Others.* Mills and Boon, Ltd., 1966.

———: *Money Management.* Mills and Boon, Ltd., 1967.

———: *Caring for Yourself.* Mills and Boon, Ltd., 1967.

Department of Education and Science Report: *Religious Education, Present and Future.* H.M.S.O. (Gp. 3319), 1969.

Devereux, Hilary: *Housecraft in the Education of Handicapped Children.* Mills and Boon, Ltd., 1963.

Donley, E. L. (Ed.): *World Traveler.* Pub. Oct. to May by Alexander Graham Bell Assoc. for the Deaf, Inc.

Douglas, J. W. B.: *Home and the School.* MacGibbon and Kee, 1964.

Furton, C.: *You and the State—an Introduction to Civics.* Understanding the Modern World Series, 3rd Ed. Allen & Unwin, 1960.

Graves, S., and Furth, C.: *Your Work and Your Wages,* Understanding the Modern World Series, 3rd Ed. Allen & Unwin, 1960.

Grosvenor, Melville B.: *National Geographic School Bulletin.* Washington.

Handicrafts for Older People. N.C.S.S. ref. 636. National Old People's Welfare Council, 1963.

Hill, W.: Social Studies in the Elementary School Programme. U.S. Dept. Health and Welfare, 1960.

Hildick, E. W.: *A Close Look at Newspapers.* Faber & Faber Ltd., 1966.

Irgens, B.: Visual Aids: An Enriching Medium. In *A Handbook of Readings in Education of the Deaf and Post School Implications.* Springfield, Thomas, 1967.

Lund, Gilda: *Manners for Moderns.* Mills and Boon, Ltd., 1964.

Manvell, R.: *This Age of Communication.* Blackie, 1966.

Marland, M.: *Following the News.* Chatto & Windus, 1967.

Marris, B. P.: *The Census,* Sec. School Bulletin Vol. 16 No. 9. School Publications Branch, Dept. of Education, Wellington, New Zealand, 1966.

Messenger, B.: *Complete Guide to Etiquette.* Evans Bros., 1966.

New Zealand Teaching Films to Help Deaf Children: *A Deaf Child in the Family* (38 minutes). 51 Clifton Terrace, Sumner, Christchurch, New Zealand.

Norton, Doreen: *Looking After Old People at Home.* N.C.S.S. (ref. 494/4), 1962.

Odell, H. J.: *Visual Citizenship,* Safety & Public Services. Evan Bros. Ltd., 1959.

———: *Bank Education Service Study Booklets.* 10, Lombard Street, London, E. C. 3.

———: *Aims and Methods* Citizens Advice Bureau Pamphlet. National Council Social Service, 1967.

————: *A Brief Summary* Citizens Advice Bureau. C.A.B. Service, 26 Bedford Square, London W.C.1., 1966.

————: *Youth Helps Age.* Standing Conference of National Voluntary Youth Organ. & Nat. Old Peoples' Welfare Council. N.C.S.S., 26 Bedford Square, London W.C.1.

Opie, J.: *Over my Dead Body.* London, Methuen, 1951.

Park, C. W.: *The Population Explosion.* Heinimann, 1965.

————: *Encyclopaedia Americana.* New York, America Corp., 1967.

————: *Encyclopaedia Britannica.* 1969.

Scheinitz, E. de, and K. de: *Interviewing in the Social Services* N.C.S.S. ref. 636. The National Institute for Social Work Training.

Sills, David (Ed.) : *International Encyclopaedia of Social Services* Vol. 2. London, MacMillan & Free Press, America, Collier & MacMillan, 1968.

Stamp, E.: *The Hungry World,* Crossroad Series. E. J. Arnold & Son Ltd., 1967.

Sullivan, N.: *101 Driving Lessons for Beginners.* Dickens Press, 1968.

————: *Car Driving for Beginners.* Assoc. of R.A.C.

————: *Know your car.* Autocar.

Tansley, A. E., and Brennan, W. K.: *School-leavers' Handbook.* E. J. Arnold & Son Ltd., 1963.

Thomas, J.: *Hope for the Handicapped.* Bodley Press, 1967.

Tizard, J., and Grad, J. C.: *The Mentally Handicapped and their Families.* Maudsley Monograph, No. 7 London, Oxford Press, 1961.

Current Events

Throughout these language outlines emphasis has been given to the invaluable role of current events—not only for its own sake but also as a practical lead-in to other subjects which are not so readily comprehended. One splendid teacher in Los Angeles based the whole of his teaching of 16-year-old deaf children on the daily newspaper. This required him to rise before 6:00 A.M. each morning so that he could read the paper carefully and make the necessary preparation. Visual aids, pictures, maps and books were found and exercises set appropriate to the needs of each child in the class. A newspaper was usually bought for every child each day.

A Television Series: People of Many Lands

(Thirteen and fourteen-year-old deaf and partially hearing children)

In this unit in a large high school there are three teachers of the deaf whose teaching commitments make it impossible for them to take this television series alone. They have shared the work and there have been advantages in this team teaching approach. As soon as they receive the TV programme they order films and filmstrips to support it. Later, books from the local library are ordered.

During the week before the viewing of a particular programme the children and teacher find out:

Where the country is on the globe and in the atlas, and relate it to England and to countries previously studied.

What the country looks like physically—flat, rolling, mountainous, etc. compared with England, using books and filmstrips as required.

What the climate is like compared with that of England and what they expect life to be like in this country.

Each 20-minute programme is seen twice—once on Monday and once on Friday. Teacher 2 supervises the first viewing. In the ten minutes before the viewing begins fairly formal factual details are given relating to population, major cities and to rivers if a river is very important. Most of this information is compared with England and this gives it more meaning. Significant language is written on the board.

If possible, the children are left to enjoy the programme uninterrupted, but if the language is at all difficult for the deaf children, the teacher interrupts to explain important points, but this is kept brief or the children miss too much of the film.

Items of special interest are discussed for the remaining few minutes of the period. This interest often continues, for example, when the children know that someone among us has been to one of the countries concerned, and they often ask about this outside the usual class periods. Teacher 1, on Tuesday, uses the booklet as a guide and asks the children what they saw and found out. This is a meaningful situation since the children know that this teacher has not seen the programme.

Each pupil is asked in turn and a variety of answers are received. Sometimes they want to know more about one of these points. This is discussed, and books already in the classroom may be used or others consulted in the school library. The supplementary film or film strip or part of same may be shown.

Further questions such as, "What sort of life do these people live? What sort of work do they do?" What about their food? clothing? houses? sports? and the way they get about? Especially, the teacher asks what the children are like: their schools, their clothes, their games, how they help their parents.

I use a variety of books such as *"Gerda Lives in Norway,"* or even the very simple "My Home" series. The pictures, the very simple factual information, and the child-centered point of view all appeal to the children. These books are then available for further reading, which may need quite a lot of guidance. I give this by means of a set of questions on a piece of paper. These questions are planned rather carefully so that the answers, which the children write in their books, make up a little summary of what the children have studied.

Towards the end, the children make a map of the country, showing some of the major physical features together with the points that seemed most important in the programme.

Occasionally, a class summary is made on the board. The teacher tries to get the children to help plan the right sequence of statements and also the priorities.

Teacher 3—Friday. As I have not yet seen the programme, I ask the children to tell me what they remember from their first viewing and what new words they have learned. I write the words on the board.

We then watch the programme, and while watching I may break in to draw attention to points not raised in the earlier discussion. These are noted on the board later.

The programme may have several themes—e.g. forest products, travel in winter, family life, learning to work in an industry—set in different countries.

While I am doing this, I may bring in additional material discovered by Teacher 2 to make clear the meaning of a word, a process, or a substance (such as paper pulp). We go to books or pictures, or get samples of the substance, to help the children understand.

Next I write on the board a set of about ten questions designed to illustrate the extent of the children's understanding, requiring them both to recall events in the programme and to explain the "how" and the "why" of these.

The programmes centre round family life and lead out, usually through the father's work, to the study of a major industry.

For the children, differences in details of family life stand out. For example, the sauna bath, in Finland, caught their attention. To begin with, whatever was different from their own way of living was inferior. But discussion of the sauna, of a French bath with a step to sit on, and of a shower, helped to modify this attitude. Similarly, they came to see sense in the use of hot springs for cooking in Iceland and New Zealand, and were interested in peat fuel in Ireland. The important ideas are that *all people have the same basic needs* and that *these needs are met in different ways.*

The interest and variety of the programmes, and the need to ask and answer questions, make summaries, look up books, interpret pictures, all result in the extension of vocabulary and the more precise use of language; the ability to observe more accurately; some ability to assess the relevance and significance of the various happenings observed. The children were able to wonder about things, to listen to other opinions; and to realise that teachers don't know everything but often have ways of finding out. Perhaps most important of all, the teachers think the children became more tolerant. They seem less inclined to see people in terms of good or bad, actions as sensible or silly, and so on.

The Beacon River Study

(Eleven fifteen-year-old partially hearing children, with average or above average intelligence)

Most of the class were town dwellers.

In four lessons, the purpose of the study was explained and discussed: to study the Beacon River and how it affected life around it. Ordinance survey maps—1 inch to 1 mile—were used, routes plotted, measurements made to scale, and the children asked to find from the maps what they might expect to see when they visited the area.

FIRST VISIT, OCTOBER. It took all day. Maps and notebooks were taken, in addition to surveyors' poles, 100 ft. tape measures, compasses, a long rope to measure the depth of the river, and a portable tape recorder. (This last was used for the teacher's comments and also for recording one or two local people.) The tape recordings proved "different" and highly stimulating. Colour slides were also made.

A minibus was taken to Beacon village, and the class and two teachers walked about 18½ miles around the area. This was a general survey to arouse curiosity. One group got lost and had to be brought back by a policeman. This resulted in a greater interest in map reading on everybody's part! The children became more independent—everybody did his or her own reading after this and discussed, argued and explained each point before setting out.

SECOND VISIT, JANUARY. This was two days after a bad flood. All knew about it, as it had been reported in the national press and on television. They found out about the damage to homes, took photographs, made drawings and wrote notes.

At times the groups were alone, and the teachers did not know what they were finding out. After this they noticed that the children were much less shy about asking questions in shops or of local people. On this visit river measurements were made at two points, seven miles apart.

THIRD VISIT, MARCH. This was made to record and check data. They visited the mouth of the river at Lytham to compare it with Beacon. Time was also spent determining the main industries and agricultural practices in the area.

IN BETWEEN VISITS. The children recorded information, talked, discussed what they should do, and did other course work.

The advantages of extending the study over a certain period were seeing the area in three different seasons, and avoiding overtiredness and boredom. It came fresh each time; and the children looked forward to it. It gave adequate time to record and discuss and absorb the material observed, to process photographs and to study maps. All the children wrote a diary account of what they did. A few also made a large chart to show the journeys to the rest of the school and demonstrate that they were really working, and not just picnicking. Special study books were made and were of interest to parents, houseparents and visitors.

One tends to think of practical projects running themselves; but they do, in fact, need more thorough preparation on the part of the teacher than most other forms of work, if time is not to be wasted.

Probably one of the most interesting outcomes of this field project was that the children's other class work improved significantly as the study progressed.

HISTORY

The Association of Assistant Masters in Secondary Schools in the United Kingdom identified three major methods employed in high schools in the mid 1960's in the teaching of history. The majority of schools relied on the *chronological syllabus.* This course begins with the prehistoric period and progresses through classical or medieval times, and reaches the present day or recent past, four or five years later. Tradition and textbooks encourage this form; and a large pecentage of history teachers approve of this approach and feel it is the only way to convey to children the true sense of time and a logical impression of the course of human development.

One alternative is what is called the *patch method.* This involves the study in some depth of certain short periods of history, e.g. seven fifty-year periods were studied in one school over four years. Each two "patches" between 350 A.D. and 1900 A.D. were separated by two centuries. The aim of this technique is to avoid the superficiality of the chronological general sweep when attempted within the confines of the modern timetable.

The third alternative emphasizes *lines of development.* Courses are planned according to theme rather than period. Topics are taken each year such as "The Story of the House," "Living Together," "The Development of Agriculture." With careful planning, interesting and successful work can be taken. In the detailed syllabus for teachers "The Story of the House" was divided into ten topics: the modern house studied first (known to unknown principle), shelters of primitive man, Greek and Roman houses, the Anglo-Saxon house, the medieval castle, the fortified manor house, the work of Wren and Nash in the seventeenth and eighteenth centuries, and a study of architecture in the present century.

In practice, few teachers adhere unreservedly to any of the three types of arrangement mentioned above. A synthesis of the most appropriate features of each is a characteristic of some of the best syllabuses in secondary-school teaching. It is suggested that a similar eclectic approach is likely to be of most value to us in the teaching of the historical aspects of a language syllabus for deaf children.

Before outlining some suggested topics for study in social history, it is felt that one criticism might be made of many of the earlier history syllabuses. There appears to have been far too much emphasis on national history to the detriment of world and local history. National bias can begin with the compilation of a syllabus, not just the emphasizing of national heroes and triumphs and glossing over people and events which were not so worthy, but loading up the timetable which implies that the home country is far more important than in fact it is. There are dangers in uncritical patriotism and insular prejudice. While wanting the children to feel pride in the contributions that their country has made to civilisation, one way of achieving a more balanced view is to spend a very considerable amount of time studying the contributions which other countries have made and are making.

The study of the history of the local area frequently has more immediate and constant appeal to young people than does that of the national community. Local history can be studied as a separate course; but often can run concurrently to illustrate events in the nation's history.

Captain Cook Discovers New Zealand

(Suitable for deaf children of twelve years and older)

It is just over two hundred years since Captain Cook first landed in New Zealand. He claimed New Zealand for Britain's King George III, and raised the British flag for the first time near Gisborne in 1769. Because of this, New Zealand became a British colony: that is why settlers from Great Britain, instead of people from other parts of the world, went to live there.

When Captain Cook left England in 1768 in his ship *Endeavour,* not much was known about the southern half of the world. Captain Cook had to take a party into the South Seas, which was what people called the Pacific Ocean, to study the stars from some of the islands. They sailed via Cape Horn. After that, he was told to sail as far as he could in the Pacific to try and find if there were any large countries in it. People in England believed there was a large continent in the South Seas. Captain Cook's journey showed that this was not so.

After they had finished their work in the islands, Cook had his men sail the *Endeavour* to the south. Early in October 1769, they thought land must be near because they saw patches of weeds and branches of trees floating in the sea, so a careful watch was kept.

Captain Cook tried to land near Gisborne and trade with the Maoris (natives) who gathered on the beaches or came round the *Endeavour* in their canoes; but they looked fierce and warlike, and Cook was so disappointed that he named the place Poverty Bay. This has turned out to be a rather strange name for the place, for Poverty Bay is one of the richest parts of New Zealand.

Captain Cook was a marvellous sailor and map maker. He sailed all round the coast of New Zealand on that first voyage and made maps of it. His map of New Zealand was a very good one, but had two bad mistakes in it. Banks Peninsula, near Christchurch, was shown as an island, while Stewart Island was joined to the South Island. It took Captain Cook six months to sail around New Zealand and then he returned to England.

Atlases and dictionaries are used by each child and a well-illustrated book such as *New Zealand, Gift of the Sea* is used by the teacher.

A passage, such as that above, is written on a chart or overhead projector reel. The teacher reads through one paragraph at a time. The children then read aloud at a near normal rate as the teacher points to each syllable.

Questions and discussion are then introduced so that the meaning of the passage becomes as clear as possible. For example, "What does 'just over two hundred years' mean?" When this has been worked out, another example is given to further clarify the concept. "If this table was 'just over four feet long' how long do you think it would be?" "If Jimmy ran a mile in 'just over five minutes' what time do you think he might have taken?"

In the second sentence, ask what "claimed" means. If there is no response, ask how we might find out. If no suggestions come from the context try looking in dictionaries. Could one country claim another today as Captain Cook did? Explain that there was a sort of "finders, keepers" approach in those early days. The countries were usually offered protection (from other races) and trade: better tools, foods, houses, etc.; but the native people usually had Hobson's choice, i.e. there was really no alternative to the offer that was made to them.

Continue this question and discussion approach to the end (probably finishing on the second session) and show the filmstrip "Captain Cook."

Life in Norman Times

(Eleven deaf children, twelve to fourteen-years-old; two partially sighted and deaf)

To stimulate interest in what it was like to live in Norman times, the teacher handed out copies of Unstead's *The Middle Ages*. The children began to look at the pictures. They would pass remarks about the clothing and homes, and soon this was developed into discussions. Then the class began to read the book to find some of the answers. Immediately they came to the date 1066 and did a sum to find out how long ago that was.

The class had only one thirty-five minute lesson a week. For four lessons the class tried to find out how the Normans lived and sometimes copied some of the drawings—of a castle for example—as a method of studying it closely.

The fifth week the teacher raised the idea of a visit to the museum in the old Norman castle at Neadham, and immediately wished it had been thought of earlier, because of the great excitement it aroused. Arrangements were made by letter and phone; and the class went in the school minibus.

In the meantime the children, from the Automobile Association's handbooks, worked out two routes for coming and going, noting road numbers and calculating distances. (On the day of the trip, they also noted the travel time.) They noted the rivers and how they affected the positioning of roads and bridges.

The class looked again at Unstead's pictures to find out what they could expect to see.

THE VISIT: Each child had made a card with a list of things to look for, and to mark them off as they were observed. The class noted signposts and road numbers, windmills, the marshes, animals, bridges and anything else of interest. The Normans were forgotten.

At the castle the guide who took the class up to the battlements talked about the various points of interest to be seen from the battlements. The teacher and companion staff member helped to get the message across.

Then, the class went down the spiral stairs in the tower, counting the steps, to the dungeon. The children were very intrigued with the torture instruments they had seen before in pictures. The darkness made a great impression, giving them an idea of life in a dungeon.

The guide then left, and the class went into the main keep They dropped pennies in the well, and discussed its depth. Then they explored one room at a time, the children followed their own interests, and discussing points as they arose.

Outside, photographs were made of the group, using the keep, the new city hall and the old guild hall as backgrounds. Everyone bought a guide book and the teacher bought some postcards.

Back at school, the children studied the guide books in great detail, read Unstead again, wrote excited letters home about the visit, made more drawings, and wrote an account of the visit in their notebooks.

The fields in which the children gained appreciably from this study included language, map knowledge and skills, library skills (reference), knowledge of the value of museums, interest in art (they had spent a great deal of time in the art rooms of the museum), a much more real appreciation of what it was like to live in Norman times, and finally sympathy for prisoners.

Sailing Ships

(A three week project for twelve deaf children, seven girls and five boys, fifteen and sixteen years of age)

A written passage was presented first to initiate discussion as the children were very poor lipreaders. This was done in four lessons on the following topics: how sailors were sometimes obtained for ocean-going sailing ships, the press gang, war-ships—especially Nelson's *Victory*, merchant ships—where they sailed and what they carried, and finally, pirates and smugglers.

During this first three weeks, one art lesson was taken with sailing ships as the subject, and part of the poem "The Smuggler's Song" was used during group speech lessons.

On the Monday of the third week the class visited the local Maritime Museum. In a preliminary lesson the teacher had explained what they would see in the museum and asked them to:

(a) Look at the flags of the fishing fleets which used to sail from Sydwash

Draw some of them, and write down the names of the owners of the ships

(b) Look at the tools used by shipwrights

Draw some of them and name them

Find out how holes were made in wood

(c) Look at the tools used by sailmakers

Draw some of them and name them

(d) Look at models of sailing ships

Draw one of them

(e) Look around the rest of the museum
Draw and write about anything of particular interest

The visit would have been more meaningful if all the children had been present during the previous week; but, nevertheless, all were able to participate and all were keenly interested.

The teacher was most impressed by their efforts to sketch and write down information while in the museum, and by the care they took afterwards with their drawings. Not all of them were able to finish everything on the list of work to be done because they were so painstaking.

Back at school they were unable to write an account of the visit without a great deal of help. Consequently, their accounts were similar. Whenever the teacher helped one child by writing on the blackboard, several other children immediately included that phrase or sentence in their accounts. Writing on scrap paper for individual children resulted in the phrase or sentence being "signed" to the others.

It was unfortunate that children of this age should still be incapable of writing a summary of what they had seen. This is clear evidence of their inadequate command of English vocabulary and syntax. It would have been better for the teacher to introduce an intensive programme of visits which were described orally, or by signs and gestures if necessary, by the children and immediately put into conventional written phrases by the teacher. After several weeks of this, the children could be gradually encouraged to begin writing in simple situations.

It is hoped to continue this project for a further week and lead up to the modern shipping which uses Sydmouth Harbour. Further lessons are planned covering:

(a) Identification of country of origin of ships entering the harbour and their cargoes.
(b) Imports and exports from and to many countries, including the geography of those countries.
(c) The uses to which the imports and exports are put, perhaps leading on to various industries in this county.
(d) Sketching and painting at the harbour.

The Christmas Story

(Fifteen year old, slow-learning partially hearing children)

Lesson 1— (thirty-five minutes)

Equipment: Ladybird book *Baby Jesus,* file paper, atlases, overhead projector and book *Camels.*

Method:

The teacher began by asking "Who knows the Christmas story? We are going to find out what it was like to live in those days, in the country in which Jesus was born."

The children found the geographical situation of the country in their atlases. The teacher asked if they could suggest the sort of climate the country would have? The type of terrain—desert, jungle, mountains, etc? Could they describe what they would expect to find? Their answers were reinforced with relevant pictures from the books. Brief descriptions were given from personal experience.

The children were asked if they could describe the sort of home Mary and Joseph might have had, how they travelled from one place to another, the sort of clothes they wore, and the food they ate. Their answers were reinforced again by showing relevant pictures.

It was suggested that the class could produce a small book on the topic, using class books and library books for reference. Suggested subject headings were homes, climate, transport, food, clothes, description of the country, etc.

The children wrote down the subject headings, decided on those in which they were most interested and briefly discussed how they might start finding out about them.

Lesson 2— (seventy minutes)

Equipment:

Filmstrips. "Life in Matarrah" (Village in Iraq) and "Edge of the Desert" (Syria and Lebanon), showing type of clothes, transport, farming methods, homes, water supply, and the people who live in the Middle East today.

Projector

Social studies books and rough notepads for class.

Method:

1. The filmstrip was set up and focused before the children came into the room. A notepad was taken out by each child.
2. The first frame of filmstrip was introduced to the class. It was explained that films had not been invented when the Bible was written, and so what they see on the films are not the exact clothes, etc., but are similar to those worn during Biblical times.
3. The first filmstrip was shown, eliciting questions and comments from individual children, to ensure that they understood what they saw. Explanations and comments were given each frame where necessary.
4. It was suggested that the children make notes to help them to remember what they had seen. The filmstrip was run through again.
5. The second filmstrip was inserted and treated in the same way.
6. Reference books were given out—one between two children looking up information about the same subject headings (which had been chosen the previous week).
7. It was suggested that the following week each child should aim to produce a drawing and a piece of writing about his chosen subject. At this lesson there had been little time for the children to do more than glance at the books.

Though the teacher was familiar with the content of the two filmstrips, she had not expected to get so much from the children. From the point of view of participation, this was a most successful lesson and to reinforce and consolidate this participation, the next language lesson was used as follow up for this topic.

Lesson 3— (seventy minutes)

Present-Day Israel

Equipment:
    filmstrip *Israel,* projector, social studies books, jotter pads, reference books listed previously.

Method:

1. The projector and filmstrip were set up at lunch time.
2. The filmstrip was introduced to the class, and it was ex-

plained that it was a film of present-day Israel. The teacher asked the children to look for things that would not have been in use when Jesus was born.

3. The filmstrip was sown, eliciting questions and remarks from the class. Brief comment was given on each frame, using the filmstrip teaching notes for reference as required.

4. On the second showing, it was suggested that the children make notes of things they wished to remember in relation to five headings: homes, transport, food, clothes and climate.

5. Reference books were allocated, one to each two children. Each group looked up the information on one of the subject headings so that the information could be pooled among them, and at least four of the headings covered. This proved too difficult for most of the class, so "clothing" was researched by the whole class. The work was written and illustrated after oral questions, answers, and a description of garments and their function had been discussed. On the following day, transport, food, homes, and climate were also considered. This went very well with a certain amount of help from the teacher.

LEARNING WITH TELEVISION

An experienced teacher using the "Television Club" series (a programme for slow learners) with a class of fourteen to sixteen-year-old boys, all partially hearing and with at least one other educational handicap.

I realise now that my original aim was to broaden the children's interests and their awareness of the world they live in. Some of the most important results, and aims, now seem to me to be:

1. A considerable stimulation of the children to express themselves and hence general language development.

2. The children certainly become more observant of things around them that are related to the programme. An accident in the programme, for example, leads to much thinking about safety in the home. They also become more critical of what people say and do, e.g. they expect more from me. (Why didn't you tell us that? etc.)

3. The children find these programmes sufficiently interesting to provide them with subject matter for their letters home. Normally, subject matter of letters relates to practical activities, e.g. football, pottery, or woodwork rather than academic work.

Preparation. I order the books (eight months ahead) and when they arrive, read all of them to get the story. I make my collection of maps and pictures, and I decide what films or filmstrips I might use with this programme, and I order some new books if necessary.

Each week I read the story aloud with the class. We then read it as a dialogue where this is possible. Everybody has a turn. I read from the booklet to fill out the dialogue.

Using the teacher's note, I mention items of interest or difficulty in the text and try to get the class to ask questions about them, e.g. a different kind of money, different houses, the use of passports. In this way, they are able to cope better with the programme when it is shown. I am, however, careful not to destroy the element of surprise in the programme. They need to know enough to follow, but not so much that they lose interest.

For ten minutes before the programme we go through our previous discussion, just to remind ourselves what to watch for.

We watch the programme, and at that time I never interfere.

Sometimes the children want to tell me all about it and ask questions about new points. I hold an open discussion and bring out the visual aids I have prepared as they become needed. This may last up to an hour if everyone is interested.

When the discussion begins to flag, I may leave the subject altogether or I may suggest some practical work, such as looking at the plumbing, measuring it, etc. copying out a recipe to be used in the next cookery class, or working out the cost of our clothes. They may write an account of, for example, what interested them most, or what they would have done in those circumstances.

On other occasions, we leave discussions until next day. Then, when they have had time to think it over, we may discuss, measure and write, or draw about what interested us."

We might use a film or filmstrip as a follow up to reinforce learning. We might do some art or craft—painting or making models. It is possible to send these to the British Broadcasting Corporation, and they *may* show them at a later date. They will always send an acknowleding letter and possibly a certificate of recognition. I now stress that the work *may not be shown* because some of the children have been disappointed in the past."

Some Results. After the Swedish programme the children seemed to be noticing Volvo cars all the time. Stainless steel, glass, and other products that were mentioned now caught their attention also, and they talked about them. They were interested in comparing life in Swedish families with their own lives, especially the country weekends in the forest house and the way the children seemed to be much more free than they are. The different food was another particular interest.

This interest does not stop when the next programme ends. The children often refer back to earlier ones, and are keen to compare different ways of life.

World History (1917–1967)

(Use of a school television series with fifteen to sixteen-year-old deaf children of average intelligence but with very low reading ages)

The lead-in to this study, which was spread over two terms, was the children's interest in television news, newspapers, and world news generally. This series would fit in with the history syllabus and would also provide focal points for geography studies.

The children's and teacher's pamphlets and other material were cut to about a page of notes for each programme. These were typed and duplicated for each child, and were used for reading at home and as a part of the record of the series.

Each précis was written on the blackboard the day before the programme, and was used as a reading and discussion lesson, using the illustrations from the children's pamphlets and other sources.

As the class watched the programme, the teacher stood beside the board and wrote a running commentary. Then they all discussed the programme together. (In two schools in England (1973), video tape recordings are made of educational television programmes and these are proving excellent for revision work.)

The previous notes were on the blackboard and the class ran through them, relating them to what had been seen. This was followed by a lot of questions and comments from the children. Usually, when a child asks a question, the teacher asks the others if they can reply. The class tries to relate the incidents to the present day situation and where possible to think about each incident personally. However the children would not discuss things unless the teacher led the discussion.

Sometimes the teacher gives questions to answer; and the answers will form a summary. At other times there may be a test to ensure understanding of vocabulary. The children also make relevant maps of diagrams.

The following week the work is reviewed, orally in the main, with a lead-in to the next programme. The class also reviews a whole group of programmes whenever a related set has been completed.

Often, arising from these programmes, an interest in some particular aspect develops, as when we were considering food problems in India. In such a case, a special lesson is given on that topic.

From this series the children have derived a great deal of factual information.

Shopping

(Fifteen-year-old slow learning partially hearing children)

First Step. With the seniors, who understand money fairly well and have learned how to behave in traffic, I first take the class as I do with the juniors but, when we get to the shops, I wait outside with one group while the others go inside and make their own purchases. If they get into difficulties they come out to me for help. If they consult me one week, I hope they will consult the man in the shop the following week.

Second Step. The pupils go shopping in two's without me. They must then help each other and do it all themselves. We teach the older pupils to use their initiative in trying other shops if they can't find what they want in the first.

THIRD STEP. We ask for volunteers to go with messages. At first the children take a note. Later they try to remember what they must buy, how much money they took, what the article cost, and what change they got.

FOURTH STEP. The pupils also keep, as soon as they are able, a little account book of their pocket money expenditure, and they are encouraged to have a savings account. Frequently their purchases will include a savings stamp. We try to get parents to allow a minimum of 25p (60 cents U.S.) a week pocket money—out of which they pay 5p towards visits to the movies and towards their own television, 3p for a stamp for their letter home, and a few pence for needlework or craft materials. (These payments are, of course, only nominal—a reminder that everything is not free.)

FIFTH STEP. The senior pupils also go in groups of three by local bus to the town a few miles away. There they can buy what they need with their pocket money, look around the shops, and think what they will get in the future.

Such an excursion, of course, also requires that they consider timetables, to be punctual, and to develop a general sense of responsibility.

The School Chapel and Local Church

(Partially hearing children aged fourteen and fifteen years)

Although many of the children had been going to school chapel for morning prayers each weekday for more than two years, it was interesting to note how little they had observed.

The shape of the inside of the roof was discussed and what it reminded one of, if turned upside down. Hundreds of years ago a roof had indeed been a boat turned upside down, as men had been extremely skilled in boat making and found this method to be equally successful for roofs.

We discussed these aspects:

The nave. The term used for the body of the church where the people sit. The word *nave* coming from the Latin *navis* meaning ship.

Congregation. The name given to the people who attend a service. An assembly of people.

The aisle. The pathway, usually down the centre of the nave.

Pews. The name for the fixed wooden seats.

The altar. A flat-topped block used for making offerings to God. A communion table, usually at the east end of the church. (Unfortunately not so in the school chapel.)

The font and its use. The name resembling a fountain, and so the connection with water.

A lectern, being a reading desk, especially for lessons, often read by pupils. (*Lecturna*—Latin for "to read.")

The chancel. The part usually railed off, at the east end of the church and where the choir sits. (*Cancelli*—Latin for "lattice, bars, a partition.")

Stained glass windows. These often depict saints and kings, and illustrate stories from the Bible.

The Lives of Saints. In the school chapel there are twelve stained-glass windows depicting ten saints and two kings. Among the saints are St. George, St. Patrick, and St. Andrew. A lesson was taken on each of them, including the banner of each; and these culminated by showing how the three banners compose the present Union Jack.

Depending on the time of the year further stories were taken about saints, such as June 24th, which commemorates St. John the Baptist (and is also the equinox!).

Art Lessons. There are ten children in the class and each chose a stained-glass window to copy and later to colour. (Copying is not entirely a good idea, but in this case it tied in well with the project.)

To copy a stained glass window has its advantages, especially for the child who is not artistically gifted. Such a window is usually divided into sections, and after a period of observation, before the drawing commences, a discussion must take place in which the children are encouraged to notice and describe what is contained in each section, building up the figure, and in a sense forming a large jig saw puzzle.

Once started, with the shape of the window and sections drawn in, the less artistically inclined children become encouraged when they find that by careful observation their pictures soon take shape.

Of the ten pupils in the class, three were reasonably artistic, five showed fair ability, and two obviously were not gifted in the slightest. After three one-hour periods, however, all had produced drawings of an exceptionally high standard. A great deal of interesting language also came from these lessons as I moved from one child to the other discussing their work.

Mathematics (measurement). The ruler was talked about; and how it was made up.

Measurements before rulers were used, i.e. the span, the cubit, the foot, the digit and the step were talked about. The children, working in pairs, were asked to use these methods in the classroom. Results were compared and the children were asked to say why they were impractical. The reason why fixed and accurate measurements had to be agreed upon was seen.

Graphs of the chapel were made after it had been measured on squared paper. It was noted that the shape was a cross.

A visit to the local church followed, after a brief history of it had been given at school by the vicar. It was obvious that within a period of only three weeks, and using the school chapel most of the time, the church could serve simply to compare sizes of different parts and to see if the children could name the parts.

With more time, the history of the church could have been taught, including the materials used in the building. As it was, we simply spoke about the French saint the church was named after (St. Stephen), noticed the flints showing on the outside walls, and that these were pieces of local stone. We observed and discussed the stained-glass windows, the font, the lectern, and so on.

Graphs were made; and it was obvious at a glance that the church was much larger than our little chapel.

A compass was used to see if, in fact, the altar was in the east— and it was.

DOMESTIC ACTIVITIES

It is in the home that real living should begin, and the house-craft centre should be a place in the school where this is continued; or, for a child of a noncaring family, it may be the only homely place he is able to experience.

In a day and residential school the housecraft teacher and matron and the children's mothers should be in close cooperation with each other on such subjects as are mentioned in Group V above.

A good example forms such a big part in the social training of young people, i.e. how the teacher behaves in various circumstances. One cannot, for example, expect a child to cross the road at a pedestrian crossing if one doesn't do so oneself.

Cooking

(Twelve and thirteen-year-old normally hearing but slow-learning girls.)

A teacher from New Zealand writes: Who did you see this morning? Where? What colour was her dress? What colour are her eyes? Gradually, I have them stumped and they realise that their observations could perhaps improve.

I have a bag of apples. We halve one, then quarter it. I then cut another inaccurately. Is this in half? Why not? What is wrong with this piece? (One child informs me that it had a grub in it!) Finally, each child is given an apple she must halve and share with her partner. This sometimes leads to arguments. "She's got a bigger half," they wail, and the lesson on accuracy begins to gain momentum.

I then mix some lemonade and short-measure the sugar. The pupils inform me that it is not sweet enough. Why? And so the need to measure correctly is emphasized. Then we begin on the actual lesson, making scones.

Having set up the boards, we examine the measuring cups. "Find the $\frac{1}{2}$; the $\frac{1}{4}$; look at the measuring spoons; note the difference in sizes."

The children then begin to measure their ingredients. I walk round, checking, complimenting, helping, until all are ready to proceed to the actual mixing. This I demonstrate while they observe.

They return to their tables and proceed to do as I did. It is extremely important to let them do it in their own time. There is no stress on speed, even if it means that they haven't a hope of getting their cooking done by the time the bell rings. It is the measuring that is important here: and I stay on during the interval to watch their cooking in the oven. These children are easily ruffled and discouraged and tend to give in if they cannot succeed. A good deal is learned during this lesson and a quiet, relaxed atmosphere is essential. The children are beginning to do things alone and most of them feel some anxiety over making mistakes.

Reaching the stage of doing things alone is quite an experience. It doesn't have the same effect as it does on other children in the school. Slow-learning children have doubts until they actually see they *can* do things—and this to them is not confirmed until they actually see their finished product. So, to relax them while the scones are cooking, I bring out an enormous chart with all sorts of amusing things drawn on it—either with parts missing or things put in the wrong place, for example, a cup with no handle, a boy with one ear, a cat without a tail, a car with no doors, etc. and we rectify this "chart of errors" which the pupils love and which causes many laughs.

Promoting discussion

The head teacher of one day and residential high school for deaf children has had some success in enabling the children to make a number of decisions after discussion in certain out of school situations.

"We usually begin preparations for a journey about two weeks ahead, as I want the children to have as large a share in the planning and deciding as possible.

First, where shall we go? I like them to suggest to me where we should go, but I do set them some limitations that will result in their choosing the place that I also would prefer! Thus, "We can go hostelling, leaving on Friday week. We can have the minibus, and we will have about two hours to get there. Where shall we go?"

A variety of ideas are put forward. Some are impractical. Someone points this out. There is argument. "Go Wales."

"Too far, silly." "Can't—takes five hours." "How far then?" "Look at map." etc.

What must we do about it? They post up a list on the wall asking who wants to go. This list must give the necessary information, so that the other children can make up their minds, e.g. date, place, cost, times of departure and return.

"We have too many names." They discuss this. "Too many." "No girls this time." "No, we must be fair." "All right, say six boys and six girls." (In such ways we help children to develop ideas of fair play, consideration, and the ability to compromise.)

We discuss food and clothing.

We consider what we will do: walking, sightseeing. For this we study the map and we decide whether to go in one party or several. We may get advice from other people. In this way we practise thinking ahead, using all the available aids we can, such as maps, books, and knowledgeable people.

On the walks we learn to use the ordinance map and compass, becoming more expert on each new occasion. Physical achievement becomes important and seven or eight miles are often covered. The children like to bring things back: stones, bones, shells, an old horseshoe, etc.

All the adults from the school, not only the teachers, take part in turn. This helps our own social relations.

On the return our children enjoy both talking and even writing about their trips. We have not had much art work as an outcome, but we expect this will come.

Doubtless, an extension of the above technique would involve suggesting to the children that they plan the next weekend by themselves. They could then go to their teacher and outline the details they had arranged.

A homecraft teacher of fifteen and sixteen-year-old slow learning partially hearing girls says, "These older children begin to discuss many small problems among themselves such as: "What material will be best for a dress? What colour suits me best for a blouse?" The keener readers look up words in their dictionaries, and some discuss the correct meaning of words when an unfamiliar one crops up. Another subject that stimulates discussion and independent thinking is their arrangement of group games, places in teams, etc., and how they play with friends at home.

Cooking and social studies

The class was doing a study of Japan. They made models relevant to their studies, and paper lanterns, fans, etc., in their room. It was quite a thorough study of all aspects of life there and the idea of a meal comprising the staple foods of the people of that part of the world seemed an appropriate way of concluding it.

The opportunity to play some part in the education of a child in some other field through the subject I teach is a chance I welcome.

The pupils brought most of the required ingredients. Large fish, some filleted fish, tomatoes, bread crumbs, butter and onions. Some of these were purchased by the form teacher with class funds.

As usual, we had a preliminary discussion. Why eat fish? We discussed types of fish, fishing, ways of cooking fish, etc.

I briefed each child on exactly what she was to do. It was important that every child do something and not just be an assistant to someone else. This was an important occasion to them, and they wanted to be able to say, "I did such and such."

We discussed the eating habits of other nationalities. Much of the discussion took place during demonstrations or while I was assisting someone. The discussion was brief, because these slow learning pupils have difficulty in concentrating for long and become bored with too much talk.

As a centrepiece, one fish was left whole and stuffed and baked. The pupils prepared the stuffing, stuffed the fish, placed it in the roasting dish, and put it in the oven. Others prepared the rest of the fish, on this occasion done in the oven with milk, butter, tomatoes surrounding it, etc. The whole fish, with their help, was placed on a large platter and decorated elaborately. I drew their attention to the need for colour in fish meals. Sliced tomato, sliced hard-boiled egg, and chopped chives were used on this occasion with a surrounding ring of rice.

The pupils took all they had prepared back to their room. There, in their oriental setting, with their project work displayed, they, and the boys and other teachers they invited, had a splendid feast.

Project On Milk

In a small secondary day school (45 deaf children) the following team teaching was done largely as a result of the lead given by another imaginative housecraft teacher. This was a project with a class of thirteen-year-old boys and girls.

Housecraft: simple food values

What we can make from milk

1. Beverages—coffee and cocoa
2. Milk puddings—rice puddings, blancmanges
3. Batters—toad in the hole, fruit batter, etc.
4. Sauces—egg with cheese sauce, macaroni cheese
5. Scones
6. Fruit cake

Each week the class had a demonstration lesson; spirit-duplicated notes of recipes and instructions were given out, and finally came the practical class. Each pupil had something to take home. General points which were made in the introductory demonstration were also made on these duplicated sheets.

The great value of cooking is that a pupil can see something made, make it herself, and then take it (and the meaningful reading material) home to show mother and father and big sister from the grammar school who probably can't cook!

This project had the cooperation of all the staff and all felt it was really worthwhile.

Mathematics: Bills were worked out; weights and capacity retaught, and then practised in the housecraft centre; cards with prices were pinned up in their classroom.

Social Studies: The language and history of the milk industry was studied; a visit to a dairy farm and milk-bottling plant was arranged.

Speech and Auditory Training: Flash cards and language master cards were used, with words, phrases and sentences.

Science: Observed the expansion of air as it is heated and related this to the action of heat on batters.

Commercial Classes: Recipes were typed out.

Woodwork: A milk bottle holder was made so that the milk could be put by the milkman in a special place away from the sun.

All price cards and word cards used in the classrooms were the same as those used in the housecraft centre.

It was not possible to visit a cheese factory, but the class made some cheese; and one day the class teacher came into the housecraft centre with the whole class and had a cheese tasting session.

First, the children tried to identify the different English cheeses (seven different varieties) from the large wall chart. Then, their list was corrected and the tasting began with each child making a note of whether he or she liked it or not. After trying out seven different English cheeses, they sampled four cheeses from other countries. One dull deaf girl left no one in any doubt that she did *not* appreciate Gorgonzola.

There was an outside demonstration from the Milk Marketing Board to wind up the project. It was good for deaf pupils to have to concentrate to understand someone who was not used to speaking to a class in a school for deaf children.

Discussion with a class of fourteen-year-old deaf boys and girls

On Blackboard

> A Housewife's work is never done!
> What do *you* think?

The class talked about the need of a timetable at home as much as at school or on the railway station; but agreed that a mother had to be only guided by a timetable and not get "het up" when she is interrupted. From this the class discussed caring for each other in a family.

Housecraft, Third Year

(Fifteen and sixteen-year-old deaf children—many from poor homes)

The pupils make dinners in turn for a small family unit of about five including the teacher (acting in the role of mother) ; and this presents the opportunity to teach good manners, courtesy, tasteful table decoration (really nice crockery, cutlery, table mats and napkins have been provided and always some flowers on the table). It is also an excellent occasion for conversation and discussion.

The teacher still gets quite a fillip from the situation when she had her group of five senior boys to dine and when she walks in they all stand up with a smile, and the nearest boy takes out her chair and graciously settles her into it. All this is done naturally and with a sense of humour, so that there is no self-consciousness.

With such a group, she doesn't have formal grace before a meal, but they are taught mentally to offer a prayer of thanksgiving to God and give a smile and a verbal "thank you" to the cook.

Fourth Year

Mothercraft is taught, with the girls going out to clinics and helping in the local nursery. The boys are also taught how to be good fathers and husbands. Discussions on marriage and sex are included.

Good grooming, in cooperation with the class teacher in hygiene, is also dealt with. A visiting representative from one of the big cosmetics firms comes to show the girls how to make up; and a model comes to give lessons on deportment and how to behave at an interview.

Home Management is a project that can start at housecraft and be continued in the mathematics and social studies lessons.

SOCIAL SERVICES. The girls have done some washing for an elderly woman living on her own and have made cakes to sell at a Christian Service Centre as well as Christmas puddings for distribution at Christmas time.

Small groups are occasionally taken out for coffee or tea. When a visit was made to a large store to see the furniture, the girls loved having coffee in such elegant surroundings.

One day, a former mothercraft health visitor who used to teach the girls mothercraft and who is now a tutor, came to school with six students. The afternoon class of four girls entertained them in the middle of the afternoon. One girl quickly made some scones, another girl cleaned the sitting room, the third laid the table and made the tea, while the fourth girl did some washing in the washing machine. Tea was served at 2:45 and the girls acted as hostesses and entertained the visitors.

MECHANICAL PROJECTS

Do-It-Yourself Projects

With the rise in labour costs in recent years, more and more people are becoming do-it-yourself conscious. Deaf teenagers can derive great enjoyment and satisfaction from studying many of the skills involved in home maintenance and decorating if it is taken as a topic in a language syllabus. The language involved is practical and useful in conversations with people whose homes they visit. If carefully planned, the results are very encouraging; and actually doing the work can be fun for both the students and the teacher. The deaf children are quick to appreciate the saving in cost; and a successful series on this topic at school may well have implications for the life time interests and hobbies of many of the class.

With the materials and tools now available, a teacher does not have to be a handyman (or handywoman) to undertake a project. As usual, however, careful preparation is essential to avoid disappointment. The first step is to obtain a reliable guide book. A good practical one is *The Complete Do-It-Yourself Manual* published by the *Reader's Digest*; but there are numerous others.

A second edition, largely concerned with modernization schemes and techniques, is well illustrated. Some of the topics covered include painting and decorating, brick and stone work, fixing and fastening, plumbing and central heating, upholstery and domestic furnishing, home electrics, glass and glazing, and handling concrete. The second section covers kitchen, bedroom, bathroom, and garden improvements, storage, children's toys, and furniture.

Cars and Car Maintenance

(Nine partially hearing boys of low ability aged fourteen years)

The first five weeks of an eight-week project concerned maintenance and how a car works. In the last three weeks it was proposed to follow up with aspects of the cost of buying and running a car, insurance, taxation, testing, and something on the history of cars.

The work was of a purely practical nature because of the low ability of the group; but it seemed that, if the boys were sufficiently interested in the subject, then the motivation to learn the associated language and vocabulary would present. This proved to be correct, and the boys were soon able to talk quite knowledgeably about the engine and its maintenance.

The project was centred round a small truck owned by a staff member. He required a complete overhaul to be done, including engine, ignition, paintwork, wheels, tyres and brakes. Two lines were followed in parallel lessons on "How a Car Works" and "Maintenance and Servicing of a Car."

Lesson 1

The explosive properties of a mixture of gas and air (exploding tin experiment) were demonstrated. This led to a consideration of how to mix a liquid and a gas (petrol and air); the idea of vapour (a fine spray) was shown using an aerosol.

Lesson 2

The word *ignite* was taught first, leading to the word *ignition*. "How can we ignite the vapour in the cylinder?" A bench mock-up of an ignition coil was demonstrated, followed by a real ignition coil connected to a sparking plug.

Lesson 3

The four-stroke cycle was demonstrated by using an old ustin engine which was found in the school grounds.

The lessons outlined above proved highly successful, and provided the groundwork for future work. Running parallel with these was the car maintenance work. The boys were taught the basic day-to-day maintenance, i.e. radiator, oil level, battery level, tyre pressure, brake fluid level. This enabled them to start work on the truck.

The routine was to make sure the boys knew what they had to do, and why they had to do it, before they began to work practically. Each day's work was followed up by either an

L.R.S. lesson based on the tasks performed, or a conversation lesson with the student teacher acting as stooge. About thirty diagrams and pictures were used.

During the three weeks, the following maintenance tasks were undertaken (here expressed in the same language that was taught to the boys) :

(a) Checking the oil level. (Dip-stick)
(b) Topping-up the radiator.
(c) Topping-up the battery. (Distilled water)
(d) Checking the tyres. (Inflate)
(e) Removing and cleaning a plug, and checking the gap.
(f) Adjusting the points. (Feeler gauge, distributor)
(g) Checking the brakes. (Brake shoes, brake drum, hand brakes)
(h) Changing the wheels round. (Diagonal, tyre-wear, jack, wheel nuts)
(i) Tyre maintenance. (Pressure, tubeless tyres, puncture, repair, tread)
(j) Body work repairs. (Rust, dents, wire brush, wet or dry sandpaper, filler, primer paint, cellulose, finishing coat rubbing down)

Thus, the boys were able to see the parts of the car, suggest ways in which they might function badly, and then suggest how this might be prevented. Wherever possible, the boys used the wrenches instead of watching the teacher use them. Speech work was all based on the topic; this lent itself particularly well to consideration of consonant clusters and stress patterns.

Written work was taken home daily for discussion with the family. An attempt was thus made to interrelate everything and this was fairly successful. The work was meaningful to the boys, with the result that they learned many new language forms and much new vocabulary.

ECONOMIC INSTITUTIONS

Investing Money

Most people try to save some of their money each time they are paid. Some save for a rainy day, i.e. if they have some bad luck, like severe illness in the family, loss of something like a car, or the house getting burned down. Some just save for a sunny day—a holiday, a party at Christmas, a new television set, etc. Perhaps the wisest people save for both rainy and sunny days.

There are a number of ways in which people can invest their money. These include Post Office Savings Bank Accounts, National Development Bonds, bank deposit and savings accounts, Building Society Accounts, Stocks and Shares, Unit or mutual trust accounts. It is rather as the Sheep said in *Through the Looking Glass* "Crabs and all sorts of things, plenty of choice, just make up your minds. Now what do you want to buy?"

Post Office Savings Bank Accounts

Most boys and girls have a Post Office Savings Bank Account at some time or another. They can be opened at nearly every Post Office and you are given a Post Office Savings Book. Only 5p is needed to start the account off. Interest is paid at 3 percent per annum, i.e. 3p each year is added to the account for every £1 held in it. Most people say that if you save regularly each week your money gradually builds up into a useful account.

One of the advantages of Post Office Savings Banks is that small amounts of money can be withdrawn "on demand" at any one of the some 21,000 Post Offices in Great Britain.

If five of the children in one class already had Post Office Savings Books, the teacher might suggest that if the mothers and fathers of the rest agreed, books should be started for them also.

A convenient time with the local Post Office could be arranged and accounts opened for children who do not already have same—and one for the teacher if necessary. Perhaps she could show the class that she is depositing £5 in her account and then say "Oh, bother! I have no money left. I shall have to take £1 out again for my bus fares and for some shopping." Let the children see the withdrawal form being filled in and used and, finally, ask for a deposit and a withdrawal slip for each child which can be used for practice back at school.

Banks

A bank is a place that holds people's money for them and pays it to them whenever they want it.

When we work, we get paid; and our money can be paid by the factory or the office or the school straight into our bank account. Nearly everyone who has a current bank account has a cheque book. A cheque is really a small letter to the bank asking it to pay the person named on the cheque the amount of money which is also written on it. The cheque is signed by the owner of the money.

We can use cheques to pay for things like groceries, the milk bill, the newspapers, the rent, or for big things like furniture or a car or our travel tickets. Another good thing about using a bank is that our money is much safer there (from thieves and from ourselves!), than if it is lying about at home.

Building and Loan Associations

These associations look something like banks from the outside and also when you go in to them. Building and Loan Associations borrow from people who have money to spare, and lend it to others who want to buy their own houses.

Later on, when you have some money to spare, or you are thinking of buying a house, you would be wise to ask your parents or your bank manager (or both) about joining a building and loan association.

They pay higher interest rates than Post Office Savings Banks or ordinary banks, but it is not quite so convenient to get your money out and you can't use a cheque book.

Next time you are in town, find out the names and addresses of two building and loan associations.

Stocks

Big stores and companies, e.g. (name some well known ones), need money to pay for merchandise and for building new shops or factories or offices, etc. This money is called *stock*. The stock is given to these shops or companies by people with money to spare.

The stock is usually divided into *shares*. The people who

have bought the shares usually receive a small amount of money for each share held (usually twice each year) if the store or company makes a profit. This is called a *dividend*. If there is a loss, no dividend is paid; and often the price of the share goes down. If a big profit is made, everyone will want to buy them, so the price of the shares usually goes up. This is the law of supply and demand.

Some people (investors) who buy stocks and shares are very wealthy men, some are in charge of other big stores and companies, but some are just ordinary people who have only a few hundred pounds to invest.

It is easy to lose money when buying and selling shares; and so you should not buy them unless you can afford to lose some of the money sometimes.

One teacher of 16 and 17-year-old bright, profoundly deaf children, when the class was looking at the format of a daily newspaper, was asked, "Why has this page all numbers?" All the children found the page in their own paper. No one knew what the figures were for, nor what a share was.

A series of lessons followed, including the concept of sharing—sharing sweets, sharing a rain coat, sharing a meal. A large picture of a factory was shown and the children were asked, "Could we share this?" "No," they replied. A model factory was then made using a cardboard box and wooden blocks, match boxes for machinery, and some toy cars as the product. Each child was given a piece of the factory and nearly all the children said spontaneously, "We have a share of the factory."

From this basis they went on to learn about profits, dividends, stock brokers, stock exchange and portfolios. Each child also had "shares" in six companies chosen from the daily press and kept a close check on the daily prices (one boy made quite substantial gains!).

THE GOVERNMENT AND ITS MONEY. Where does money come from? Where does it go?

The time-honoured practice of working from specific and practical examples, rather than from abstract generalizations, is essential.

A teacher's first step might be to obtain some of the helpful literature on the subject and after becoming reasonably well informed about governments and the fields in which they spend money, to select practical examples in each of these areas that will help to lead the children to an appreciation of what is involved.

For example, a picture of an aircraft carrier might be shown to the class and an attempt made to guess how many sailors were on board.

Teacher: Who pays all these sailors their wages?

Class: The government.

Teacher: Who pays for all the food they eat at sea?

Class: The government.

Teacher: Who pays for all the fuel?

Class: The government.

Teacher: Who pays for the aircraft carrier? The airplanes? The guns?

Another picture of a flight of fighter aircraft and perhaps a convoy of trucks loaded with soldiers could be treated in a similar manner and then the children asked where the government gets all this money from?

Three major sources of revenue—income tax, sales tax and customs duties—may be dealt with before going on to consider the other fields of government expenditure.

Some of the estimated British Government spending for 1967 to 1968 in millions was as follows:

Defence	£2,321
External relations—including aid to overseas countries	279
Roads and Transport—road building, grants to railways and waterways, and spending on airports and ports	451
Agriculture, Fisheries and Food—including money paid to farmers to help to keep down the cost of food	335
Employment, Industry and Trade—grants and loans to industry and investment in industry	569
Industrial Research and Medical and Scientific Research—including atomic energy and aerospace, and research in universities and laboratories	183

Housing—and things like public parks and swimming pools	176
The Arts—including help for orchestras and theatres, national museums and libraries	14
Law and Order—the police, prisons, and Parliament and the law courts	188
Education—schools, training teachers, further education, universities and technical colleges	325
Health and Welfare Services—including the hospitals	1,171
Children's services—including school dinners, milk and welfare foods (dried milk, cod liver oil, orange juice), and family allowances	222
Social Security benefits—old age pensions, war pensions and Government payments to the National Insurance Fund and the Industrial Injuries Fund	862
Grants to local councils—other than grants tied to a specific service, like education or highways or health	1,410
Other Services—like tax and license collection; the BBC; the Stationery Office; the Central Office of Information; the Meteorological Services; and paying compensation when property is bought and demolished for new building schemes	324
TOTAL	£8,830

EXCURSIONS

Weekend Excursions

While school journeys of a week or more have great value, some schools find that a series of weekend journeys, conducted several weeks apart, can be very useful. There are some practical advantages, e.g. less money has to be found at any one time and they enable the children to make visits to a number of contrasting areas.

Camping

During recent years, school journeys involving camping are becoming increasingly popular in most countries. Camping sites today usually possess good toilet facilities, a shop (often with a postal section), and not infrequently a central hall with television in the evenings. The equipment for camping, too, has become much easier to manage during the last few years, making the whole project far less effort. If teachers of the deaf have been put off camping through some traumatic childhood experience of leaking tents and wet firewood, they might well take another look at the modern facilities for this form of school excursion.

As with most things in teaching, careful preparation well in advance is of prime importance. Points to consider include:

1. Do we want to go for educational or vacational purposes, or both?
2. What staff members will be available and where should we go?
3. What transport should we use?
4. What maps are available?
5. Will passports be necessary? Or insurance?
6. What would be the cost, and is financial help available?
7. How much camping equipment would we need?
8. Hearing aids—will maintenance and storage be possible?
9. Photographic equipment—what type is most suitable?
10. What books and colour slides of the area are available? Also tourist office material?
11. Emergency precautions—home telephone numbers, etc.
12. First aid—what facilities are there?
13. Identity cards if children become lost?
14. What clothing should be taken?
15. Is the children's behaviour compatible with such an outing?

Visits to Factories

(Ten multiply-handicapped deaf children, aged thirteen to sixteen, of average ability)

Preparation

1. Arrangements with the factory must be made at least six weeks ahead.
2. In the classroom, locate the factory on the map, trace out the bus routes. The teacher asks, "Which way shall we go? Which way is shortest? Easiest? Quickest? Costs the least?" They measure the distance on the map. The teacher explains the problems of time and tells them the fares, which come out of their own pocket money. Sometimes if it is far, they go in a chartered bus and the teacher explains the cost of this.

3. The day before the visit, brochures from the factory are studied. The class is asked: "How do you think this is made? What is it made of? Where does the raw material come from? (These places are located on the map.) Forms are filled in each visit (See App. 4a and 5).

The aim is to *make the class think,* not just to inform them. They do not always agree. They may argue and correct the teacher. There is some real discussion, however simple. We have a good talk on how we will behave.

The Day of the Visit

Discuss behaviour, check appearance, and then board the bus in an orderly fashion.

At the Factory

The class is received, greeted, and feels at ease. The children do not all remain with the teacher. Three or four go with a factory worker; and the teacher goes with the less able group.

They have been told to ask questions, to observe, to find out specific information, to talk to the men who are actually at work. They do this. Even with their speech difficulties, they get most of their questions understood and answered.

Back at School

The class has a question session—they provide their information in writing or drawing, or speech, or mime. The class analyses the information to determine if it is general knowledge or social knowledge.

Results

They see and meet the men on the job and learn about other people's lives and work, about life in a factory, the amenities. They broaden their knowledge of adult working life.

They become more independent and self-reliant in their dealings with adults.

They learn how to find out detailed information that they need—by asking and observing the right people. This results in stimulation of language development and widening of vocabulary, as well as skill in expression. They develop skill in discussion—mainly pertaining to wages, piece work, flat rate, overtime, etc.

They learn about the wage packet—deductions for withholding tax, medical insurance, union dues, etc.

They learn about imports and exports by observing where the product is sent etc.

FURTHER PREPARATION FOR THE ADULT WORLD

In the last two years at school, the first few years of post-school life are kept particularly in mind.

The pupils need to go out having some confidence to cope with the outside world and the information needed to handle the more immediate problems of life: job, board, taxes, insurance and so forth. They cannot possibly prepare for every emergency, so a major aim is to give them sufficient independence to be able to meet new problems in a sensible way.

Teaching Children How to Find Out

One of the threats to a deaf person's development is the overprotection to which he may be subjected by parents, friends, teachers, or welfare officers. A number of teachers try deliberately to help pupils to establish, by a series of experiences, the idea that they can cope with all the ordinary events of life by themselves but that they do have the security of knowing who they can fall back on and where they can get help if necessary.

These are some of the experiences:

1. A movie show was coming. The class wanted to get details of it.

Mrs. C.: How shall we find out about the movie?

Class: Look at the newspaper.

Mrs. C.: Which one, national or local?

Class: Local paper.

Mrs. C. How else?

(At first they didn't know.)

Mrs. C.: Could we try the library? And is there anywhere else that we can get information?

Class: Office by the station.

The group was divided in three groups of four children to follow each suggestion.

Group 1. Newspapers—Went off to our school library.

Group 2. Library—"What shall I say?"

Mrs. C.: Write down what you think you should say.

(They write it down. Mrs. C. corrects it. They copy it on to a clean piece of paper, and go off with it.)

Group 3. Information Bureau: same as Group 2.

In about half an hour all returned to the class. Each group told the others in turn what it had found out, and whether the source of information was useful. They now know the sort of places to look for information on some other questions.

2. The class wanted to go on a boat trip. They needed to know the schedule and the prices.

Mrs. C.: How shall we find out?

Class: Look in the paper.

Mrs. C., Which?

Class: Local.

Mrs. C.: Where in the paper?

Class: At the back.

Mrs. C.: Yes. At the back. But what heading?

(They do not know. But they look and find out. After a discussion on headings they concluded that there is a special place for each kind of advertisement.)

Mrs. C.: Where else could we find out?

Class: Blackboards on the "front." (waterfront)

Mrs. C.: Yes. Where else?

Class: Information office.

Half go to the waterfront to check; and the other half go to the information bureau. Back at school they compare results. They are learning to look for information in the appropriate advertising places.

3. For many of the problems that will crop up after leaving school we use the television series "Going to Work," "You and the World," and others as relevant.

4. Fairly frequently the class wants to go on a bus or train trip.

They discuss what must be done. Two pupils go with their queries written down, find out the time and the point of departure, and buy the tickets. Any mistake will obviously effect the whole class.

5. Sometimes one or two pupils need to go by train or bus to another school for a course. They use their own money, ascertain their timetables, and so on. Later, they fill in a claim form to receive the money. They take lunch with them; and this is either bought or prepared at school.

6. In many discussions about interviews, meeting people, and emergencies, the pupils consider what they should say or do. They like to write down suitable sentences to use in the introductory stages of meeting a stranger.

With these real experiences, television programmes, discussions of situations, and notes of what to do, the pupils seem to go out fairly confident. But this confidence can only become secure when they have found that they can, in fact, cope with "real" life.

Your Pay Packet

1. Wage Slips.

When you get your pay packet, look at the wage slip. Look at your *net wage,* then count the money to see if it is correct.

After working through three wage slips with the class, the teacher gave out further slips which were incomplete (sample shown below) and the pupils were asked to answer them on blank forms which had been duplicated, to initial them, and pass them on, until they had completed eight of the nine slips. The teacher checked as this was being done. The children took the ninth slip home to show their parents and to fill in for homework.

WORKS No.	Name	Code No.	Rate per hour	Basic Wage	Tax	Gross Wage	Over-time	Nat. Ins.	Other Deds.	Tot. Ded.	NET WAGE
264	Mr. Smith	360	20p for 40 hrs.	?	50p	?	NIL	?	25p	?	?

The precise reasons for taxation and national and medical insurance schemes are not easy to explain to deaf children. One teacher used the following techniques.

1. We visited the local library, looked inside the newsroom and saw a number of elderly people reading. When we returned we discussed this. How old were the people? Were they working? Where did their money come from? The old age pension. How much is paid to old age pensioners? From that we worked out a budget for such a person, using income against costs, such as rent, food (and what kind of food they could afford), heating, clothing, etc. And from this the children better understood the real meaning of the term "old age pension," and the problems facing the aged.

   They saw, for example, that perhaps some of these old people go to the library as much to keep warm and for company as for reading the newspapers.

2. From the newspaper I took a clipping about "Mr. Brown" who is, say, a truck driver. He has an accident, cannot work, and has no earnings. He has a wife and two children at school. Where does the money come from for food, rent, etc? I then go into the procedure for obtaining sickness and other benefits.

3. We may go to the Labour Exchange and see a small crowd outside. What are the men doing? They are fit and strong. Why aren't they working?

   We discuss this and many questions arise about problems of employment, unemployment benefit, and so on. The discussion may lead in many directions, such as security and the question of changing jobs.

4. We visit the hospital to see the working of the National Health Service, and discussion follows.

   I tried getting the pupils to make a full record to which they could refer after they left school, but I felt that while this could be important to some, it was often not very meaningful to the poor readers and the amount of time spent in writing, copying and correcting was not felt to be warranted.

   I now try to keep records to a minimum of essential information, and to spend the time developing understanding through questions and discussion.

The contribution of pupils who left the school and started work the previous year, should never be underrated A visit from one or two of them can be a great stimulus to the pupils in their final year at school. One visit by ex-pupils should take place fairly early in the school year and, if possible, another towards the end. Questions previously prepared by the class can be put and after, suggestions and points can be made by the ex-pupils and a general discussion held to conclude the session.

Employment

The teacher of one senior class received the following reply from a large drug company near to the school, and gave spirit duplicated retyped copies of it to the class. The letter was used as a group reading for the class, and the meanings of the words in italics were worked out by the children from the context or, if that failed, with the aid of their dictionaries with the teacher checking the accuracy of the class's findings.

Dear Mr. Armstrong,

Thank you for your letter of the 1st May (1967). We have pleasure in providing the information which you requested.

All our *employees* in the Benton Factory work from 8 a.m. to 5 p.m., Monday to Friday, with an hour for lunch each day. Lunches are obtained in our *canteens*. *Staff* members under age 18 years, have a special *lunch permit,* which entitled them to a hot lunch, costing between 10p and 25p, depending on what they selected from the menu. A coffee break is given in the mornings from 10:20 a.m. until 10:30 a.m.

All staff members receive three weeks holiday with pay after working for a full year. If a girl joins the company after August, she receives only two weeks holiday the following year.

The rates of pay in the factory depend on age. For example: a girl aged 15 would receive £9.40 per week; at 16 she would receive £12.50p per week, and so on.

We do not pay piece rates, but *on occasions* we do pay *overtime*. The hourly rate for overtime depends on whether the work is done evenings, Saturdays, or Sundays.

Until they reach age 18, our girls have *day-releases* to attend the college at Benton.

A Discount Card is given to all staff members, which enables them to obtain a *discount* on goods *purchased* in our retail stores.

Yours faithfully,

F. Sullivan (Mrs.)

Women's Employment Officer

One worthwhile method of helping pupils take a balanced view of job prospects before finally making their minds up, is to study the situation with them as objectively as possible. More careful assessment of abilities and aptitudes and job prospects is necessary than is usually the case in many schools (App. 6).

Choosing a Job

In a few months you will be leaving school to start work. Last October, Mr. Daniels and Mrs. Brit, the Youth Employment Officers, came and talked to us about jobs for boys and girls. We have looked at books, films, and filmstrips about different jobs. We have visited several offices, factories, hairdressing salons, and construction works.

You have all been thinking hard about the job you would like to do. Your parents, the Youth Employment Officers, Mr. Razzell (the headteacher) and I have all been thinking a lot about the jobs for you too.

The Youth Employment Officers will be coming to school again on Friday, 15th May (in one week's time). Remembering the things we have talked about when choosing a job, such as:

    That you really like to work
    That you are reasonably good at it
    That it has some sort of promotion in it, i.e. it is not a
        "dead end"
    That there are such jobs available,
we want you to try to decide what three jobs you would like to

do most, i.e. your first, second and third choices. Your parents and the others who are interested will talk things over with you and try to help you select the best one.

On the 15th May, the Youth Employment Officer will *interview* you. What will you say? (Each child is given a list of questions and replies in gaps left for him or her.)

Youth Employment Officer: What is your full name please?
You: My name is James Murray Dowling.
Y.E.O: I'm sorry I don't understand.
You: My name is James Murray Dowling.
Y.E.O: I'm sorry, I still can't quite follow.
You: I'll write it down.
Y.E.O: Thank you. What is your address?
You: 14 Cameron Road, Belmont.
Y.E.O: Could you write that too please? Thank you. Now, could you give me your age in years and months?
You: 16 years 8 months.
Y.E.O: I see you are wearing a hearing aid. Can you understand everything I say to you?
You: No, some.
Y.E.O: Would you tell me how to speak so you can lipread?
You: Speak slow, but clearly.
Y.E.O: (Shouting) Which-subject-do-you-like-best-at-school?
You: Don't shout please. Art, history, woodwork.
Y.E.O: Sorry! Have you a hobby?
You: Woodwork, chess, plasticine modeling.
Y.E.O: Do you belong to the Boy Scouts or any other boys club?
You: I belong to Youth Club.
Y.E.O: Where would you like to work—in a factory, in an office or outside?
You: I would like to work in a joinery factory.

The day before the interview, notes, such as the following, might be given to each child, and discussed and dramatised where necessary.

ABOUT THE INTERVIEW: Wear smart clothes but don't over-dress. Be polite and friendly. When you sit down don't flop like a sack of potatoes! Whatever happens, try to be calm. The

Employment Officer is a friend who wants to help you. If you keep calm, you will be able to think more clearly and sensibly.

If he doesn't understand you, try to speak more clearly. If he still doesn't understand you, try to explain by writing or drawing. It's a good idea to carry a pencil and small notebook in your pocket or handbag. If there's a suitable map on the wall you can use it to show him where your home is.

If you don't understand him, say, "I beg your pardon," the first time. If you don't understand the second time, say, "I'm sorry, I don't understand. Please try again." Or "Please write it for me."

These interviews with the Youth Employment Officers are felt to be of great importance. It is an opportunity for a young person to "try himself out" with a comparative stranger in a one to one relationship. If the pupil's speech and/or lipreading is very poor, it will, of course, be mainly a written dialogue; clearly an interpreter must go with this type of pupil when real decisions regarding vocational guidance and placement are concerned.

If the employment officer has not helped formulate the questionnaire that the pupils have been studying in preparation for the interview, he or she should at least see it before the pupils are seen and then will be able to include some of these questions. From this beginning it will be possible to extend each pupil and conduct a more complicated and searching type of interview according to the oral and intellectual ability of each.

One last point—where it is necessary to use a teacher or parent or welfare worker as an interpreter (and at such an important event in a young person's life this is almost certain to be the case), the interpreter should ensure that the discussion of the child's future is held up at very frequent intervals while he or she summarises what has been discussed.

Work Experience

Some students during their last year at one school spent two days each week in technical occupations. (Bartlett, 1968). After a four week period they moved to another occupation for the next four weeks, and so on. Care was taken to select tasks which the boys and girls were likely to be able to manage. Within each trade the simplest duties were tried first. In engineering, for example, a boy began working on an assembly line and progressed from this to operating a lathe or to the drafting division.

While at work the students were expected to conform to the conditions laid down for the permanent employees. They had to clock in on time and work the full eight hours each day. The insurance carried by each firm covered the deaf children who received no wages.

Regular contact between the school and the firms employing the children was essential. On the first day a teacher accompanied each child to ensure that he or she was acquainted with such things as toilets, time clock, lunch rooms, and so on, and was introduced to some of the workers. Following frequent discussions with the manager or foreman during the four week period, each trainee was assessed and the form (App. 6) was retained by the school after discussion with the child.

One teacher of a senior class in a school for deaf children gained valuable experience from a visit to another class in a school for slow-learning boys and girls. As a result, he modified his whole approach to teaching. He observed that the teacher felt her task was almost entirely to prepare the pupils for leaving school. She tried to encourage the feeling that the classroom was a sort of annex, a base from which the pupils could explore the outside world, that they must see themselves no longer as children and members of a school, but as trainee adults.

The teacher refused to do any remedial work in reading or arithmetic. It was too late; and in any case, there were other matters which ought to take priority. With special reference to mathematics, she felt that the need to work out wages, deductions, and bills acurately would be a better stimulus to growth of skill.

They did learn thoroughly all sorts of facts they would need as adult workers: wages, piece rates, deductions, social security deductions, insurance, etc. The teacher also tried to get them to shoulder the responsibility for their own affairs. Hers was a sympathetic but serious programme, making demands in the way that adult life does. She gave them a weekly quota of work to do. The order in which they did it was left to them; but it had to be done. They clocked in and out of the classroom and used the time clock record cards to work out their wages for the week. There was no question about the pupils' seriousness when they took part in this apparently play activity. They believed in it, because they saw it as a valuable preparation for their working life.

Having calculated their wages, they worked out a budget; trying to find, for example, if they could afford the payments on a motor bike, in view of their other weekly commitments. They made regular visits to local shops, by themselves, to find out the prices of various goods and the credit terms. They used the telephone which the teacher had installed in the classroom to make appointments at the hairdresser, and so on. The teacher had written, and the local education office had printed, two information-cum-work books, based on the *School leavers' Handbook* published by Arnold.

A number of deaf boys and girls who were also crippled have had very considerable success through a careful evaluation made by the Tower System (App. 7). One wonders whether a similar type of assessment procedure might not be designed for many deaf people who are not crippled, but who require special vocational placement.

Censuses

A government needs to know how many people in each age group there are in the country. The government can then plan ahead what services will be needed. For example, if an extra 20,000 children are born one year, the government knows that enough extra teachers will have to be trained before the children go to school at age five years. Counting up all these people is called taking a census.

Censuses are usually taken once every ten years in large countries and each five years in smaller rapidly developing ones. A census form is sent to every household and hotel in the country; and on one night—say 14 October—all the house-holders (usually the fathers) fill in the form, stating how many people were in the house that night, what their ages were, their religion, whether they were married or single, where they live, and how they earn their living. The householder also says what salaries the people in the house earn and what type of house they live in—large or small, brick or wood or stone, etc. No names are given, so people usually don't mind filling all these details in.

The earliest census we know about was taken in the Babylonian Empire about 6,000 years ago. This one, like most other early ones, was to help the king collect taxes. The information (or statistics as the figures are called) is very helpful to present-day governments for planning new schools, knowing how much will have to be paid out for each child or in old age benefits in coming years, where and when extra hospitals will be needed, and the number of boys and girls who will be leaving school soon and wanting jobs. The statistics from the census are also of great assistance to local-authority planners, to manufacturers, to teachers, doctors, architects, journalists and banks—in fact to almost everyone in the country.

Taking a census of a country involves a great deal of work and expense (the 1950 census in the United States cost ninety million dollars) but the different countries of the world realise that they can't afford to be without the information that a census gives.

NOTE: The best known of the various censuses mentioned in the Bible was that instituted by the Roman emperor Caesar Augustus. Luke 2:1 "There went out a decree from Caesar Augustus, that all the world should be taxed." Every man had to take his family with him and return to the place of his birth so that he could be registered there. Joseph and Mary returned to Bethlehem, and finding no room at the inn, had to sleep in a stable.

The ideal time to consider this topic, of course, is when an actual census is taking place, but children from about the age of ten years, can become interested in the subject at other times.

Some information such as the above passage, could be introduced, either as an LRS lesson or worked out as far as possible, by the children's contributions.

A spirit-duplicated copy of a modified census form can be filled in by all the children and two 'clerks' can collate the figures and place them on the blackboard. Parents should be informed of the results.

The Duke of Edinburgh Award

This scheme offers young people, both in the United Kingdom and in other Commonwealth countries, a challenge to endeavour and achieve. An award may be obtained by anyone, between their fourteenth and twenty-first birthdays, who qualifies in four sections of the Scheme. The sections are Service, Expeditions, Interests (hobbies, etc.) and Design for Living (for girls) and Physical Activity (for boys). Physical handicap should not deter anyone from taking part and a number of deaf boys and girls have achieved awards. Details can be obtained from The Duke of Edinburgh Award Head Office, 2 Old Queen St., London S.W.1.

In one school, seven boys and three girls are attempting the bronze medal of the Duke of Edinburgh Award. The social value lies in the development of confidence and independence, the ability to give something to others in the community and a wide range of contacts with hearing people, both during and after school.

Some progress towards these aims is already to be seen, for example:

1. The children are learning first aid for the service section of the award. Minor playground accidents—grazes, splinters, etc.—are handed over to their care automatically by all the staff. The children obviously enjoy doing this and are proud to be able to do it.

2. For the expeditions, we plan a fifteen mile hike over unfamiliar country, staying out one night under canvas. The children have to prepare their own equipment, food, menus and routes. They do a practice journey with an adult. The journey has to have a purpose and they must propose it.

This all adds up to increasing the children's responsibility, and can only result in growing self-confidence.

3. For the interest section the boys are doing marksmanship at the police range and this brings them into contact with people outside the school. One has chosen chess and joined a club in town.

4. The physical development section requires the children to achieve a standard, or attend a minimum number of training sessions. This, again, may have socially useful results.

An important aspect of this scheme is that after leaving school the children are encouraged to compete for the other awards, the silver, and the gold (up to their twenty-first birthday). The silver they might achieve before they leave school. The gold involves almost entirely their own planning but requires them to go to at least thirty people for help and advice. Such an exercise must result in a larger number and a greater variety of social contacts than they would otherwise make.

Over My Dead Body

(A story for fourteen to seventeen-year-old deaf children)

A teacher of speech, June Opie, had a very severe attack of poliomyelitis and was in a hospital in an iron lung which helped her to breathe. She could hear, but could not see properly and could not speak except to say "ar." She could not move her arms or legs at all. A clever nurse had a good idea. She said to June Opie, "Can you wink?" June closed and opened her left eyelid.

"Splendid!" said Nurse Farley. "When you want to say 'Yes' you wink that eye; and when you want to say 'No' leave it open—Now, can you see me?"

June winked. Nurse Farley moved, "Can you see me here?" There was nothing but a blur so June kept her eye open. "Here?" Her eye remained open. "Here?" June winked quickly, twice. Nurse Farley moved about asking how well June could see her in different places. June responded with a wink when she could see and kept her eye open when the nurse was in a place where she could not see her at all well.

When Nurse Farley stood to the left of June and leaned over the corner of the iron lung June winked twice.

"Right," said Nurse Farley, "I get you. You can see me best when I stand here?" June winked again.

As time went on June Opie learned to control her breathing so that she could speak, first in single words and then in short phrases. Today she is a qualified educational psychologist and although she still cannot walk, she drives her own car and lives independently in her own home.

The children can be asked to act out the above scene and make up other questions that Nurse Farley might have asked.

The following points can be taken as discussion:

1. Can you imagine what life would have been like for June Opie before Nurse Farley spoke to her? Or if she had not spoken to her at all?

2. Do you remember ever feeling something like June Opie when you were little? Or now?

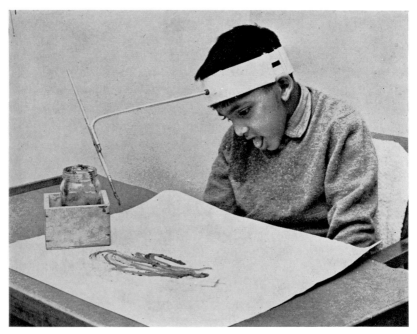

Figure 17. A 9-year-old boy learns to paint without using his arms (double hemiplegia and bulbar palsy).

3. What ways can deaf people with poor speech use to communicate with others?

4. Although deafness is a serious problem, can you see that someone who cannot speak at all and is confined to an iron lung is worse off? Why? (No communication at all unless someone comes near, no joy in movement, no independence, i.e. dependent almost entirely on other people's goodwill not able to do anything for anyone else, unable to sign, gesture, or fingerspell or even to laugh. Perhaps deafness isn't quite so bad after all when you think of all the things you can do.)

Visits to meet some other handicapped children always serve to make adolescent deaf children feel genuine compassion (and vice versa). Such comparisons and meetings with sufferers of other handicaps are among the few things that can encourage handicapped people when their own disability depresses them. Another excellent book for this purpose is *Hope for the Handicapped* by Jessie Thomas.

Old Age

Another group of handicapped people are the very old. Why are they handicapped? Their overall health is often poor. They have poor sight so that they can't read, poor hearing so that people can't talk to them so easily, arthritis in their joints—knees, hips, hands and elbows—so that they can't walk about freely, poor bladder control so that they have to go to the toilet very often, and poor digestion so that they must be careful what they eat. When, to these physical problems, one adds perhaps worries about money and the death of a wife or husband and of friends, the life of an old person can become very miserable. They can feel frustrated, humiliated, intimidated, and desperately lonely. The worst feeling of all is probably that they are no use to anyone, and that no one really cares about them.

An eighty-six year old man in London was moved to a new home in an area where he knew nobody. He became so lonely and depressed that he tried to commit suicide. He was then admitted to a mental hospital. After some months he was discharged and returned to his apartment. A kind neighbour "adopted" him; visited him daily, encouraged him, talked to him, played cards with him, and helped him to cope with his life. He was able to stay happily in his little flat until he died some years later.

What can we do to help old people?

A Party for Elderly People at Christmas

"It is a pleasure to give as well as to receive." Every year the older pupils (sixteen to eighteen years) in one school for deaf children give a party to a group of ten or twelve elderly people from the neighbourhood.

One year, four of the children wrote letters of invitation which, though on school stationery, were signed by the children. We had a preliminary lesson on writing such letters, including some thinking about the feelings they wanted old people to have when they received the letters and the detailed information they would need. We developed a pattern which the children used.

> Dear Mr. and Mrs. Brown:
>
> The children of Heaton Street School are having a Christmas lunch on 17th December. We should be very glad if you could join us.
>
> If you could arrive here by twelve noon, we would show you a short film first; then we will all go down to lunch. When lunch is over, some of us will do folk-dancing for you, and after that we have some gifts for you on our Christmas tree.
>
> If you live some distance away, our staff have offered to take you home in their cars.
>
> Do let us know if you can come.
>
> Yours sincerely,

The writers of the letters received replies accepting, or in one case, regretting inability to attend.

During the next two weeks the staff members in charge discussed with the children what might be done to entertain their guests, how they should be received, and how they should be looked after. It was decided that the guests should be met at the door by children who would act as their escorts or guides throughout. The children would sit and eat with the guests and see to their needs.

The parcels contained sweets and groceries; but also cushions or hot water bottles which had been collected partly from the staff and partly from the children. The children took a lot of pleasure in making up the parcels and in presenting them.

During previous years these older pupils had learned to welcome guests and look after people. No special lessons were needed, though there was some discussion as a way of giving a few reminders. The response of the guests and later their letters of thanks, gave great joy to the children.

BIBLIOGRAPHY

Armstrong, J.M.A.: *Projects and their Place in Education.* London, Pitman, 1950.

Association of Teachers of Social Studies of the City of New York: *Handbook for Social Studies Teaching,* 3rd. ed. New York, HR&W, 1967.

Barker, M.L. (Ed.) : *Pears Cyclopaedia.* London, Pelham Books, 1964.

Barnes, D., Britton, J., and Rosen, H.: *Language, the Learner and the School.* Harmondsworth, Penguin, 1969.

Bartlett, S.J.: (1968), Work experience programme for deaf children. In *Proceedings of 10th Triennial Conference.* Australian Association of Teachers of the Deaf Inc. Ashfield, Sydney, James and James Printers.

Bernstein, B.B.: Class, Codes and Control. In *Theoretical Studies Towards a Sociology of Language.* London, Routledge, 1971, Vol. 1.

Bowker, R.R.: *Audio Visual Market Place: A Multi Media Guide.* New York, Bowker, 1969.

Bruner, J.S.: *Toward a Theory of Instruction.* Cambridge, Harvard U.P., 1966.

Burston, W.H., and Green, C.W. (Eds.) : *Handbook for History Teachers.* London, Methuen, 1962.

Chapman-Taylor, R., and Clark, H.V.: *Thinking about Education: An Introduction to Curriculum Studies in the Primary School.* Auckland (N.Z.) , Collins, 1968.

Carlyle, Thomas: *The French Revolution.* London, J. Fraser, 1837.

Chomsky, C.: *The Acquisition of Syntax in Children from 5–10.* Cambridge, M.I.T., 1969.

Clarke School for Deaf Children: *Language—Curriculum Series.* Northampton, 1971.

Clarke School for Deaf Children: *Reading—Curriculum Series.* Northampton, 1972.

Connor, L.E.: (1971), *Speech for the Deaf Child.* Washington, A.G. Bell Association, 1971.

Connor, L.E., and Rosenstein, J.: Vocational status and adjustment of deaf women. *Volta Review.* 65: 585–591, 1963.

Cornett, R.O.: Cued speech. *Am Ann Deaf.* 112: 2–13, 1972.

Cornett, R.O.: *Cued Speech, Parent Training and Follow-up Program.* Washington, United States Department of Health Education and Welfare, 1967.

Cory, P.B.: *School Library Services for Deaf Children.* Washington, A.G. Bell Association, 1960.

Croker, G.W., Jones, M.K., and Pratt, M.E.: (1967), *New Language Stories and Drills*. Bks. I–IV. Brattleboro, The Vermont Printing Co., 1967.

Crone, G.R.: *The Explorers: an antholoy of discovery*. London, Cassell, 1962.

Dale, D.M.C.: *Applied Audiology for Children*, 2nd Ed. Springfield, Thomas, 1969.

Dale, D.M.C.: *Deaf Children at Home and at School*. London, U London Pr, 1971.

Dale, D.M.C.: Individual auditory training schemes. In *International Conference of HEAR Foundation*. Springfield, Thomas, 1973.

Dale, D.M.C.: Social Aspects of Speech. In Connor, L.E. (Ed.) : *Speech for the Deaf Child*. Washington, A.G. Bell Association, 1971.

Dale, E.: *Audio-Visual Methods in Teaching*. New York, Dryden Press, 1954.

Darrow, H.F.: *Social Studies for Understanding: (Practical suggestions for teaching)*. New York, Columbia University Teachers College, 1964.

Davies, L.: *Some Problems of Parents of Deaf Children*. Unpublished dissertation. University of London Institute of Education, 1966.

Department of Education and Science: *A Survey of Children born in 1947 who were Educated in Schools for the Deaf*. London, H.M.S.O., 1962–63.

Douglas, J.W.B.: *The Home and the School: a study of ability and attainment in the primary school*. London, MacGibbon and Kee, 1964.

Encyclopaedia of Myths and Legends of all Nations. London, Edmund Ward, 1968.

Ewing, A.W.G. (Ed.) : *Educational Guidance and the Deaf Child*. Manchester, U Manchester Pr, 1957.

Ewing, A.W.G., and Ewing, E.C.: *Teaching Deaf Children to Talk*. Manchester, U Manchester Pr, 1964.

Ewing, A.W.G., and Ewing, E.C.: *Hearing Impaired Children Under Five*. Manchester, U Manchester Pr, 1971.

Ewing, A.W.G., and Ewing, I.R.: *New Opportunities for Deaf Children*. London, U London Pr, 1958.

Gardner, D.E.M.: *Education of Young Children*. London, Methuen, 1956.

Garretson, M.D.: (1969), The Simultaneous Method. In Powrie Doctor (Ed.) : *Communication with the Deaf*. American Annals of the Deaf.

Gentile, A., and Di Francesca, S.: *Academic Achievement Test Performance of Hearing Impaired Students*. Crallendet College, Washington, D.C., 1969.

Ginsberg, V.S.: (1960), An experiment in teaching preschool children a foreign language. In *Soviet Education*. Vol. II.

Goddard, N.L.: *Reading in the Modern Infants' School*, 3rd Ed. London, U London Pr, 1969.

Gorman, P., and Paget, G.: *An Introduction to the Systematic Sign Language*. London, 8 Iverna Court, London W.8., 1969.

Graser, J.B.: *Der durch Gesicht—und Tonsprache der Menschheit Weider-gegebene Taubstumme.* Bayreut, Grau'sche Buchhandlung, 1829.

Griffiths, C.: *Conquering Childhood Deafness.* New York, Exposition, 1967.

Groht, M.A.: *National Language for Deaf Children.* Washington, Volta Bureau, 1958.

Hall, T.R., and Broome, E.B.: *Language Journeys.* Grade 5. Toronto, MacMillan, 1953.

Hamp, N.E.: *A Reading Vocabulary Picture Test.* Unpublished M.Ed. thesis. England, University of Leicester, 1970.

Hansen, M.: *A Citizen of Today.* London, Oxford U Pr, 1957.

Hardy, W.G.: Trends. In Connor, L.E. (Ed.) : *Speech for the Deaf Child.* Washington, A.G. Bell Association, 1971.

Harrison, M.: *Learning out of School: a brief guide to the educational use of museums.* London, Educational Supply Association, 1954.

Hart, B.O.: *Teaching Deaf Children to Read.* Washington, Volta Bureau, 1962.

Hill, W.: *Social Studies in the Elementary School Program.* Washington, Department of Health Education and Welfare, 1960.

Holcomb, R.K.: The total approach. In *Proceedings of the International Congress on Education of the Deaf—Stockholm 1970.* Vol. I., 1972.

Illinois Annual School for Mothers of Deaf Children: *If you Have a Deaf Child: A Collection of Helpful Hints to Mothers of Preschool Deaf Children.* Urbana, U Illinois Pr, 1959.

Ivimey, G.P. The development of English morphology—an acquisitive model. *Br J Psychol* (In press) .

Jones, H.: *Sign Language.* England, English Universities Press, 1968.

Lack, A.: *The Teaching of Language to Deaf Children.* England, Oxford Pr, 1958.

Leitman, A.: *Science for Deaf Children.* Washington, A.G. Bell Association, 1969.

Lenneberg, E.H.: A biological perspective of language. In Lenneberg, E.H. (Ed.) : *New Directions in the Study of Language.* Cambridge, M.I.T., 1964.

Lerman, A.: *Vocational Adjustment and the Deaf.* Washington, A.G. Bell Association, 1965.

Lewis, M.M.: *Language and Personality in Deaf Children.* Slough, (Bucks.) , National Foundation for Educational Research, 1968.

Lloyd, G.T.: *International Research Seminar on the Vocational Rehabilitation of Deaf Persons.* Washington, Department of Health Education and Welfare, 1968.

Lorton, M.B.: *Workjobs.* California, Addison Wesley, 1972.

Macauley, T.B.: *The History of England from the Accession of James II.* London, Longmans, 1848.

Madeley H.M.: *Time Charts.* London, Historial Association and George Philip & Son, 1954.

Michaelis, J.H. (Ed.) : *Teaching Units in the Social Sciences, Grades III–IV.* Chicago, Rand, 1966.

Miller, G.W.: *Educational Opportunity and the Home.* London, Longmans, 1971.

Minor, E.: *Simplified Techniques for Preparing Visual Instructional Materials.* New York, McGraw, 1962.

Morkovin, B.V.: *Through the Barriers of Deafness and Isolation.* New York, Macmillan, 1960.

Mosley, P.J.: *Lipreading with Video-tape recordings.* Unpublished Diploma dissertation, Univ. of London, Institute of Education, 1974.

National Coal Board: *Film and Filmstrip Projection.* London, National Coal Board, Hobart House, Grosvenor Place, London S.W.1., 1962.

National College of Teachers of the Deaf, *Manners Matter.* Nova Scotia; Printed Interprovincial School, Nova Scotia, Canada, 1968.

National Council of Social Service. *Help for the Handicapped.* London, National Council of Social Service, 1958.

Newton, M.G.: *Books for Deaf Children.* Washington, Volta Bureau, 1962.

New Zealand Department of Education. *Suggestions for Teaching Social Studies in the Primary School.* Parts I–IV. Wellington (N.Z.) .

Norwood, M.J.: Captioned films for the deaf, a program for today and tomorrow. In *Voix de Silence.* 1966. Vol. 10, pp. 534–539.

Opie, June: *Over my Dead Body.* London, Methuen, 1957.

Peters, R.S.: *Ethics and Education.* London, Allen and Unwin, 1966. pp 292–295.

Philips, H., and McInnes, F.J.C.: *Exploration in the Junior School,* London, U London Pr, 1965.

Plowden, Lady, B.: *Children and Their Primary School: a report of the Central Advisory Council for Education (England),* London, H.M.S.O., 1967.

Powell, L.S.: *A Guide to the Use of Visual Aids.* London, British Association of Commercial and Industrial Education, 1961.

Ragan, W.B., and McAulay, J.D.: *Social Studies for Today's Children.* New York, Appleton, 1964.

Richards, D., and Hunt, J.W.: *An Illustrated History of Modern Britain (1783–1964).* London, Longmans, 1967.

Rutter, M., Tizard, J., and Whitmore, K.: *Education, Health and Behaviour.* London, Longmans, 1970.

Scouten, E.L. (1969) English Through Fingerspelling in *Communication with the Deaf.* Ed. P.V. Doctor Am. Ann. of the Deaf.

Sevante, D.: *A Survey of Educational Visits Made by Schools for Deaf Children.* Unpublished dissertation, London University Institute of Education, 1966.

Speak, P., and Carter, A.H.C.: *Map Reading and Interpretation.* London, Longmans, 1964.

Stuckless, R.: Planning for individual instruction of students at N.I.T.D. in *Am Ann Deaf. 114:* 5, 1969.

Templin, M.C.: *Certain Language Skills in Children.* Minnesota, U Minnesota Pr, 1967.

Tervoort, B.: The effectiveness of communication among deaf children as a contributor to mental growth. In Ewing, A.W.O. (Ed.) : *Modern Educational Treatment of Deafness.* Manchester, U Manchester Pr, 1960.

Tizard, J.: *Community Services for the Mentally Handicapped.* Oxford U Pr, 1964.

Tizard, J.: Foreword to *Deaf Children at Home and at School.* Dale, D.M.C. London, U London Pr, 1971.

Townsend, P.: The institution and the Individual. In *The Listener.* London, B.B.C. Publications, 1960.

Tracy, Mrs. Spencer: *John Tracy Correspondence Course.* Los Angeles, John Tracy Clinic, 808 West Adams Boulevard, Los Angeles 7, U.S.A., 1970.

Treasure Chest for Teachers: Services available to teachers and schools. London, Schoolmaster Publishing Co. Ltd., 1967.

UNESCO: *History, Geography and Social Studies. Paris,* UNESCO Publication, 1965.

Unstead, R.J.: *Teaching History in the Junior School.* London, A. & C. Black, 1965.

United States Department of Health, Education and Welfare: *Catalog of Captioned Films for the Deaf.* Washington, Government Printing Office, 1969.

Van Uden, A.M.J.: A model of teaching a mother-tongue to prelingually deaf children based on psycholinguistic principles. In *Proceedings of the International Congress on Education of the Deaf—Stockholm 1970.* Stockholm, Pedagogiskaskrifta, 1970.

Van Uden, A.M.J.: *A World of Language for Deaf Children.* Holland, St Michielsgestel, 1968.

Watson, T.J.: *The Education of Hearing Handicapped Children.* London, U London Pr 1967.

Wedenberg, E.: Auditory training for deaf and hard of hearing. *Acta-Otolaryngologica.* Supp. 94: 1–130, 1951.

APPENDIX 1

Language through Art

References

Author	Title	Publisher and Date	Comment
1. Gombrich, E.H.	*The Story of Art*	Phaidon	In paperback. Especially good text on background to works of art, sculpture and painting. A history of art. Excellent.
2. Janson, H.W. and D.J.	*The Picture History of Painting*	Thames and Hudson	A history of art with many very good and varied illustrations.
3. Murray, P. and L.	*Dictionary of Art and Artists*	Penguin books	Good for quick reference on artists lives, style and dates. Deals chiefly with painters. In both illustrated and only text editions.
4. Clark, K. (1969)	*Civilisation*	BBC and John Murray	Personal views of civilisation introducing major works of chiefly western art. Architecture, Sculpture, painting and the applied arts in historical setting. Some very good illustrations. Very readable.
5. Copplestone, T. (1966)	*World Architecture*	Paul Hamlyn	Excellent for pictures. Some large, in colour.
6. Museums			Useful for good illustrations in postcard and larger form. Can illustrate social life as well as the arts.

Games—Leisure

Illustration	Period	Reference
1. Girl dancers and musicians	Egyptian, c. 1400 B.C.	Janson, pl. 16
2. Greek vase Achilles and Ajax playing draughts.	540 B.C.	Gombrich, pl. 48, p. 53
3. Musicians	Etruscan, Tarquinia, Italy. 480 B.C.	Janson, pl. 36
4. Knucklebones Game	Greek 1st century, A.D.	Janson, pl. 28
5. Lady Musician and young girl	Roman 1st century, A.D.	Janson, pl. 34
6. Très Riches Haures Hawking Party	c. 1415	Clark, p. 77
7. Card Sharpers	1593	Janson, pl. 250
8. The concert	1655–60	Janson, pl. 290
9. Card Players	17th century	Clark, p. 199
10. Music lesson	17th century	Clark, p. 220
11. Dancing at Fete	early 18th century	Clark, p. 236
12. Reading Molière	18th century	Clark, p. 252
13. Boys fishing	early 19th century	Clark, p. 283
14. Boating Party	mid 19th century	Clark, p. 289
15. Cafe Life (French) Moulin de la Galette	1876	Janson, pl. 399
16. Japanese boy Painting	19th century	Gombrich, pl. 99, p. 108

Work

Illustration	Period	Reference
1. Scribes of the Church	10th century A.D.	Clark, p. 16
2. Très Riches Heures	c. 1415	Janson, p. 85
3. German merchant	c. 1532	Janson, pl. 205 / Gombrich, pl. 231, p. 275
4. The Scullery Maid	18th century	Clark, p. 254
5. Stone breakers	1849	Janson, pl. 381
6. Gleaners	1857	Gombrich, pl. 320, p. 382
7. The Man with the Hoe	1863	Janson, pl. 380
8. Monet working in his boat	1874	Gombrich, pl. 325, p. 388
9. Self portrait van Gogh with palette	19th century	Clark, p. 336

Eating, Utensils, etc.

1. Family portrait	c. 1530	Janson, pl. 224
2. Meat Stall	c. 1551	Janson, pl. 229
3. Still Life	1634	Janson, pl. 284
4. The Cook	c. 1660	Gombrich, pl. 270, p. 322
5. St Carlo (eating)	17th century	Clark, p. 174
6. Kitchen Still Life	1735	Janson, pl. 327
7. Back from Market	1739	Janson, pl. 328
8. Lunch	18th century	Clark, p. 260
9. Fruit Bowl Glass Apples	1879–82	Janson, pl. 412
10. Boating Party (French)	19th century	Clark, p. 343
11. Potato Eaters	1885	Janson, pl. 420

Dress

1. The Emperor Charlemagne	Early 9th century A.D.	Clark, p. 28
2. Très Riches Heures	c. 1415	Janson, pl. 85 Clark, p. 73 and p. 77
3. Knight Asleep	15th century	Clark, p. 68
4. Giovanni Arnolfini (Flemish)	1484	Clark, p. 105
5. Portrait of Young Girl	c. 1465–70	Janson, pl. 117
6. Sir Thomas More's Dauguhter	1528	Gombrich, pl. 230, p. 274
7. Lady with the Unicorn	16th century	Clark, p. 60
8. Young Man	c. 1588	Janson, pl. 225
9. Henry VIII	c. 1540	Janson, pl. 228
10. Francis I	1525–30	Janson, pl. 238
11. Eleanora of Toledo	c. 1550	Janson, pl. 237
12. Dutch Interior	17th century	Clark, p. 198
13. The Jewish Bride	17th century	Clark, p. 208
14. Self portrait of Rubens with wife	1609–11	Janson, pl. 257
15. Infante Carlos	c. 1625	Janson, pl. 299
16. Jan Six	1654	Gombrich, pl. 265, p. 316
17. Young Men	c. 1638	Gombrich, pl. 254, p. 304
18. Prince of Spain	c. 1660	Gombrich, pl. 257, p. 307
19. Louis XIV	1701	Janson, pl. 308
20. Madame de Pompadour	c. 1755	Janson, pl. 312

21. Mrs Siddons	c. 1785	Janson, pl. 321
22. The Graham Children	1742	Janson, pl. 331
23. Portrait of a Girl	1780	Gombrich, pl. 296, p. 351
24. Mounted Officer of the Guard	1812	Janson, pl. 350
25. Sunday Afternoon	1844–86	Janson, pl. 414
26. Artist's mother	1871	Janson, pl. 406

Living

1. Port du Gard	Roman	Clark, p. 5
2. Viking Ship	9th–10th century A.D.	Clark, p. 15
3. Horsemen with Stirrups	9th century A.D.	Clark, p. 19
4. Très Riches Heures	c. 1415	Janson, pl. 85
5. Medieval town	c. 1460	Gombrich, pl. 173, p. 198
6. Peasant Wedding	c. 1565	Janson, pl. 233
7. The Young Mother	c. 1660	Janson, pl. 296
8. Experiment with Air Pump	1768	Janson, pl. 324
9. Portrait Group	18th century	Clark, p. 249
10. Local Election	18th century	Clark, p. 248
11. Morning Toilet (dressing a child)	18th century	Clark, p. 261
12. Third class carriage	1860–70	Janson, pl. 362

War: Death

1. Warrior's leave-taking	Greek 500 B.C.	Gombrich, pl. 49, p. 54
2. Viking Wood Carving, Dragon's Head—warship	820 A.D.	Gombrich, pl. 107, p. 110
3. Bayeaux Tapestry	1080	Gombrich, pl. 102, p. 111
4. Triumph of Death	c. 1350	Janson, pl. 91
5. Battle of San Romano	c. 1455	Janson, pl. 139
6. Knight in Armour	c. 1513	Janson, pl. 218
7. Surrender of Breda	1634–5	Janson, pl. 287
8. Goya (Deaf) The Third of May 1808	1814–15	Janson, p. 349 Clark, p. 306

APPENDIX 2

SOME FAMOUS ARCHITECTURE, SCULPTURE AND PAINTINGS

References as for Appendix 1

Architecture

Title and Place, Date	Architect	Reference
1. The Parthenon, Athens c. 450 B.C.	Iktinos	Gombrich, pl. 45 World Architecture, pl. V
2. Colosseum, Rome c. A.D. 80		Gombrich, pl. 72
3. Santa Sophia, Istanbul, 532–37 A.D.		World Architecture, pl. 488 xxvii
4. Notre Dame, Paris, 1163–1250		Gombrich, p. 123
5. St. Peter's, Rome 1506–1626	Bramante, Michaelangelo and Maderna, Bernini, etc.	Clark, pl. 120 Clark. pl. 132
6. Monastery of Melk, on Danube River, 1702	Prandtauer	Gombrich, pl. 287
7. St. Paul's, London 1675–1710	Wren	Gombrich, pl. 291
8. Versailles, France 1655–1682	Le Vau and Mansart, J.H.	Gombrich, pl. 282
9. Guggenheim Museum, New York, 1943–59	Frank Loyd Wright	World Architecture, pl. 1020
10. Church at Ronchamp, France	Le Corbusier	World Architecture, pl. LVI

Famous Sculpture

1. Discus thrower, c. 450 B.C.	Myron	Gombrich, pl. 53
2. Parthenon frieze, c. 440 B.C.	Pheidias	Gombrich, pl. 61 British Museum, London
3. David, c. 1444	Donatello	Clark, pl. 68
4. David, 1501–4	Michaelangelo	Clark, pl. 84
5. Ecstasy of St. Teresa 1645–52	Bernini	Clark, pl. 134

249

| 6. Sculptor Jules Dalon 1883 | Rodin | Gombrich, pl. 326 |
| 7. Recumbent Figure, 1938 | Henry Moore | Gombrich, pl. 366 London, Tate Gallery |

Famous Paintings

Name or Title, Date	*Artist*	*Reference*
1. Mona Lisa, c. 1505	Leonardo	Janson, pl. 164
2. Birth of Venus, c. 1480	Botticelli	Janson, pl. 137
3. Self portrait, c. 1660	Rembrandt	Janson, pl. 279 Clark, pl. 143
4. 3rd May 1808, 1814–15	Goya	Clark, pl. 210 Janson, pl. 349
5. The Fighting Téméraire 1838	J M W Turner	Janson, pl. 372 Tate Gallery, London
6. Road with Cypresses 1889	Vincent van Gogh	Janson, pl. 430
7. Waterlilies, 1916	Monet	Clark, pl. 42 National Gallery, London
8. Three Musicians, 1912	Picasso	Janson, pl. 471 Museum of Modern Art

APPENDIX 3

Visit to the Barclay Museum (Work Sheet)

On the way in, look at the Mosaic floor.

Now go into the "Belsize Archaeology Room."

Can you find out about these things?

1. The first people to make pottery in England lived at _____

2. To heat water in a leather bowl, they _____

3. What do you notice about the two skeletons? _____.

4. All the tools in Case 3 come from _____

5. On your plain paper, draw 2 Mesolithic Axes.

6. A shoulder blade of an ox used as _____

7. To make skin clothes, they used

    1.   2.

8. Draw 3 different arrow heads.

9. What were Hammer Stones used for? _____

10. How did they grind corn in the Stone Age? _____ Draw something they used.

11. Deer antlers were used as _____

12. Write down the names of 6 Prehistoric Sites in Sussex.

    1.   2.

    3.   4.

    5.   6.

Find them on the map when you get back to school.

APPENDIX 4

(To be filled in before and during each factory visit)   No. 1.

Occupations Form

Name of Firm or Place of Work:

Address: City Map Reference:
                                                             (Number and letter)

How to get there from the
   City Bus Centre:

Name of Occupation:

Machines or tools used:

Training for the job:

Wages   Piece Work/Hourly Rates/Fixed Wage
        (Cross out the ones which are not applicable)

Amount per week:

Overtime Rates:

Promotion Prospects:

Hours of Work:

5-day week?   Yes/No

Lunch Break: From.....................to...................... _____hrs. _____mins.

Tea or Coffee Breaks?

Facilities? (e.g. Sports Grounds, Clubs, Special Cheap prices)

Holidays:

APPENDIX 5

(To be filled in after each factory visit)

Employees' Application Form

Surname (BLOCK LETTERS PLEASE) ....

Christian Names...

Home Address...

....

Age....................yrs....................mths

Date of Birth...

Married/Single...

School last Attended..

....

Name of Last Employer...

Address...

....

When did you leave?...

Reason for leaving...

....

Occupation..

Are you on the Disabled Persons' Register?..

State Nature of Handicap, if any...

Name of Welfare Officer or Other Person who might help you

....

Address...

Do you suffer from Industrial Dermatitis?..

Date..Signed...

APPENDIX 6

Report on 4 Week Work Experience Period

WORK

Dexterity	S	AA	A	BA	IF
With tools					
Without tools					
With machines					

Work tolerance
Reaction to environment
Attentiveness
Endurance

Work habits
Neatness
Carefulness
Industriousness
Retains instructions
Punctuality

Comprehension
Follows written instructions
Follows oral instructions

Personal

Attitudes	S	AA	A	BA	IF
Alertness					
Resourcefulness					
Initiative					
Self-confidence					
Cooperativeness					

Appearance
Personal hygiene
Grooming

Relationship
With fellow workers
With foreman
With others

Communication	S	AA	A	BA	IF
Use of oral language					
Use of written language					
Use of gesture					

Rating of characteristics   S—superior
AA—above average
A—average
BA—below average
IF—inferior

WORK EXPERIENCE ASSESSMENT

Name:
Firm employed with:
Type of work:
Work period..to..
General remarks:
Recommendations:

APPENDIX 7

The Tower System of Vocational Evaluation

S. H. WARD: Vocational Evaluator

Dadley Foundation for Crippled Children, Mount St., Auckland, New Zealand

Vocational Evaluation is achived by means of an organized series of simulated work situations where candidates are exposed to the actual activity of a trade by utilizing the basic hand tools, materials and techniques of that trade. Their performance in these work situations is measured by standardized rating criteria which have been based on normal employment standards.

The TOWER System includes thirteen broad work areas of Vocational Evaluation. These are Clerical, Drafting, Drawing, Lettering, Leathergoods, Electronic Assembly, Sewing Machine Operating, Jewellery Manufacturing, Mail Clerk, Receptionist, Welding, Workshop Assembly and Optical Mechanics. All areas, with the exception of Optical Mechanics, are used in the work evaluation programme at the Dadley Foundation.

The system on an average requires four weeks, five hours per day, five days per week, during which the work sample technique is employed. There are over 100 work sample tests which apply to the different job areas. The disabled person is exposed to as many of these areas, and tests within the areas, as possible, and as consistent with the medical social adjustment and vocational findings prior to admission. The candidate need not take all tests in a chosen area if the earlier tests in the area indicate unsuitability in relation to his capabilities.

Before admission to TOWER Evaluation, each disabled person previously has been given a medical examination, has been interviewed in the intake process by the Field Officer or Social Worker, has had a psychological review, vocational counseling, and has completed a period of three to four weeks prevocational assessment in the Occupational Therapy Department.

The primary purpose of vocational evaluation is the selection of an occupation for each handicapped person that is within the range of his abilities and which is available in his locality. The TOWER graduate can be presented to an employer with proven aptitudes and abilities and with defined personal and work characteristics. This tends to eliminate the trial and error method of gaining employment based on vocational interview technique alone. From experience already gained with the Dadley Foundation post-TOWER placements, it has been evident that employers welcome the TOWER job assessments as a worthwhile advance in personnel selection.

Case Example

This young man, aged 23 years, suffers with Myotonia Congenita. He is fully ambulent, but unable to handle heavy physical work. He was frustrated and discouraged following several job failures. His Evaluation Report showed above average aptitude for Jewellery Manufacturing. He was successfully placed in a 5-year apprenticeship in Jewellery Manufacturing. Continuing reports from his supervisor rate his aptitude for the work in line with the TOWER report.

SUBJECT INDEX

A

Accidents at home, 126–127
Activity lessons, 17, 18, 86–87, 100–105
Adhesive boards, 48–50
Alexander Graham Bell Assoc., 167
Animals and pets, 58–61
Art, 245–250
Assemblies, 82–86
Audio-visual aids, 56

B

Birthdays, 86
Blackboard, 47–48
Bus depot, visit, 109–111
Buttermaking, 105–109

C

Camping, 220–221
Censuses, 232–234
Cine-loop, projectors, 69
Cities, 166–167
Class newspaper, 123–124
Classroom walls, 94–100
Compass points, 143–144
Conversations, 4
Country code, 115, 185
Courtesies, 90–93, 130
Cued Speech, 12–13
Current events, 74, 142–143

D

Daily routines, 32, 93
Diaries, 35–37
Direct speech, 4
Discussion, 207–209
Domestic activities, 96–97, 205–207,
    209–212
Duke of Edinburgh Award, 234–235

E

Economic institutions, 215–220

Emergency services, 138–140
Emotional adjustment, 39–42
Employment, 225–232

F

Fathers, 32
Films, 145–148
Flowers for Mother, 89–90, 94
French, 155–156
Fruit, 149–152

G

Geography, 162–167, 185–190
Ginger beer, 127–129
Group stories, 22–23

H

Hearing aids, 7–8, 9, 10, 31, 37
History, 167–177
House Parents, 5, 6
House, the, 89

I

Integration
    hearing impaired children in
        ordinary schools, 62–71
    individual, 66–71
    with normally hearing people, 38

L

Language
    masters, 57, 68
    topics, 74–78, 115–122, 161–183
Latitude and longitude, 144–145,
    147–148
Lipreading, 8–9, 13, 14, 15, 56

M

Maps, 34, 130–134, 144–145
Mathematics, 98–99

257

Meals, 96–97
Mechanical projects, 213–215
Methods
  activity centered, 10–12, 17
  auditory, 7
  conversation, 20–21
  developmental, 9
  finger spelling, 13
  listening-reading-speaking (L.R.S.),
    7–8, 37–38, 104, 150, 151, 215
  mothers, 8
  out of class activities, 25–30
  seizing, 16
  sign languages, 14–15
  simultaneous, 15
  total communication, 15–16
Milk, 210–211
Mother's Day, 125–126
Music, 38, 148–149

N

Nativity play, 87–89
Nature rambles, 100–105
News, 123
New words, 95–96
New Zealand, 163, 191–193
Nouns, 4
Nurse, 140–141

O

Occupations, 181–182
Other handicaps, 235–239

P

Parent guidance, 68
Parents, 5, 6, 31–46
Pay packet, 225–228
Pictures and photographs, 34, 50–54

Post office, 137–138
Projected visual aids, 54–56

R

Reading, 34–35
Reference books, 24–25
Relations, 99
Religious knowledge education, 87, 157,
    197–198, 203–205
Residential care, 42–46

S

Sailing ships, 195
Shopping, 135–136, 202–203
Slides and filmstrips, 69
Social living, 178–181
Speech, 5, 34
Stone-Age People, 154, 155
Story telling, 21–22
St. Patrick's Day, 124–125

T

Television, 56, 95, 154, 185–8, 199–200,
    201–202
Topics, 6, 72, 74–78, 115–122, 161–185
Tower System, 256

V

Verb Tenses, 141–142
Video-tape recorders, 56
Visits, 25–30, 220–223, 251–252
Visual aids, 47–57

W

Walls, 94–100
Weather, 78–83
Work experience, 254–255

AUTHOR INDEX

B

Barker, M. L., 173
Bellugi and Brown, 17
Bernstein, B., 5

C

Case, S. L., & Hall, J., 170
Chapman-Taylor, R., 6
Connor, L., 62

D

Dale, D., 5, 7, 14, 67, 71

E

Ewing, A. W. G., 5
Ewing, E. C., 21
Ewing, E. C. & A. W. G., 4
Ewing, I. R. & A. W. G., 8, 19

G

Gardner, D. E. M., 5
Gentile, A., 67
Ginsberg, V., 4
Gorman, P., 15
Grammatico, L., 9–12, 17–18
Groht, M., 19, 78

H

Hamp, N., 67

J

Jauhianen, T., 71

L

Lack, A., 141
Lenneberg, E., 5, 17
Lorton, M. B., 11

M

Macaulay, T., 168

N

Nässtrom, E., 71

R

Ragan, W. & McAuley, J., 144, 148
Rutter, M., 5, 71

S

Strong, C. F., 168–171

T

Thomas, J., 237
Tizard, J., 5, 6, 62
Tracy, Mrs. Spencer, 19

U

Unstead, R. J., 167

V

Van Uden, A., 16–17, 19, 20–21, 147

W

Williams, G., 169–172